T0327184

From the Ramparts

ASHOK MITRA

From the Ramparts

ASHOK MITRA

Tulika Books

Published by **Tulika Books**
35 A/1 (third floor), Shahpur Jat, New Delhi 110 049, India

First published in India 2006

ISBN: 81-89487-05-1

Typeset in Sabon at Tulika Print Communication Services,
New Delhi, and printed at Chaman Enterprises, 1603 Pataudi
House, Daryaganj, Delhi 110 002

In remembrance of
ALICE
who was fond of these pieces

Publisher's Note

Tulika Books would like to express its thanks to Mihir Bhattacharya, for editing for publication these essays which first appeared in the 'Calcutta Diary' column of the *Economic and Political Weekly* during 1999–2003; and to Prabhat Patnaik and Rajendra Prasad for initiating the idea of this collection.

Contents

ONE

To be as free as the Caribbeans

8–14 January 2000

Even as the final year of the twentieth century makes its presence felt, those in the age group of 70 and above shrink further into a frail minority. Some amongst them will perhaps still remember the Government of India Act, 1935. The statute incorporated provisions that were intended to mark a new beginning in central–provincial relations in imperial India. The reluctance of the national leadership to admit the fact notwithstanding, large chunks of our post-independent Constitution, drafted during 1947–49, were lifted straight out of the 1935 Act. The nation's leaders, there is no question, were great copycats. And they obviously held in great reverence the just-departed colonial masters.

Thereby hangs a tale. In quite a number of instances, the 1935 Act was actually more forward-looking than the Constitution which we, the people of India, gave unto ourselves, or the leaders gave on our behalf. To pick just one example, the 1935 Act ordained that a provincial government would be allowed to start a broadcasting station on receipt of a licence from the central government. The text of the Act could not be more explicit: yes, the centre would have to issue a licence before a provincial regime could begin to operate a broadcasting station, but this was just a formality; such a licence should be issued as a matter of course to whichever provincial regime applies for it. This was an eminently sensible approach. The British knew their oats. India constituted a far-flung empire; decentralized arrangements for broadcasting would promote more effective administration. Some provinces in the proposed Indian federation would, in fact, have a population far exceeding that of Great Britain itself. Cultural and linguistic diversities were of a pronounced order. Taking into account these considerations, His Majesty's Government in London thought it proper that in the new Act, the end-product of Sir Samuel Hoare and Sir John Simon's labours to accord India the status of a dominion, broadcasting be delegated to the care of the provincial governments, and the statute says so explicitly. It is a different matter that the second world war intervened, the native princes had mixed views about the federation, and the 1935 Act met a dead end. Despite the sentiments reflected in the Act, no province actually embarked on any broadcasting on its own between 1935 and the transfer of power in 1947.

The 1935 Act was dead and gone, those who wrote the Constitution of India took a different view on the issue of according broadcasting rights to the states which supplanted the provinces of the pre-independence days. Lazybones, they bodily lifted the major features of the 1935 Act to give shape to centre–state relations in the new Constitution. But the prerogative of issuing licences for broadcasting was firmly reserved for the union government; the discussions in the constituent assembly made it amply clear, this prerogative was not going to be an idle formality either. The liberalism reflected in the 1935 Act would have no echo in the Constitution of the independent democratic federal republic of India.

In the half century following the introduction of the new Constitution, broadcasting has therefore continued to be under the sole surveillance of the centre. Of late, broadcasting has been overshadowed by the new electronic medium, telecasting; the same regulatory provision has hemmed in telecasting too. True, globalization has led to the opening of private telecasting channels in the country, including a number of foreign channels. They operate on the basis of uplinking facilities granted to them by New Delhi; since private, and especially foreign, parties are involved, the facilities sought have been granted with great alacrity.

The position obtaining at this moment can be easily summed up. A private entity can proceed to start a television channel of its own, New Delhi will be quick to arrange uplinking facilities for it. This government at the centre is however based on principles. It will frown upon public sector initiatives at all levels. It will encourage only private sector activities; since the state governments do not belong to the private domain, they will not be given permission to promote television channels on their own.

At least, such is the conclusion derivable from the response of the union government to the request of the government of West Bengal for permission to operate a satellite telecasting channel of its own, thereby enabling it to telecast programmes which, apart from disseminating local news, would lay stress on encouraging regional languages and cultures. New Delhi will quote the Constitution and admonish the states to dismiss all notions about opening their own television channels with the concurrence of the centre; such concurrence, it has been made clear, will not be forthcoming. New Delhi has however been generous with its advice; should a state government feel the need to do something in this direction, it could buy time from a private television channel.

It will be pointless to rake up ancient history and remind those in authority that where this particular matter is concerned, the Constitution, as drafted in 1947–49, was much more regressive than even the Government of India Act, 1935 drawn up by the colonial masters. Given the stockpile of first-rate technologists and engineers the country possesses, it should be possible for a state government, if it so wills, to make an outlay of Rs 50 to 100 crore to establish its own television facilities. The need for uplinking will however still be there. The *firman* of the union government appears to be unwavering at this moment: no uplinking will be made available to a state government channel. The situation could not be more absurd. A private television channel can claim – and receive – uplinking facilities as a mater of course; a state government is to be denied this privilege. A fiat of this nature is not just because of hauteur or spite; it is also presumably influenced by dollops of ideology. The government of West Bengal, which has applied for the uplinking facilities, flaunts a Left ideology. Such a government is dangerous: if granted the permission it has sought, it might use its television channel to propagate the vicious cult of Marxism. That cannot be allowed, period.

Is this going to be the final verdict of history? There are member-countries of the United Nations whose population will not amount to even 1 per cent of the population of West Bengal or Andhra Pradesh to Uttar Pradesh or Bihar or Madhya Pradesh or Maharashtra. And yet, these countries not only have each a vote in the United Nations. They have their own radio and telecasting facilities. They do not have to beg permission from any external authority to broadcast and telecast programmes of their choosing and in their own languages.

So what a teeny-weeny Caribbean island can enjoy will be denied to a state in India, notwithstanding its impressive size and population. The government of India will not permit Bihar, West Bengal, Uttar Pradesh, Madhya Pradesh, Maharashtra and other states the necessary licence to own and run a television channel. When the matter is discussed in private with representatives of the centre, the latter will go to great lengths to draw attention to the potential peril to the nation if freedom is granted to state governments to launch their own broadcast and telecast programmes. Unlike the private – including foreign – channels, a state government, channel, it is hinted, cannot be quite relied upon to behave responsibly. The prerogative private channels are currently being granted – and what was granted one and a half decades ago to the LTTE – is yet to be accorded to a state government howsoever densely populated it might be and howsoever rich its language and culture may be. Liberalization signifies freedom of action for private entities, not for a state government.

Does the centre realize, though, that its obstinacy is an invitation to disorder? The wobbly alliance the Bharatiya Janata Party has formed a few months ago is already experiencing troubles. Despite its concordat with the class fraternity, the Indian National Congress, as, for instance, in the matter of the passage of the insurance, FEMA and patents bills, it will hardly be a tranquil time. To ride roughshod over the demands of states of the most commonplace kind, such as for opening a separate television channel, is insensate provocation. By not granting the permission the government of West Bengal has asked for, the centre is tempting fortune. And if the reason underlying the decision is ideological, the sense of outrage will be more widespread: X-rated films are okay, so are displays on the television screen of orgies of violence, but narrations of supposedly socialist morality are to be proscribed: such an attitude of mind is not defensible on any ground. Those who nonetheless defend it are genuine enemies of civilization.

Having said all this, it is equally necessary to invite attention to an inexplicable failure on the part of the state government of West Bengal. It had all the time in the world, it could have applied for the television licence when the alliance it was supportive of – the United Front – was in power at the centre during 1996–98. It did not do so, it preferred to procrastinate. The wages of laziness too is death.

Books: the great alibi

2 March 2002

That venerable eccentric, one of the earliest of women's libbers, Virginia Woolf, has made the assertion somewhere: an age of genius is followed by an age of endeavour. She could have added as an afterthought: an age of earnestness is followed by an age of frivolity. The Calcutta Book Fair is now a formidable institution and has completed a quarter of a century's existence. In the beginning, it was the transcription of an interesting concept: books are to be brought to the people; a mountain of books will come face-to-face with a mass of people; readers will meet other readers as well as authors; authors will meet other authors and publishers; publishers will meet, and snoop on, other publishers. A certain grandeur will mark the proceedings. Men and women are wont to commune with nature; let it be the turn for communing with books. A subterranean flow of Bengali sub-nationalism was soon discernible, though, in the mêlée of fair-mongers: those unable to feel superior to the rest of the nation on any other cognizable count experienced a catharsis of emotions via the snobbery over books: look at us, we are special, we are given to reading, and browsing in, books, unlike you philistines who while away time and money in the pursuit of wishy-washy, pedestrian pastimes; please come, visit us at the Calcutta Book Fair. We of course adore books, but we love this occasion all the more because it makes all of you feel small, while we look tall and taller during the ten days of the Fair every year.

The Bengalis, that is, those taking their snobbery about books as a serious social attribute, possessed one initial advantage; they knew little about what was happening in other neighbourhoods. Only a handful amongst them had a modicum of an idea of the goings-on in the rest of the country in scholastic fields or in literature and the arts. What they were unaware of, they had few reasons to worry about; developments in the various sectors of knowledge in the wide open world they could ignore with comfort. That state of being hoity-toity continues:

whatever the Bengalis do not read is not worth reading. The company of books, so is the assumption, widens the mind; in the case of Bengalis, it is the pretext for displaying a vacuous superiority complex. The snobbery had little leg to stand upon to begin with; the circumstances are far worse now. The Left, who take pride in their eclecticism, have been in charge of administration in West Bengal for the past twenty-five years. Whatever their other achievements, they have taken it for granted that those who dabble in books need to be handled with conventional absent-mindedness. Books are now a fixed coordinate. The Bengali middle class is smug, breathtakingly so. The mixture of snobbery and smugness can be a deadly chemistry. The awe this class has for the English language has a *sui generis* quality; otherwise its constituents nurture an impressive disdain for things not on the agenda of the daily Bengali routine. The Calcutta Book Fair exemplifies the phenomenon. It draws participants from across the country and sometimes from overseas as well. Even so, it is an overwhelmingly Bengali affair; the fare served is quintessentially Bengali. Books are only one item for transactions taking place within the precincts of the Fair. You have tea and coffee stalls, you have eateries serving varieties of savouries. Football and cricket stars hop from stall to stall parading themselves as intellectuals; failed poets wander about in the manner of aspiring politicians; film personalities commingle with English Channel swimmers, mad philosophers and fake physicists. All this is supposed to build an appropriate atmosphere of hoopla. Icecream parlours abound, along with purveyors of *mishti doi*. In case you are a seeker after hooch, you will not be disappointed, all you have to do is to look for a discreet corner. Every now and then, rock bands will regale or torture you; now that the copyright on Rabindranath Tagore's intellectual property is off, they are determined to convert *Rabindrasangeet* into delicious ragtime. Habitual oglers can hardly be missed, even as lovers and would-be lovers furtively look around in search of nooks and crannies where they can coo at one another without getting interrupted. The instant revolution-makers discovered the Fair pretty early, right in the hazy 1970s. The fundamentalists too have now arrived. The Fair, besides, is considered to be a prized picnic spot; families invade it in hordes. And with children swarming all over, fun and games of different kinds are regularly catered to. Books are sold, but the turnover of books is, in monetary terms, appreciably lower than the turnover of the coffee, milk, icecream and snack bars. Books provide the façade, carnival reflects the *esprit de corps*.

Frivolity is as frivolity does. This year there was some initial furore adding to confusion, or perhaps it was the other way round, confusion contributing to furore. Waging battle for expanding civil and political rights is reduced to a dim Calcutta memory. Talk of class struggle and of an impending bloody uprising raises a horse laugh, but the Bengali *bhadralok* can still work up an ersatz passion. It was Calcutta Book Fair till last year. The organizers offered some resistance to change over to Kolkata Book Fair. Hackles were raised: how dare they cling to the last vestiges of colonialism and imperialism! Such regalia as Mayor and Sheriff are all right, Calcutta however has to be out. The organizers capitulated, the crisis blew over. There was nonetheless never a dull moment. Since Tagore is now a liberated commodity, the free market principle took charge, fierce competition ensued between publishers, many of whom belonging to the fly-by-night brigade, to print Tagore's prose and poetry in the shoddiest hurry and within the fold of the luridest covers and dust jackets. In due course, Tagore will survive the assault of perfect competition. Bengali smugness, though, will have the better of Bengali snobbery, and Calcutta, by whatever name you call it, will continue to welcome the transition of flippant seasons.

Other species of entertainment are not *verboten* either on the Fair grounds. An interesting departure in recent years is the explosion of 'book-release' ceremonies; it has emerged as the latest status symbol in Calcutta society. Politicians of other breeds vie with one another in presiding over the 'inauguration' of community worships, such as on the occasion of Durga or Kali Puja. But those whose political affiliation or ideological belief prevent them from participating in events of this nature, have now discovered the modality of how to lick the problem. In Book Fair time, they compete amongst themselves in the intense sport of book releases. Snobbery within snobbery; the more new publications one releases in the course of a single evening during the Fair, the greater is the spread of one's fame as an 'intellectual politician'. One particular politician has created a record of sorts this year; on the closing day of the Fair, he, scurrying from one stall to the next, managed to release twenty-three books. If it were the Soviet Union 70 or 80 years ago, he would have been pronounced a Stakhanovite.

Persons who have safely left behind their halcyon days of activism used to migrate in the past to the quietude of library and write books, either memoirs of their distant exploits and disappointments or arcane philosophical tracks on *shruti* and *smriti*. No longer. These days they invade the Calcutta Book Fair and preside over book releases. Whether you read the books you release, is a different matter. Besides, is not the precious point elegantly stressed in the process: the Calcutta Book Fair is for ever, it will bore you to death for ever.

To confess, there is a further cloud in the horizon. The economic holocaust that has hit the Indian economy could not sidestep West Bengal. Apart from the hard datum, referred to earlier, of the turnover of icecream, coffee, tea, chocolate, savouries and fowl curry far exceeding the turnover of books sold, there is another reason for concern. Although the monetary value of book sales has been nominally higher than what it was last year, the actual number of books sold has in fact declined this year. A much more fearful omen, the information technology books and journals sold extremely poorly, while sales of tracts on philosophy and psychology have shot up. Investigative reporters are currently hard at work to unravel the implications of this state of being.

It is however not wholesale gloom. The Book Fair is, by now, established as the greatest promoter of conjugal relationships in these parts. So, even in case, in the coming years, the crowd thins and the transaction of books declines precipitately, prospective brides and bridegrooms and their guardians and friends are bound to compensate for the loss, at least to some extent. On the other hand, some people's meat is always some other people's poison. There is a deep furrow along the forehead of the marriage bureaus; they are fast losing their clientele to the Book Fair. A second point to note is that the Bengali middle class no longer believes in presenting books on wedding occasions; the standard gift these days is compact disc recordings of breakdance music.

Re-writing history

25 May 2002

History is the story of the past. How this history is written, that is, the method or manner or approach for chronicling the past, is historiography: a mind is at work, and this mind determines the approach to history-writing. Sometimes history can be written on the basis of total mindlessness as well. But not applying the mind is also a method; mindless historiography can therefore not always be discarded as junk.

In the olden days, a distinction was made between historians and historiographers. History as authorized by the rulers was historiography. The official historian was the historiographer. He had no competition, because none was around to question the writ of the rulers. When ancient Greeks such as Herodotus, Thucydides and Xenophon wrote history, they wrote the official version; the plebians did not occupy any space in it, or rather, they occupied whatever space the rulers permitted the historiographers to set aside to describe the life and living of the section of human species condemned to slavery. The circumstances were not any different in the case of Roman history; Sallust, Cicero, Livy and Tacitus concentrated on the goings-on in the palace and its vicinities: some of them were verbose in the manner of Cicero, while some others were as tight-lipped as Tacitus. The central point of history-writing however remained unchanged: to describe a universe revolving round the axis of the dominant class or classes. Plato's *Republic* was not exactly history, it presented a concept of what history ought to be; it nonetheless underlined once more the supremacy of those situated at the top of the social pyramid.

Pluralism in history-writing is a development of the latest half-a-millennium. Even the nature of society changed and it tended to assume a more complex shape, historians too began to embark on separate heterogeneous sojourns. Different streams of historiography emerged. Historians came to contend with one another alongside groups and classes clashing with one another. The world lost its unilinear flavour; so did its scripted annals. It was henceforth not only his story vis-à-vis her story, it was also my story versus your story versus the story of our nephew or niece thrice removed.

Fortunately or unfortunately, the matter did not quite end there. The *Dead Sea Scrolls*, for instance, do not describe merely a particular format of history; they proceed beyond and give rise to theory or theories on the basis of which policy is formulated either to guide contemporary action or to project the course of the future. About everyone can play the game: my history is superior to your history and I derive policy prescriptions accordingly. A very recent episode comes to mind. The airport at Port Blair in the Andaman Islands has been renamed after V.D. Savarkar, the Hindu Mahasabha ideologue who had been banished to the cellular jail there by the British authorities in the early decades of the twentieth century. The Bharatiya Janata Party has reasons to be beholden to the memory of Veer Savarkar. The redesignation of the airport at the Andamans will however be regarded by many as a mischievous act of the first order. Usually firebrand revolutionaries, who swore to oust the foreigners from the country by whatever means, including armed manoeuvres, were sent to the Andamans. They spent long years, sometimes stretching to even twenty, in solitary cells with shackled hands and feet. In subjugated India, they were acclaimed as the greatest of heroes. In this slot of heroes will certainly fall the prisoners transported for life to the Bay of Bengal island because of their culpability for the uprisings in Chittagong, in the 1930s. The BJP, for its own excellent reasons, chose to ignore them while mulling over the issue of giving a name to the Port Blair airport. In its lexicons, heroes are perhaps anti-heroes. It opted for Savarkar.

V.D. Savarkar was by no stretch of the imagination a vanguard the revolutionaries were proud of. According to their light, he was a renegade. From his prison cell in the Andamans, he used to write ingratiating letter after letter to the British masters: he was repentant, he promised to turn over a new leaf, from now on he would cooperate with the authorities and unearth all conspiracies against the empire, would they kindly release him forthwith? He pledged to be, on repatriation, a ceaseless champion of British imperialism. All this is well-documented.

Admirers of the men and women who participated in the raids on the Armoury and the European Club in Chittagong could justifiably feel chagrin. The Port Blair airport could have been named after the great revolutionary heroine, Pritilata Waddedar. It could have been named after Ganesh Ghosh, or collectively after all the participants in the Chittagong operations. It could have been dedicated to the hallowed memory of the *guru* of these heroes and heroines, Surya Sen, who was sent to the gallows by the foreign rulers in 1934. They naming it after Savarkar, at least some people would conclude, is a deliberate affront to India's war of independence.

Getting worked up over the issue is however neither here not there. Less than a quarter of the national electorate might have voted for the BJP in the 1999 elections. But it succeeded in gathering a number of calculating hangers-on to go along with it, and who, by implication, endorsed the Hindutva agenda. Therefore there is not much point in zeroing in on the BJP or its ministers. They have the votes in the Lok Sabha which enable them to rewrite Indian history and change the syllabi in schools, colleges and universities. Facts are not to be considered as any problem; in case necessary, the Ministry of Human Resources Development might even order the manufacture of a certain genre of facts. If, for reasons of state, it is important to coopt Harappa as an integral part of Hindu civilization, why, facts should not stand in the way. That is historiography for you. In any event, the theory has already been sponsored in diverse quarters: faith overrides facts; where so called forth, faith is capable of creating facts.

Please hold your horses, there is little scope for any sense of outrage here. Was not *Rashomon* a much hailed film, and accepted as a trendsetter? The same datum, the datum of a murder, is interpreted in several ways, and you are welcome to take your pick: all that is needed is cultivation of an appropriately cynical frame of mind; things will then fall in their respective places.

Once the British empire qualifies for a reverential reassessment, a consistent pattern emerges all over the system. Rewriting history is rendered into an absorbing occupation. Thomas Babington Macaulay is no longer the planter of the poison tree which weeded out the Indian languages from official deliberations and ensured the sprouting of English education so as to provide the rulers with an ample supply of clerks and scribes. Sociologists and historians in institutes of higher learning in India are at work to magnify the role of Macaulay in charting the route map of Indian emancipation. Economic historians are not lagging behind either. Liaquat Ali Khan, the first native to be installed as Finance Minister of India, albeit in the interim administration of 1946, was unspeakably bad; he was a Muslim Leaguer and prepared a budget which proposed to soak the Hindu capitalists. Instead, Jeremy Raisman, the Finance Member in the Viceroy's Executive Council, who preceded Liaquat Ali Khan as helmsman of the finance department, must be extolled: his budgets were relatively soft on the rich and, what is more important, he had the reputation of being anti-Muslim, both impeccable credentials.

In this brave new century, all is right with the world, theology will dominate history as well as economics. Both areas of study will be recognized as offspring of beliefs and prejudices. A dear departed friend, who spent long years in the Pakistan administration, was a besotted non-conformist: he was in the habit of regaling the company on evening occasions at his house with pontifications on the nuances of economics. Islamic economics, he would explain, could be summed up as *insha-allah*, price falls, *suhan-allah*, demand increases. Dictatorial economics, on the other hand, was delineated by the following outburst: if the president so orders, the blooming price has jolly well to fall, and the blighted demand better rise, for, if neither does as bid, the benign president with the clipped accent is going to shoot both of them dead. To dispute the departed friend's descriptions would have been pointless: he witnessed manifestations of both kinds of economics in Pakistan in the 1960s. He was just illustrating facets of the same theology – one facet representing wishfulness, the other the authoritarian propensity.

We would like to smile, but can we really afford to? Consider the grand credit policy pursued by the government of India and the Reserve Bank over the past few years. The price of money is being lowered, the availability of credit is being liberalized. The demand for money should therefore go up; investment too must rise, since lowering the price of money and widening its availability are bound to expand the demand for goods and services. The expectation aired seems to be a joint supply of prayer and enjoining. And now the ultimate theological instrument is proposed to be put on display. The price of money will very soon be determined, the Finance Minister has announced, through free competition among the commercial banks, the state will be a recluse. Politicians are by definition incapable of thinking, but in-house economic practitioners are expected to possess a trained logical mind. Suppose, given the structure of distribution of land and other assets in Indian society, the demand for goods and services fails to pick up whatever the inducements from the supply side, what prospect will the banks face were they to follow the grammar of the official prescription? They compete with one another, lower the rate of interest to entice new demand into their parlour; new demand still plays hooky; the banks lower the interest rate further. A sort of trade war ensues among the banks and the rate of interest touches the nadir of zero. Will the monetary system survive such a denouement? Even if it does not, we will conceivably be told not to worry; upholding the principle of the free market is the essence of the matter.

Enrich thyselves

14 September 2002

An esteemed colleague, himself resident in Gujarat, was commenting on the shameful events in the state six months ago. He was particularly distressed at the phenomenon of supposedly sophisticated women from affluent families actively participating in the vandalizing of shops owned by members of the minority community. This development, he felt, provides concrete evidence of the growing materialism of the Indian middle class.

The colleague went a bit further. He wondered whether this materialism is not the outcome of the process of globalization the country has been going through since the early 1990s, and just stopped short of suggesting a direct link between globalization and avarice. Even this half-inference is significant, for it amounts to a half-confession: the colleague has been one of the most prominent votaries of global integration.

Whatever that be, why blame the Gujarati gentry alone? The urge to indulge in the good things of life is a ubiquitous propensity in the country. Worn-out cliches of the genre of plain living and high thinking now raise a horse laugh. The pristine example of the new national culture is the demeanour of our top-notch cricketers. They had recently engaged in a major hassle with the Board of Control for Cricket in India. A mini-World Cup championship competition is scheduled to begin in Colombo from next week. The International Cricket Conference, of which the BCCI is an affiliate and which is organizing the event, has set some ground rules for players participating in the competition: for one month preceding and one month following the mini-World Cup matches, the players will not be entitled to enter into any separate contractual arrangements with their own sponsors; the ICC has its sponsor and its writ must be obeyed by each and every player. That is to say, no player will be permitted to benefit from double sponsorship, the ICC sponsor's endorsements will be the only ones on display.

This will, without doubt, cause some inconvenience, including monetary loss, to some players. While initially the grumbling with the terms set was fairly widespread, players from other contesting countries nonetheless decided to fall in and abide by the ICC rule. Not the Indian players. They held out and refused to sign on the dotted line till the very last hour. They were served an ultimatum by the BCCI, which went to the length of choosing a substitute set of players to go to Colombo in case the senior players continued to be adamant. Of the eighteen Indian cricketers currently touring England who refused to sign, a handful of three or four 'star' players, in fact, took the initiative to organize the stand-off.

The front-rank players carry considerable weight. Because of the dazzle of their performance, they have emerged as outstanding crowd-pullers: sponsors make a beeline for them. The BCCI shows them deference; gate receipts and revenue from the sale of television rights, of which the BCCI gets a hefty share, are correlated to the performance of these cricketers on the field. It is a heavenly situation for the prima donnas in the team. They are pampered and coddled by the cricket authorities, by advertisers and by the general public. Those players who are yet to receive recognition as master performers also bank on the patronage of the stars, who can help them during the team-selection process. Besides, the seniors are in a position to place the juniors in touch with sponsors; proximity to sponsors is crucial for money-making from advertisements and endorsements. It is therefore virtually impossible for the lesser players not to agree with what the seniors say. The star players come to assume that the universe revolves round them. They earn fabulous sums. They think they have the divine right to such fabulous money-making.

The fact that players from other countries have signed the ICC pledge but Indian cricketers have not, is not much of a puzzle either. The relative size of the Indian consumer goods market counts. Ours is a poor country – one of the poorest in United Nations ranking – but at least 10 per cent of Indian citizens, one hundred million people or thereabouts, have a comfortable level of living comparable to, and sometimes superior to, that enjoyed by the average population in quite a few advanced industrial countries. None of the other cricket-playing countries can boast of an affluent citizenry of near-equal size able to bid for consumer goods and services from the market. The players from the other countries have obviously less bargaining power than the Indian players. Cricketers from Britain, Australia, New Zealand, Pakistan and South Africa caved in, in no time: the Indian players did not.

The latter have been most forthcoming in expressing their views. It is they who represent Indian cricket, and not the BCCI. Men and women flock to the ground or sit glued to the television screen to watch them play and marvel at the quality of their performance. The profit which the ICC will make from holding the mini-World Cup business will be partly distributed among the cricketing authorities in the different member-countries. The BCCI will be one of the beneficiaries. The Indian Board of Cricket Control, however, the players complain, is likely to pass on to them a bare 5 per cent of what it will get from the ICC. In the circumstances, to prohibit them from entering into separate contracts with their personal sponsors is, according to Indian players, unjust in the extreme. They who sow should reap, at least should reap a reasonable share of the crop. If the players refused to sign the bond and opted out of the mini-World Cup, gate receipts and revenue from television rights were bound to tumble. The BCCI should, therefore, see reason and join with the players to present a united front against the International Cricket Conference. It is, the players have suggested, an immense tragedy that, instead, the BCCI should decide to combine with the ICC for the purpose of doing in the poor players.

Maybe the players have a point, perhaps they deserve a bit more generosity from the ICC and BCCI, although one can never be sure whether they are virtue personified. They certainly have been overdoing their show of intransigence. Self-righteousness should not go too far. The cricket stars are of course blessed by ethereal talent, the exhibition of this talent dazzles spectators and telly-watchers. They therefore have the right, they argue, to set their own price. If the ICC and the BCCI would not listen to them, they would refuse to cooperate; if they did not cooperate, the mini-World Cup, they were sanguine, would be a flop.

India's cricketers were suffering from a handicap though. Players from all other participating countries had signed; the Indian players were the only deviants. The absence of the Indian stars would have detracted from the worth of the event to Indian viewers. Even so, the Australians, the Pakistanis, the West Indians, the New Zealanders and the English teams would have been in Colombo in full strength. The Indian absence, or the presence of a second-grade Indian team, would not have made much of a difference. Television watchers elsewhere in the world would hardly miss the Indian superstars. The Indian players matter, but they largely matter for the Indian consumer market. The potential loss in case the Indian stars boycotted Colombo would have affected mostly the sponsors in India; and had they been adversely affected, the money flow to the Indian stars would have thinned out too.

But leave all this aside. Does not the ego of India's cricket divas richly deserve to be brought down a peg or two? They have a market value only because the Indian economy has been so organized as to ensure the availability of roughly one hundred million comfortably placed people in a position to acquire and enjoy consumer goods of all descriptions. The economy is what it is since the system is what it is, ravaged by inegalitarianism, with horrid inequalities in income and assets distribution. The poor starve, they go without clothes, they lack shelter, they do not get the opportunity to elementary education, they are denied minimum health facilities including supply of potable water, they are deprived of cultivable land and adequate employment opportunities. On paper, India is a democratic socialistic republic. But both democracy and socialism are most peculiarly defined: the top decile of the nation grab all the goodies. They are able to do it at the courtesy of the rest of the population. The rest of the population are not even rudimentarily organized and bereft of the awareness which could spur them to fight for and win their rights.

The inequalities in the distribution of income and assets constitute the key element enabling the setting up of an alluring consumer goods market made up of one hundred million luxury-loving Indians. Our star cricketers, some of whom reputedly earn anything between 20 and 50 crore rupees annually, should have the modesty to admit what they owe to the nation's poor. It is because the poor are oppressed and exploited that the cosy consumer goods market, backed by ample purchasing power, has emerged. The cricketers may have divine talent, but it would not have earned them their living had the poor, by their abnegation, either voluntary or forced, not paved the way for the creation of fabulous wealth on the part of the nation's cricketers.

One final matter. True, in the post-globalization era, morality is a dirty word. Never mind, what about a sense of aesthetics? Does it not sound obscene to the cricket prima donnas that, while drought and other afflictions scorch the land and nearly one-third of the nation have not the means to buy even subsistence food, they engage in bargaining bouts to raise their own annual income from 5 to 10 crore rupees, or from 10 to 20 crore? But, then, aesthetics is a matter defined by narrow subjectivity: these young men, earning astronomical sums of money, feel terribly exploited; therefore they are exploited.

It was perhaps ego that was proving the stumbling block, but finally, latest reports indicate, the Indian players too have capitulated and signed the document they were asked to sign. The particular chapter may have ended for the present. The issue nonetheless remains: the cricketers need to be taught the facts of life.

The miracle-maker

18 January 2003

. . . where angels fear to tread. But in case an angelic occasion presents itself, why shy away from the act of indiscretion? So here goes.

The Calcutta élite are in a tizzy. They are agog at the prospect of experiencing what in American parlance is known as a 'double-header'. Mother Teresa was already a Calcutta-based Nobel Laureate. She might soon be a Calcutta-based Saint too. According to reports, the Congregation for the Cause of Saints recently met in Vatican City and took a decision to beatify the Mother, that is to say, to declare her to be a Blessed of the Church. This is one step forward to the

attainment of Sainthood. To qualify for beatification, the saintly person concerned is supposed to accomplish two miracles, one after another. There is a
further conditionality: these miracles are to be performed after the person has
shuffled his or her mortal coils and retired to heaven. Mother Teresa died in
1997. Two years after she passed away, that is to say, in 1999, Monica Besra, a
thirty-year-old adivasi woman in the district of south Dinajpur in northern Bengal was, it was stated, blessed by a miracle performed by the Mother. Monica
was undergoing treatment for a tumour in her stomach in the Nabajiban Ashram
of the Missionaries of Charity, the network of succour built by the Mother. Monica's
story is short and simple. One September night, she prayed and prayed to Mother
Teresa to relieve her of her illness; suddenly the Mother appeared in her dream
and took charge. When Monica woke up next morning, the tumour was gone.
The sisters in the Ashram cried in ecstasy: it was a miracle and instantly became
international news.

The cardinals, bishops and priests who met earlier this year in the papal
headquarters deliberated over the happening and formally recognized it as a
miracle. Mother Teresa has, in a way, therefore reached the half-way house
towards the attainment of sainthood. All that the cardinals, bishops and priests
constituting the Congregation for the Cause of Saints have now to do is to scrounge
for another miracle attributable to the Mother and, whoa, Calcutta's élite would
have their prayer answered. The Mother, who publicized the city's squalour,
poverty and heartlessness to the world in a uniquely humanitarian manner, would
be a Saint on top of being a Nobel Prize winner.

There is a hitch though. The woman who was said to be cured by the
miracle, Monica Besra, had been admitted as a patient earlier, in 1997, in the
government hospital at Balurghat, the district headquarters of south Dinajpur.
Her medical records are fully available. These records indicate that she was
cured of her 'tubo-ovarian mass' in the hospital itself in May 1999, at least three
months earlier than the date on which she and the Missionaries of Charity claimed
the miracle to have taken place. According to the hospital superintendent,
M. Murshed, an ultrasonography of her stomach done on 29 May had established the disappearance of the tumour. Such ovarian masses, Dr Murshed explained, were common amongst women suffering from tuberculosis. Induced by
malnutrition, Monica was suffering from tuberculosis.

This is therefore a sort of tussle between two assertions, one claiming
healing by medical care and the other claiming faith-healing. The medical records
at the hospital are proving to be a nuisance. Since they suggest that Monica
Besra was actually cured three months ahead of that prayerful night, professional cynics can now indulge in the prank they are so good at: they can question
the authenticity of the miraculous act and, adding insult to injury, pass a Henry
Fordish judgment: all miracles are bunk.

Come to think of it, the villain of the piece is information technology.

Thanks to the technological revolution that has overwhelmed the world in recent decades, information travels further than sound, and sometimes further than light even. The Middle Ages and the more primitive times did not suffer from this disadvantage. Holy persons had then all the time and space available to them to perform a miracle and have it duly recognized by the Congregation at Vatican City. A couple of such miracles, and the imprimatur of sainthood would descend upon the miracle-maker as a matter of course. For hundreds of years on end, the papacy has created such saints, and no family planning programme had intruded either. The medical profession was not sufficiently advanced. Medical records were non-existent. Information technology was yet to be. What is most important, cynics could be summarily beheaded.

Unfortunately, the Monica Besra episode cannot be just brushed aside as an ordinary happening. It has a relevance in the context of Gujarat. Religious fanaticism has climbed inglorious peaks in this western state in the country in the course of the past few months. Reasoning has been forced to take a back seat, and faith is being claimed to be, without question, superior to objective reality. Sophisticated circles in urban circuits, proud of their faculty for rational cerebration, are generally disdainful of Hindu obscurantism. They are, they profess, prepared to fight to their last breath, the excesses of the puranic tribes. They are, all of a sudden, in a jam. During all these years, it was as smooth as it could be. Mother Teresa was the in thing; seasonal donations to the Missionaries of Charity would be flaunted by this species with a somewhat superior air. The virus of sectarianism and narrow-mindedness would be condemned. Such alumni of, for instance, the Calcutta élite now face a dilemma. Saints from the distant past were innocuous idols. Ordinary folk, and even the cream of society, did not have to bother over the details of the circumstances which took them to sainthood. Miracles, as long as these happened in the remote past, were phenomena one did not need to take seriously, nor was there any compulsive need to scrutinize the credentials of such miracles. Missionary people could therefore spread themselves across the world and open schools, hospitals and charitable homes in the name of assorted saints. The apostles and their preachings were taken for granted, and, along with them, saints and the marvels and miracles attributed to them.

Glory by association, the Calcutta crowd would dearly love their city to qualify as the abode of a Saint. Mother Teresa's beatification and prospective sainthood are therefore deliriously welcome tidings. On the other hand, the intellectual hurdle cannot quite be surmounted. The moment you express jubilation over the Mother's forthcoming near-certain attainment of sainthood, you also have to bear with the embarrassment of tacit acceptance of the genuineness of the Monica Besra miracle. The claim of the miracle cuts across the nitty-gritty of the data enshrined in the medical records of the Balurghat hospital. It cuts across the evidence of medical diagnosis and therapy. Either the doctors in that hospital are impostors, or those putting forth the claim on behalf of Mother Teresa are. Even honest impostors are, after all, impostors.

We cannot, alas, slip into the comfortable security of ancient times when miracles were dime a dozen and few, or perhaps none, had the guts to question their authenticity. In this first decade of the twenty-first century, with IT to the right of us, IT to the left of us and IT in front of us, it is impossible for us to accept miracles qua miracles. They have to be scientifically established. Should we try to cut any corners here, the Vishwa Hindu Parishad and the Bajrang Dal will jump on us. Mother Teresa's miracle and the disowning of Ram Janmabhoomi cannot quite go together. If the latter is a hoax, the former too is.

It is in fact a problem facing all Indians. The twenty-first century and puranic fervour are impossible fellow-travellers. One has to choose in life, particularly if one claims to be a rational human being. Either the twenty-first century exists, or Lord Rama with his kingdom does. For the Calcutta gentry, the problem is even acuter. They feel most comfortable with Mother Teresa. The dear lady has been gone for the past five years, but she continues to be very much *à la mode*. She coexists, snugly and simultaneously, with the state administration's supposed devotion to Left radicalism and the scientific spirit. Gujarat has to be countered, on to battle; the Bengali vanguard are desperately anxious to mount the barricade of reason and secularism. In the given situation, what are they going to do with the miracle ascribed to Mother Teresa? Debunk it? But were they to treat it with contempt, they have to say goodbye to the Mother herself and the pride and glory she has brought to them. This is, let us admit, an archetypal instance of the prisoner's dilemma referred to in the preliminary textbooks on game theory. The mathematicians do not mind being occasionally checkmated. It is because of seemingly intellectual *culs-de-sac* that we come across unsolved puzzles in mathematical sciences. A non-solution of this nature will not however do for the Bengal gentry, or, for that matter, any conscientious Indian. The option has to be exercised, either for rationality or for black magic. Should you want to vote for the Left Front in West Bengal and, at the same time, be besotted by the Missionaries of Charity, let us then talk turkey, you might as well join the *parivar* presided over by the Singhals and the Togadias.

Facets of civilization

12 April 2003

How unfair, how mean on the part of the Iraqi tyrant. The holy Anglo-American expedition is yet to unearth weapons of mass destruction supposedly stashed by Saddam Hussein. Iraq is being razed to the ground; men, women and children of the country are being butchered hour by hour and minute by minute; but the hidden armoury cannot be traced. What do you expect the Anglo-American junta to do in the circumstances? As far as verified data go, they – Bush and his gang – have the monopoly of weapons of mass destruction. These weapons have now been deployed to ferret out Saddam's weaponry. The effort though is a failure. Doesn't all this prove that Saddam is a blackguard of the first order? He has, in fact, no cache of the prohibited weapons. He has, however, been behaving in a manner which made Bush-men believe that he possessed such weapons. What a scoundrel he is! He deserves to be hanged and shot, guillotined and garroted for his knavery.

Things have started going awry. The wretched Iraqis are not behaving like meek lambs arriving for the slaughter. The junta is slaughtering them all right, but, what cheek, what audacity, they are not submitting themselves like lambs. Even their women have taken to small arms and guarding streets, lanes and by-lanes. Such demeanour is leaving the Anglo-American invaders with no alternative; they have to intensify their barbaric operations. The Anglo-American establishments, everybody knows, are not by nature savage beasts; it is ill-mannered provocation indulged in by the Iraqis which is forcing the envoys of civilization to have recourse to satanic murders and destruction. The end-product is black humour of the luridest kind. By exhibiting four captured American soldiers on television, the Iraqis have breached the Geneva Convention protocol. The allegation is posted by George W. Bush, the gentleman who has made smithereens of the United Nations and its laws, and engaged in committing genocide in Iraq.

Civilization obviously has several facets. Even as the two self-appointed leaders of the Christian west are embarked on their killing spree, the law of dialectics too has set at work. Dissent and protests are over-running Europe, the Americas, Australia and considerable segments of Asia. Even the snooty Oscar Awards ceremony has been spoiled. The processions, rallies, demonstrations and day-and-night vigils seem unending. This is a disastrous development. How could you, for Christ's sake, liquidate the last vestiges of the Babylonian civilization if your own backyard is so uncivil and treason-bent? The junta is therefore being forced to fight on two fronts simultaneously: silencing Saddam, and disciplining the backwoodsmen devoid of all patriotic virtues, which poses a genuine long-term problem.

At a certain point of time sooner or later, if not sooner at least an expense-laden later, the land mass known as Iraq will perhaps disappear from the face of earth and only a cluster of craters, hollows and spent missiles will make up the shrivelled concourse of the Tigris and Euphrates valley. That is to say, Iraq will be a closed chapter and a new one, the phase of 'reconstruction', so-called, will begin. Contracts are already being doled out by the US administration. The multinational oil and energy corporations have been invited in and fat contracts have been assured, a splendid opportunity for the tycoons to pick easy money. Provided one still retains both a sense of humour and a proper perspective, the *modus operandi* adopted will assume a family resemblance to what was once proposed by that departed gay fella, John Maynard Keynes. Keynes had a bee in his bonnet. Creation of effective demand, he thought, was the key to licking the problem of mass unemployment and aborted economic prosperity. Bush–Blair are following the Keynesian prescription in the minutest detail. They are deploying troops, marines, fighters, bombers, aircraft carriers and the rest to reduce Iraq to nothingness, thereby to conjure an effective demand for labour, steel, cement, mortar, concrete and sundry other building materials needed to rebuild Iraq in the Anglo-American image. All this is in addition to stimulating activity and income for the oil and energy companies. New oil reserves will now come under the control of the Anglo-Americans, providing fillip for their exploitation. Oil fields set on fire by the Iraqis will also need to be rekindled; work and profits will then soar further, taking more than adequate care of the problematic of effective demand.

Come to think of it, the wholesale – and wholesome – destruction of Iraq will have other advantages. The rest of the world, not possessing enough of a Christian pedigree, are a moody lot. They have strange notions in regard to the content and meaning of human civilization. Some of them claim, raucously, to be worshippers of peace. Such peace-mongers are fifth columns at work. Do you not remember those pre-Gorbachev days, when the communists would organize fakeries such as the World Council of Peace? The moment you hear the word 'peace , you should therefore rush for the protective missiles lying in repose next to your *chaise lounge*. Peace is evil and the peaceniks have to be disarmed in country after country. Matter always prevails over the mind. One effective way of neutralizing the peace-mongers is to offer them lollipops, for instance, a share of the reconstruction loot. It is in human nature to be generous in victory, even France and Germany could have been invited to partake of the booty. But there is a limit to courteous behaviour. Since the governments of these two countries opposed the putsch into Iraq, we will not, repeat will not, allow them in the neighbourhood of Iraq's oil installations and reserves, where the real gravy lies.

Besides, one never knows, odd elements here and there are not always as worldly-wise as the parliamentarians of Turkey. The latter had initially turned down the American request to use their air space in the war against Iraq. Swiftly followed a curt communiqué from Foggy Bottom, cancelling five or six billion dollars worth of economic and military aid to Turkey. Within twenty-four hours, the Turkish parliament came round and accorded the hitherto withheld permission. Unfortunately, several other countries are reluctant to learn from the example set by the descendants of the Ottomans; they are proving to be bribe-proof. They talk an altogether strange language, with a surfeit of such words as humanity, kindness, empathy, love, justice, restraint from greed and avarice, and so on. What is worse, these species are attracting adherents within the United States itself. Their number growing with every day, the make-peace-not-war brigades are ferociously active everywhere. Iraq will be obliterated in due course, leaving only a trace of its ruined oil reserves. Even then, this army of vigilantes will perchance continue to be on the march. They will be constant thorns in the flesh of imperialists and colonialists. No respecters of military might, immune to seduction by offer of a share of the Iraq reconstruction pie, they will persist in their nagging opposition to imperial lust. The nagging will soon assume the form of a permanent rebellion. This particular collateral damage has the potential of turning out to be the mother of all collateral damages. Developments of this nature will make it impossible for those bestowed with a Bush–Blair mindset to relax their guard. They will, every moment, be the target not just of 'friendly fires', but unfriendly fires as well. The sum of these moments will constitute their existence. The fires could begin with the revolt of a bunch of MPs or assorted members of the House of Representatives or one or two diplomats manning foreign missions. Rebellion is a contagious disease, more so when the rebels choose to flaunt a conscience. Nothing could be a greater human tragedy. Men like George W. Bush and Tony Blair are in a position to forsake their conscience, or, still better, they never had one. Others are not so fortunate.

All told, we could enter the Age of Guerrillas. Osama bin Laden will be the role model for the millions of rebels in every land. Terror will be rendered into a common daily experience. The technology of terror is advancing with such rapidity that, give or take a short interval of time, the assembling of nuclear, biological or chemical weapons for mass destruction might become child's play. Weapons are neutral-minded instruments of devastation: they can be directed against anybody, including tribes swearing allegiance to the likes of Bush or Blair.

There is however always a silver lining amid the darkest constellation of clouds. The Indians, as a people, are made of a different stuff. They are not given to sentimentalities; they have denuded their constitution of the milk of human kindness. A single-minded community, they live for cricket and they die for cricket. The good imperialists could please relax, Indians will not die for

Iraq. Sunday, 23 March, was the litmus test. In towns and cities and open spaces all over the world, including of course the United States, anguished, restless millions marched, demanding the cessation of war and praying for the outbreak of peace. India and Indians refused to keep such disreputable company. It was World Cup day at Johannesburg, South Africa. It was a matter of life and death for Indians and they refused to fall prey to any diversionary tactics. The rest of the earth's population are welcome to fight their great battle for peace and against the bestial Anglo-British aggression against the hapless Iraqis. The Indians have other priorities. Every Indian habitat that Sunday was given to extraordinarily special prayers, including prayers for the fulfilment of wishes that were horses. The Vishwa Hindu Parishad and the Rashtriya Swayamsevak Sangh were present in full force at the Wanderers cricket ground in Johannesburg, performing regulation *yagnas* for Indian success. Members of the Indian cricket team were given the treatment; they were consecrated as direct *avatars* of Brahma, Vishnu, Maheshwar rolled into one. Prominent political personalities flew in, including one or two Left parliamentarians. India Incorporated was present in full strength, occupying fantastically high-priced box seats. So too present was the Bombay filmdom in its entirety. The rituals accompanying the World Cup final were adequately anaesthetized, that is, Hinduized. A savant has recently made the important observation that whatever is happening around us is a part of the great Indian national revolution initiated by Indira Gandhi, subsequently further advanced by her successor son. Even the World Cup encounters must have reminded the savant of Indira Gandhi and her achievements: cricket is synonymous with the Indian national revolution. On a different occasion, when asked what precisely in the proceedings stirred in him memories of the late lamented prime minister, pat came his response: 'Don't cross-examine me, everything I see reminds me of Indira Gandhi.' The World Cup final must have evoked the same emotions in the savant.

All is well that does not end well. The rest of the world marched against war and for peace; Indians, proud and different, glued their eyes on the television set. The architects of destiny did some clever conspiring, India was mercilessly cut down in the final encounter. Perhaps that was humanity's revenge.

The colonial bug for ever

13 September 2003

If a town cynic is not around, does he not deserve to be invented? Consider the piquancy of the situation. The populace of Calcutta is split down the middle. They were, till now, ensconced in the belief that their credentials were impeccable: what glory, that seventeenth-century merchant-adventurer from British shores, Job Charnock, had established this settlement some 300-odd years ago; the day he arrived was therefore the birthday of Calcutta. The pride had kept swelling in the breast: they were no dispensable category, their pedigree was pucca colonial. The patter of little boys and girls attending English-medium schools had a quality of conditioned reflex: Christopher Columbus discovered America, Job Charnock discovered Calcutta. Independence came and went, the Left movement grew from strength to strength in the neighbourhood, but the pride in the pedigree remained undiminished. Then something funny happened. A landowning family, at present in somewhat diminished circumstances, suddenly got incensed; its lineage, it claimed, was at least two centuries more ancient than Charnock's; it had documentary evidence, from the Mughal days, to prove its ancestry. The family got highly indignant at the spectacle of Anglophile Bengalis making asses of themselves. No, not that English rogue, it is they, the Roy Chowdhurys of Savarna, who were the original settlers of Calcutta, these days aka Kolkata. The Roy Chowdhurys moved a writ petition in the High Court; the honourable judges were made to sit up. The High Court bench appointed a committee consisting of eminent historians to look into the matter. Perhaps the composition of the committee had its particular bias, perhaps it was yet to come out of the haze of anti-colonial blues, perhaps it merely wanted to double the fun. After deliberating for more than one year, the committee conceded that the Roy Chowdhurys had a point, their arrival in Calcutta in fact preceded Job Charnock's. The honourable judges did the honourable thing. They accepted the committee's recommendations and declared that, sorry, Charnock had to be deprived of his claim of parentage in the light of the DNA test by the history experts. And once the city was without a founder, it was without a date of birth too; the schoolchildren are currently confused beyond words.

This is a development which many amongst Calcutta's choicest citizenry consider to be a major calamity. A city without a birthday is like a Verdi opera without Maria Callas. Never mind the High Court dictum, never mind if Job Charnock has been officially dethroned, the day Charnock anchored his boat at the Kidderpore marshes would still continue to be observed by them as the city's birthday. Calcutta urchins had once scribbled in bold calligraphy on their city's walls: China's chairman is our chairman. Calcutta's sophisticates are determined to chant in similar vein: Charnock's advent was Calcutta's as well.

Call it a facet of cultural anthropology, call it the colonial bug for ever. The Bengalis remain incorrigibly provincial-minded, and the province of their mind is etched in loving colonial colours. No Sherwood forest girdles the city, it nonetheless flaunts a Sheriff, who is selected on an annual basis and consecrated with symbolic bread and wine. The Sheriff may be without any occupation, but the ritual is embedded in firmest colonial antecedents. Colonialism is dead, long live colonialism! Buttonhole a Calcutta householder holding a petty clerical job in some decrepit attorney's office; he would reel off, agog with excitement, his family history, his great-great grandfather was invested with a Rai Bahadurship way back in 1893; the great-great grandfather's name actually occurs in the roll of the first sixteen Rai Bahadurs thus honoured by the British crown.

No question, the Bengalis are a tribe deserving more pity than ridicule. But why pick on the Bengalis alone? Indian academia is currently overwhelmed by a ferocious tidal wave. The corpus of post-colonial and post-modern scholasticism expands with every day. This distinguished set has cornered a substantial chunk of research money afloat in the system. They abide by no nonsense, they have contempt for discourses which keep referring to the country's, and for that matter the world's, colonial and imperial past. They, and their like-minded comrades in residence in foreign universities, have outlived such puerility. The colonies and the empires ended nearly half a century ago, even the Soviet empire is dead and gone. The time has come for social scientists and others engaged in the pursuit and dissemination of knowledge, to grow up and cultivate a proper post-colonial/post-modern mind. This genre of mind is not easily definable. It is possible, though, to identify it by a number of tendencies and symptoms. It takes a dim view of class analysis of any phenomenon – just any phenomenon, whether belonging to the past or the present, whether taking place here or anywhere. All collectivities of a 'political' nature are invalid, problems and issues need to be explored in their micro-forms, groups and movements are bunk. Civil society is the only hegemony allowed *laissez-passer*. Governments and groups aspiring to capture governmental power are condemnable. Non-government organizations alone are worth reposing trust upon. The world admittedly must be reformed from time to time, but political formations are bound to make a hash of it, leave the task to the NGOs.

Anarchists of nineteenth-century vintage would surely have felt comfortable in this milieu of post-modernism. Be nihilistic; if you feel the urge to cite an authority in support of your own proposition, quote a fellow-nihilist; he/she will of course bear you out, and return the compliment. The post-colonials/post-moderns have set up a tightly knit, closed shop; solely those who are already in can be given admittance. Theories aired require to be either outrageously obfuscating, or outrageously original. For example, finance capital is hardly something to worry about; since colonies never ever conformed to a specific pattern, colonial exploitation is invalid as a concept; objective or scientific rules are, per se, obnoxious; categories are a hoax, class and class conflict too are unreal; all value systems are flawed; progress is undefinable, and therefore progress-mongers are to be mocked at.

Supply creates its own demand. Even the most preposterous nihilism sells. As a new book is spun out every couple of years, the fund-givers begin to be in awe of the author; she/he receives cross-country invitations to attend a breakfast or a lunch or a dinner discussion on an otiose theme; he/she is provided with at least a club-class return air ticket, accommodation in a luxury hotel and not pressed to speak beyond fifteen minutes. The author has arrived; she/he is a post-colonial/post-modern deity; whatever he/she says straightaway enters the scriptures.

Problems nonetheless threaten to rear their head. The post-moderns have nothing but contempt for the traditionalists who create concentric circles of acolytes and devotees, much in the manner of feudal lords and capitalist tycoons. Such dynasty – or empire-building – is a colonial concern, and must not detain the ideological nihilists. At the same time, be reasonable, it will be a cardinal sin to let dry up the intense gushing creativity of the post-colonial and post-modern oeuvre. Other lines of studies might shrivel up, post-colonialism and post-modernism could not. Thereby emerges the awareness of the necessary evil. The post-moderns too must organize themselves in caucuses and cabals, and engage in some demure empire-building. Empires are out, empires are the *élan vital*. International conferences multiply.

An additional uneasy question nags. Is not post-modernism too of respectable colonial heritage? It spread its wings in the 1970s and 1980s in the cosy havens of western universities, in Europe and North America. True, stray academics away from their native shores in Asia and Latin America found a niche in these locations and contributed their mite. But the working environment was quintessentially colonial; barring a few exceptions, the ideological roots too were overtly colonial, and, more importantly, the ventures were lavishly blessed by colonial cash. The tyranny of inheritance could not be got rid of. It is the erstwhile colonial masters who have laid the foundation stone of the new academic culture; the new nihilism suits them well. Even Afghanistan and Iraq have failed to rattle the post-moderns. American imperialism is a passing episode, leave it to the loose-limbed NGOs to tackle the difficulties that ensue. Global political mobilization is both futile and impractical.

The curse of the empire will not leave us. The curse of the empire has rendered existence in Calcutta into a mournful colonial experience. Much worse, it has kept in bondage the scholars and scholastic pretenders across the entire country even after more than half a century of formal political freedom. It is, in any case, a pretty long legacy. Charvaka, let us admit, was the last original thinker this land has produced. The succeeding crowd of alumni through the centuries have been basically synthesizers and copywriters of various shades and descriptions. The recent spate of midsummer and post-Christmas visitors – many amongst them expatriates – from European and American academic sites are no different. There is little original in their pontifications. Besides, they have deserted their countries; yet they hanker after recognition in the countries they have deserted. A hunger is at work. Evidently not quite recognized as progenitors of original thinking in the countries they have settled in, they shuffle back home to receive accolades from the colonial-minded natives. The post-colonials, post-moderns including, are as much lush colonial foliage.

There is a danger of being torn to pieces by *éminences grise*, but temptation is great for raising yet another query. Is the proliferation of faculties and departments on women's studies in Indian universities an altogether different kettle of fish? The Germaine Greers and the Gloria Steinems are supposed to be the ones who declared the global war of women's independence some forty years ago; the war set the continents ablaze one after another, western universities had a new occupation. It was inevitable that India did not remain unaffected for long. Centres for women's studies soon became *à la mode*; the syllabi, the research topics, even the clichés and jargons, are characterized by heavy American influence. But do not the Madam Camas and the Pandita Rama Bais pre-date these recent war heroines? A strong women's movement existed in the country long before the post-moderns arrived on the scene. Although not in English, a considerable body of literature developed in the nineteenth century itself in Indian languages: reports of episodes, incidents and law cases, biographies and autobiographies, semi-fictional accounts. These works were never extinct, even if not known to the university academics. Even French and Italian designers in the world of *haute couture* sooner or later reach the end of their imagination; at that point, the models are shuffled, but the designs only get new names. Post-colonials, please be not proud, scratch your heart, you too are lousy colonial hacks.

The conundrum of Nepal

8 November 2003

The Vishwa Hindu Parishad cannot understand it. Nepal is the only Hindu kingdom in the world; substantial sections of the people there are of north Indian ethnicity and bear names of Hindu gods and goddesses; the ruling family has long-time links with India and marries into the Rana clan dispersed along the higher and lower reaches of the Indo-Gangetic valley. And yet Nepal is hardly a benevolent land for Hindu chauvinism. Maoist communists, who are engaged in a relentless guerrilla war against the country's regime for the past seven years, control most of the countryside. Even in the national parliament, the second largest party happens to be the Communist Party of Nepal (United Marxist–Leninist). So, irrespective of whether one applies the criterion of parliamentary or extra-parliamentary influence, Marxists, and not revanchists of the Togadia–Singhal brand, reflect the overwhelming *vox populi* in Nepal.

This clinches several points. Not rapid religious sentiments, but hard economic realities, mould the psyche of a nation. If the chemistry is different in Aryavarta, that is because of an unnatural hiatus between people existing under today's canopy and their consciousness lagging millennia behind. To argue that British colonialism was the albatross which prevented the Indian mind to swim away from the corrosive waters of obscurantism, would be altogether banal. Hindu feudal ethos successfully resisted contamination from the spirit of enlightenment that was the major spin-off of British rule. The Mughals too had tried earlier to wear down this resistance, and failed. India obviously is an exceptional case defying the dynamics of history. Part of the responsibility for continuation of the same stagnation in the post-independence period has to be shared by the orthodox proletariat-loving parties. They have exhibited a fetish for verbal callisthenics, but failed to delve into the metabolism of either class realities or forces which could disturb such realities. The leaders of the parties belonging to the Left might well ponder over the fact that, at the dawn of independence, the Communist Party of India, though relatively small, was still the second largest party in the country; the situation is now qualitatively different, both ordinally and cardinally.

Nepal did not suffer from the India malaise. A book recently published, *The Nature of Underdevelopment and Regional Structure of Nepal: A Marxist Analysis* (Adroit Publishers, Delhi), offers some clues as to why Nepal could escape India's fate. The author of the book, Baburam Bhattarai, happens to be one of the top leaders of the Maoist guerrillas currently on the rampage across the length and breadth of the country. That does not diminish the book, it actually adds lustre to it.

Some irony, Bhattarai's life story bears a strong parallel to that of Indian students who once travelled to Great Britain for higher studies. The worldwide depression was at its worst in the 1930s. Europe was seething in discontent. The British empire was still a non-negligible political entity. For Indians, Britain was the metropolitan centre. It was easy for the bright generation of young Indians coming from affluent households to transit to radicalism, often to membership of the Communist Party of Great Britain, to join the global struggle against fascism, from there to comradely solidarity with the Republicans in the Civil War in Spain. For the earnest young Nepalese in the second half of the twentieth century, the metropolitan centre was India. They would travel to Chandigarh, Delhi, Lucknow, Allahabad, Patna and Calcutta for higher studies. *En route*, they would pick up ideas and assorted titbits of revolutionary praxis. Bhattarai found himself first in Chandigarh and then in New Delhi. He took a bachelor's degree, and subsequently a Ph.D., in architecture in Indian universities. He lingered at Jawaharlal Nehru University, honing the ideology of activism. These details however are a frivolity. Much more relevant is his success in organizing the Nepalese students in India into a radical political formation, and his contribution towards giving Marxism–Leninism–Maoism a Nepalese face. Bhattarai, of course, has had comrades equally steeled in activism. He is nonetheless different: he leads a ferocious rebellion and at the same time writes a treatise on facets of dialectical materialism, including its application to particular circumstances and events, such as the state of development, or, if you will, underdevelopment, in Nepal.

Even this two-in-one role of scholar–politician bears a strong resemblance to the perambulations of the first batch of the CPI leadership. B.T. Ranadive actually started life as a proper academic in the Bombay School of Economics and Sociology. He and such others as E.M.S. Namboodiripad and P.C. Joshi never discarded their thinking caps even in the most turbulent times; they set aside a certain time of each and every day for reading, thinking and writing – and producing books. The tradition has died out in India: a notion has struck roots that theorization is by and large a dated modality, one does not need to be literate – and learned – to understand socio-political realities. Nepal politics is in its early phase, the Baburam Bhattarais are therefore not yet deterred from reading, thinking and writing. Whether this trend will continue, only the future can tell. Were the Marxist movement in Nepal too to lapse into relative illiteracy, that would be a tremulous prospect. If conformity claims radical groups, could the spread of Hindu fundamentalism be averted for long in that country either?

Nepal is therefore a land of both hope and apprehension, depending upon where one's allegiance lies. Feudalism has an ancient history in the country, strongly resembling the annals of northern India. In a still overwhelmingly primitive economy, feudalism, if left undisturbed, leads to smaller and still smaller sized holdings, and to increasing fragmentation of land. Poverty is endemic in such a system, and as the decades roll by, the ancillary aspects of poverty – malnutrition, lack of literacy and high infant mortality – overwhelm the milieu. Surplus accumulated through ground-rent, usury and unfair terms of trade might have risen over time if land productivity had displayed a secular upward trend. That did not happen since there was little feedback from the capital extracted from land, while progressive fragmentation militated against efficiency per labour unit. Till 1950, the situation was complicated by two exogenous factors: (a) imperial presence, even if indirect, asserting itself through treaty arrangements with the British crown, and (b) the intrusion of Indian capital, mostly in trade and services. The export of Gurkha contingents to the British army could have turned the face of Nepal's villages and lifted it from the quagmire of underdevelopment. The reality bites were different; what was directly transferred to the Nepalese royal family by the British far exceeded the sum of subsistence wages paid to the Gurkha recruits, very little of whose income could filter back into the Nepal countryside. On the contrary, the degree of monopoly power exercised by the royal family and its appendages, such as the Ranas, increased significantly, intensifying the rate of exploitation of Nepal's masses.

Bhattarai draws attention to yet another datum. Perhaps because of his background in architecture, he has a searching eye for spatial arrangements. He points his finger at a riveting home-truth: not only is the long, thin territorial strip consisting of the Kathmandu valley and the lower Terai in the grip of the landed gentry, this class has spread its tentacles across the whole country. That is to say, apart from the standard phenomenon of inter-clan income inequalities, Nepal has to bear the cross of spatial inequalities, what many others would choose to refer to as regional inequalities. Trade, transport and commerce are also concentrated in Kathmandu and the Terais, partly because the latter region ensures a natural linkage with India. Tourism, including casino culture, suffers from a similar bias. Little of capital goods industry has developed in any part of Nepal. The consumption goods industries too are concentrated in Kathmandu and the Terais, and therefore emerge as a further instrument of spatial exploitation. Bhattarai articulates yet another lament: whatever cottage crafts were once located in the outlying provinces have tended to disappear due to intrusion of Indian imports and import substitution mostly centred around the Kathmandu valley: de-industrialization with a vengeance.

Poverty in Nepal, it is hardly surprising, has grown exponentially. There are, as yet, no safety valves to take care of the anger increasingly churning among the Nepalese peasantry and lower middle classes. Conceivably, this statement is only partly correct in the historical sense. In the early phase of the post-1950 era, the Nepal Congress Party and the Koiralas provided some hope. However, as the decades succeeded one another, both got gradually assimilated into the ruling class. For a while, radical presence from the middle classes, exemplified by the Pushpa Lals and the Sahana Pradhans – who too had earlier taken shelter in India and were proximate to communist formations – offered a second layer of hope. Things are moving fast and the generation of the Prachandas and the Bhattarais is apparently outflanking the senior radicals. On paper, the Communist Party of Nepal (UML) has a larger membership roll than the Maoists have. The ground reality in the villages tells a different story though. At least, this conclusion seems legitimate in the light of the extent of hold the Maoists have been able to exercise in the remote provinces.

Some quarters would love to look at the Nepal dilemma through the prism of a China–India face-off. It is hardly so. The Maoists have not as yet succeeded in attracting much sympathy from the Chinese Communist Party. As of now, China has other preoccupations. At the same time, part of the tilt of ordinary citizens towards the Maoists must be on account of the strong relationship, whether real or imaginary, between elements of the royal household and the Nepal Congress on the one hand, and Indian ruling groups on the other. Metropolitan capital to the Nepalese is, for all practical purposes, Indian capital; the paradigm of British colonial hegemony has faded into oblivion. Bhattarai's book has many theorizations, some ingenious and some not so, concerning the penetration of north Indian capital into the land-locked country and the material and moral havoc it has rendered. One does not necessarily have to agree with each of these propositions, but India's anxiety to keep Nepal out of China's sphere of influence has had several deleterious consequences. Add to this the other indubitable fact that the ingress of north Indian finance has the marks of footloose predatory capital, with insidious impact on the terms of trade between the two countries.

The intrinsic merit of *The Nature of Underdevelopment and Regional Structure of Nepal* is somehow diminished by Bhattarai's fondness for ideologically tilted terminology. One wishes there was another, shorter version of the book with the hierographics rendered into simple everyday language, so that it could have a wider reach amongst the struggling masses in Nepal. Others who should read this book are the mandarins in the Ministry of External Affairs at South Block, New Delhi – and, in addition, the cloak-and-dagger retinue in the Ministry of Home Affairs who love to flog the thesis that the Nepal Maoists too are a constituent of Pakistan's Inter-Services Intelligence.

TWO

TWO

Staying away from the nitty-gritty

22 January 2000

Details that are inconvenient are pushed aside. About half a dozen years ago, when the government decided to privatize insurance on the insistence of the International Monetary Fund and the World Bank, it went about the task according to strict grammar. The hoary custom had been set up during the Raj; the government constituted a committee to look into the problems afflicting the insurance industry and to recommend measures towards their solution. The committee was expected to put in a command performance and pump for wholesale denationalization of the insurance industry, thereby making it easy for the authorities to proceed in the manner foreign financial institutions had wanted them to proceed. The denouement was somewhat anti-climactic. The committee produced a modest-sized report stretching to 150 pages, of which only one-and-a-half pages concentrated on the issue of insurance denationalization. The rest of the report went to great lengths to extol the performance of the LIC and the GIC in the post-independent decades. And a number of chapters dealt with their future programme of work. But since the purpose of setting up the committee was clear-cut, the chairman, one presumes, persuaded his colleagues to add a brief, somewhat disjointed chapter, recommending the entry of private entities in the insurance sector.

In the course of the attempt to pass the insurance bill in the previous parliament, which failed, and the renewed attempt in the current parliament, which succeeded, there was not one reference from the treasury benches to the committee's report. The authorities must have been embarrassed no end that the committee was so inept while drafting its recommendations; its obfuscation of the issue was, to say the least, most disappointing. Not that it really mattered much. For, meanwhile, the message had gone down the line: it is the old liberal house, whatever the foreigners want to denationalize, please adhere to their *firman*; even more generally, whatever instructions the foreigners transmit, blindly conform to them without asking any question; you will be rapped hard on the knuckles should you have the temerity not to do so.

Given the class concordat between the two principal political parties, this time it was smooth sailing for the insurance bill in parliament. Important leaders of the Indian industrial world were present in full strength in the Lok Sabha galleries to witness the historical event. Some representatives of American insurance companies were also present. The tycoons from New York and Chicago could not be blamed for their exuberance, they only wanted to make an advance survey of the new property they were acquiring, and *gratis*. They had in fact also flown in two years ago at the time of the earlier endeavour to pass the bill; things however went awry on that occasion. This time, thank god, there was no mishap.

The entry of American and other foreign insurance companies, argue the spokesman of those favouring privatization, will, apart from contributing to an increase in available resources which could cater to faster economic growth for the nation, promote competition within the industry, and thereby raise efficiency as well. The unit cost of insurance will therefore come down; it will be without question a great boon to Indian citizens belonging to the middle and more humble classes.

Many of these assumptions belong to the realm of pure fiction, though. Bunches of Indians occasionally travel to the United States; some of them have relatives too more or less permanently settled in that country. Almost all of them have horrid experience of being at the receiving end of unkindness and worse whenever insurance cover was sought for a sudden illness or reimbursement claims filed for medical expenses incurred; dealing with the private insurance companies has proved to be a nightmare. Maybe Indians as a community are inclined to be emotional and lack in objectivity. Why not therefore switch over to pucca American testimony? John Grisham, the best-selling writer of American thrillers, spun out a story in the late 1980s chronicling in meticulous detail the shenanigans indulged in by American health insurance outfits. The unholy alliance between the insurance companies and the American Medical Association has also been widely commented upon in diverse discourses.

But since the authorities in New Delhi have already entered into commitments, philosophy will render its quiet verdict: what has to be done will be done; the dictum of the season needs to be accepted, with or without grace. Both earned profits and accumulating premium receipts will add to the coffers of the foreign insurance companies. According to one's judgment, receipts from premium payments will be wheedled out of the country. Nonsense, say the protagonists of the new economic order, this cannot happen; a specific provision in the new bill prohibits such transfers. Naiveté could not stretch any further. With the scrapping of the FERA, what was known as '*hawala*' till yesterday will henceforth constitute a most respectable category of international transfers; sifting illegitimate laundering of funds from legally valid transactions will be an impossibility; foreign insurance companies, rest assured, will once more have a whale of a time.

The nation has to go through the experience of a return to the pre-1955 conditions as far as the insurance industry is concerned, just as it has to cope with some of the other slings and arrows of fortune following the onset of globalization. Consider the brand of black humour the country's banking industry is exemplifying. Financial sector reforms must not be interrupted in any manner. Two widely circulated reports sponsored by the Reserve Bank of India at the command of foreign financial institutions had earlier ensured the entry of foreign banks and the beginning of the process of progressive denationalization of the public sector banks. The intrusion of foreign equity has also been simultaneously permitted in these banks; statutory restrictions on foreign entities acquiring majority share of any domestic bank, including the State Bank of India, are being winked at. If reliance is to be placed on market gossip, the State Bank of India has already slipped under total foreign control; it is a matter of a few moments before it is renamed the Imperial Bank of India.

The moving hand nonetheless continues to write, and official committees continue to dole out recommendations. An official working group was asked to suggest measures for restructuring weak public sector banks. The group has persevered with the task assigned to it, and has come up with a coherent logic for reorganizing the so-called weak banks that are beset by the overwhelming burden of non-performing assets. These banks, the group has proposed, should be helped by an Asset Reconstruction Fund to be set up by the government; the banks must, at the same time, shed excess manpower through the introduction of a voluntary retirement scheme; if such a scheme cannot be made to get going, the alternative has to be a reduction by 25 per cent in emoluments for the employees.

There are certain other suggestions, no doubt equally well-meaning; the bull, nonetheless, deserves to be taken by the horn. At no stage has the working group dared to enumerate the factors responsible for the creation of non-performing assets and which have led to the ruination of the banks concerned. It is easy to take it out on hapless employees, but they have not been responsible for either the creation or the proliferation of NPAs. In a class-driven society, the banks have to ditch the notions of grammar and listen to the diktat of the authorities. They have done so; credit has been advanced to politically favoured parties without questions being asked. A very large proportion of the advances made to these parties – individuals, private firms or corporate entities – have not been paid back, or paid back on time; other things being equal, the poor banks can do nothing in this situation; the defaulting parties have the strongest possible nexus with ministers and senior civil servants.

The hypocrisy in the ongoing discussions can therefore only nauseate. Times without number, academicians and members of parliament have suggested a few straightforward steps for discouraging defaults in the banking sector: (a) do not allow the defaulting parties to open another account in the same bank in another name; (b) do not allow the party concerned to open a line of credit with another bank; (c) do not permit bank credit to an entity – any entity – in which the defaulting party has an interest; (d) where it can be established that a defaulting party has close family and business links with any other party enjoying credit with this or any other bank, cut out such credit for this party too; (e) revise the statute making rigorous imprisonment mandatory for habitual bank defaulters.

It is still an integrated banking system: the Reserve Bank of India provides guidance to the banks and the Ministry of Finance is the supreme authority entitled to take any decisions for enforcing improvements in the general health of the overall financial system. The present Finance Minister has, however, the temerity to pretend in parliament that decisions in such matters are best left to the individual banks, and the government is in no position to issue directives in the matter. New Delhi's officialdom, *babus* for ever, have also alluded to the statutory provisions whereby there can be no public disclosure of a bank's transactions with individual customers, including those who are habitual defaulters.

As if such colonial statutory provisions cannot be altered; as if the Reserve Bank of India, under instructions from the Ministry of Finance, has not disclosed to the public on innumerable occasions the quantum of overdraft run up by individual state governments with it, thereby technically infringing the confidential relationship between itself and its customers, the state governments. Military dictatorships are to be strongly disapproved of, but record is record; the authoritarian regime in Pakistan has declared, of late, two significant economic measures: (a) it has publicly disclosed the names of all bank defaulters, and (b) it has slashed the country's defence budget by Rs 700 crore.

Ours is a more responsible regime. In any event, it is against our principle to follow the example set by a military junta responsible for the gross misdoings in and around Kargil. Our rulers have raised our defence expenditure for the current year by Rs 4,000 crore; what the next year's budget will feature is, for the present, a tantalizing secret. The government has also stuck to the old statutory provisions in order not to let out the names of the rascals who have walked away with the nation's resources by defaulting payments to the banks.

Pipe down, these rascals are as of now the principal decision-makers for the nation. Some of them took umbrage at the suggestion of an Asset Reconstruction Fund to assist the revival of three of the weakest public sector banks. Nothing doing, thundered a committee of the CII top brass, these banks do not deserve to be kept alive. The fact that these very dignitaries from the CII were the major defaulting parties responsible for the swelling of the proportion of NPA of these banks is neither here nor there. For, did not rapists in the medieval days sit in judgment on the moral waywardness of the rape victim and despatch her to her death?

An imperial NGO?

5–11 February 2000

No question about it, major confrontations henceforth, whether globally or within the precincts of individual countries, are going to be between NGOs and other NGOs. Country governments will, for their own reasons, recede into the background; the proxy war between non-governmental organizations will be the real thing.

Already, Seattle has presented a preview of the future awaiting the world. Years of preliminary soundings with friendly governments notwithstanding, the American administration was feeling extraordinarily shaky about the outcome at Seattle; the combined weight of the western nations and Japan was no longer considered adequate for swinging decisions in international fora in favour of unbridled capitalism. Quite apart from the fact that the majority of the membership of the WTO belong to either the developing or the underdeveloped category with short as well as long-range interests mostly in conflict with those of the industrial west, even within the west confusion prevails on a fairly large number of important issues, including, for instance, agricultural subsidies. Romping in the free market is all right as a concept, which has its direct lineage from the works of David Hume and Adam Smith. Interpretation of what the original *gurus* had meant has however tended to vary from epoch to epoch, and from country to country; the articulation of class attitudes has often overshadowed other aims. Contentious domestic issues have sometimes goaded private pressure groups in a particular country to strike out on their own. The purpose has been to persuade the government of the country to decide in this manner rather than that of a seemingly grave systemic problem. Or, what has been on is the phenomenon of a non-governmental organization mobilizing a movement for introducing a piece of social or economic reform, or against the continuation of a set of archaic laws and regulations offending the soul. Many of the NGOs of this genre have been frightened at the prospect of being dubbed as camp-followers of any political group. They have, in fact, insisted that they be allowed to display their equidistance from established set-ups of all descriptions, and have taken pride in stressing the nuances of an approach to life that is wrapped in a philosophy which distinguishes it from similar other ideological positions. At least the attempt has been to emphasize this distinction.

The NGOs had actually already been around for some while: Salvation Army or Boy Scouts types of various nomenclatures, or lobbies in support of women's suffrage or demanding abolition of capital punishment. They and the twentieth century have provided sustenance to each other. The reason for the convergence is not far to seek. In most western societies, stability of a sort began to mark the polity once the embers of the second world war died down. The phase of post-war reconstruction too was soon over. Social and political controversies would, it was thought, conform to a given set of rules; everyone, barring the incorrigible revolution-mongers, were expected to adhere to this basic grammar, irrespective of substantive differences in ideological stance. Revolution was no longer the order of the day in such polities; neither the social infrastructure nor the legal superstructure, it was held, needed any drastic reorientation. By and large a congenial milieu, it expressed its preference for the craft of persuasion. Pressure-groups emerged so as to propagate a special cause, perhaps the enactment of a new statute, or abolition of a statute whose relevance was long over. One never knew what would lead to what. A small group, intensely believing in the genuineness of a certain point of view, would conceivably mobilize support and offer battle to the old fogeys arrayed against them. Things would warm up in due course, and ideologues would join in. Bizarre developments could follow and a purely local issue might begin to attain political overtones. And it was a matter of a brief interlude before NGOs were organized to preach causes that directly contradicted one another. Alongside NGOs opposing the Sardar Sarovar project are now others which are supporting it. Big money has a way of infiltrating itself in these situations.

Getting Internationalized

Times are a-changing, globalization is the password, NGOs too are getting internationalized at a scampering speed. The immediate inspiration could be the tail-end of a happenstance. Or perhaps deeper motivations are at work. Charity-minded groups, the milk of human kindness spilling over, with their base of operations in advanced industrial countries, are massively afflicted by pricks of conscience. They did not have any intention per se to disturb the imperial–colonial system that featured the inter-war period. Some of the grosser irrationalities of the system however stirred their conscience, they launched a reformist movement in the country they had chosen for their beneficence. A pattern of cross-country assistance soon took shape. In case a sufficient number of enlightened people in a colony or dominion would succeed in mobilizing local effort in support of some stated objectives, a generous flow of funds would ensue from the overseas NGO, accompanied by dosages of counsel and advice, *loco parentis* being *lexo parentis*. Scan the history of the past half-century. It took only a while before several of the freshly independent countries in Asia and Africa latched on to the basic knowledge of how lucre accompanies the accord of formal recognition to an international NGO operating through a local chapter or branch. A convulsion occurs; the NGOs turn over a new leaf. Or perhaps they do not. Anyway, they learn to campaign furiously for a public cause in the nearly liberated lands. These NGOs generally acquire any of the following three forms. First, they build on the infrastructure set up by a pioneering group of kind-hearted citizens keen to advance a civic cause or lobby on an economic issue. They have their pride and raise funds from membership subscriptions or from donations forthcoming from private, unquestionably untainted sources. They would not dream of accepting money from a government agency, for that would endanger their objectivity. They would be even more shocked at the suggestion that they seek assistance from a foreign government or an international agency.

But times change, so do social cultures. The second genre of NGOs came into prominence by the middle decades of the twentieth century, in the aftermath of John Foster Dulles's tenure as Secretary of State. Scores of voluntary groups began to prosper in the developing countries. They had outposts in different parts of the country, even though their activities, to begin with, concentrated on only some parts. Enlightenment is a function of time. A few amongst these NGOs were excited at the prospect of establishing international links. They built bridges of hope on the assumption of large-scale donations from affluent patrons in rich foreign lands. They hastened to establish such foreign links and saw nothing wrong in case money received overseas were brought back home and used for social and humanitarian purposes, including relief in the wake of a natural calamity or for financing more enduring types of social services, such as women's and children's education and nutrition or technical education at different levels. Some of these agencies did succeed in attracting considerable international attention in the course of the past few decades. They have been at the same time in a position, perhaps on account of their international clout, to throw their weight about within the country too. The home government learnt to respect these organizations, and also nurtured a quantum of fear and apprehension given the network of connections, domestic as well as foreign, built by them. But let us not wear any blinkers. While persons heading these NGOs have, more often than not, been well-meaning individuals, there were, and continue to be, many others with their eye on the main chance.

Interesting Group

On to the third, and perhaps the most interesting, group of NGOs which have come into prominence in recent times. Many of the NGOs referred to above were not initially involved in direct politics. As creatures of circumstances, they nonetheless found themselves in a position where they could exercise considerable political influence from behind the scenes. They were, and continue to be, in receipt of government bounty as well as international assistance flowing in from diverse sources. The official bounty often assumes curious forms. There was the celebrated instance of equipment purchased and installed in a government hospital at considerable cost being resold within a few months at a nominal price to a non-governmental organization. Connections matter; commercial ventures

41

embarked upon by NGOs have also been winked at by the government. For example, cinema shows organized on a regular basis by a well-known NGO in a certain country have been exempted from payment of entertainment and amusement taxes.

Not surprisingly, *hauteur* has turned out to be an enduring way of life with many of the NGOs of this species. Their sovereignty, some of them have come to presume, runs parallel to – or even exceeds – that of the government of the country. A few of them have acquired the notion that they deserve the benediction that the country's written Constitution offers to minority religious groups. By virtue of their being a voluntary non-governmental organization devoting itself to spiritual activism as well as various forms of social service, so went the claim, they ought to be treated as constituting a distinct and separate denomination of a religious minority, and therefore not subject to the normal laws of the land. The plaint received short shrift from the judiciary, though.

True, NGOs as a rule are hardly any different from ordinary pressure, groups, such as the oil and natural gas lobby or the farm lobby or the website lobby. There has however been, in the recent period, a qualitative change in the picture. The traditional agendas have been divested of relevance; the confrontation is increasingly between different social groups for cornering markets for their respective bill of goods in a more or less tariff-free world. The help of the NGOs is being enthusiastically sought so that these trade wars can be won.

On all sides, there is evidently no sense of shame in unalloyed self-seeking. Each group is keen to have an assured market all over the world; that is how employment could be promised both to domestic capital and the domestic working class. Each party wants to penetrate into other people's markets; pressure has to be applied so that international rules of the game are bent in our favour. At the same time, strategies must be evolved so as to ensure that the domestic market is saved from intrusion by foreigners. Situations of this nature are shot full of absurdities. All countries have to behave in identical or near-identical fashion; this is what the pursuit of the profit motive has boiled down to. One wants a free market overseas, but will not offer a free market to foreigners within one's own country; foreigners must take off all trade barriers, one's own trade barriers must however remain. Not that seemingly good, solid reasons cannot be proffered for such bizarre stances. The free market, after all, is the progenitor of market monopolies.

The proffering of sound or unsound rationale makes little difference. Two categories of problems unfold themselves. First, in a confused international situation, who is to decide whether the claim adduced on behalf of a country is full of truth and justice, or whether it is pure fake? How is the judgment to be reached whether it is worthwhile to purchase goods at relatively low prices from an underdeveloped country on the ground that such purchases would be instrumental in providing a morsel of food to millions and millions of undernourished women and children, despite their being paid sub-standard wages? Or should the argument be dismissed with contempt? What is the criterion for deciding that in case low-priced imports from developing economies lead to lay-off of workers in the advanced industrial economies, the trade unions in the latter countries must put up with this bitter experience for the sake of international brotherhood of the working class? On which side does the claim of genuine humanitarianism lie?

The new generation of NGOs blooms in this climate of confusion. Many of them have, these days, a strong network of associates in all the five continents; they also happen to be in command of enormous resources. If a government feels it imperatively necessary to counter the activities of any such NGO, it might be seriously urged to sponsor a parallel NGO of its own: Bill Clinton apparently knows all the ropes. Steel will then clash with steel. The two NGOs would fight it out, country governments and scheming capitalists would watch on benignly, condescendingly.

This, then, is what state-of-the-art phenomenology is about: NGOs to the right of you, NGOs to the left of you, NGOs in front of you. You survive because the NGO concerned permits you to. The final year of the twentieth century, which this world has just entered, is going to fade out soon and joustings will take place to push the human species, with rude remorselessness, to the uncertainty of the next century; the century where the agenda for all the months of the year, for all the days of the month and for all the hours of the day will be reduced to thousands of NGOs engaged in the battlefield trying to annihilate thousands of other NGOs. What else do you expect when governments, in country after country, are being privatized wholesale? Only NGOs are henceforth likely to matter. It is little use complaining that these are dangerous, faceless entities. You made the bed and you have to lie in it; is that not the essential free market philosophy? In some of the poorer countries, resources originating annually with the NGOs are four or five times the size of the country's government budget. The law of monopoly capital will however come to operate. One of the NGOs will swallow the rest of them. That will then be the day of the imperial NGO. And it will be no surprise if the face behind the mask is that of either Monsanto or Unilever.

Re-dreaming futile dreams

29 April 2000

The unnamed spokesman of the Ministry of External Affairs was obviously trying to be too clever by half; as is usual in such cases, he however did not realize the dangerous implications of his wit. He buttonholed a member of the entourage travelling with President Bill Clinton, enlightening him on the basic reason impeding India's signing the CTBT. In other circumstances India would have, he explained, complied with the American request, but there is a snafu. The country's nuclear '*bundobast*' is not directed against this particular ally of the United States, Pakistan. Its target, really and truly, is the People's Republic of China. India must don the nuclear role, and indefinitely stay donned that way, to ensure that the Chinese dragon does not misbehave with the world. The Americans must not mind the brisk nuclear activities on India's part and New Delhi's refusal to sign on the dotted line as far as the CTBT is concerned. It is all for the great, noble, global cause: to bring down Beijing a peg or two.

Should the Americans be amused, or, better still, appreciate admiringly this latest apologia for India's nuclear adventure? All we have to do is to imagine a revival of the cold war climate, the Indian reluctance to sign the Treaty will immediately fall into place. The Americans, the world's only superpower, may not straightaway express their delight at the splendid initiative displayed by one of their global subalterns. The imbibement of awareness is however a function of time. If the Soviet Union is simply not there and its supposed successor, the Russian Republic, is not worth a brass farthing, so what; the People's Republic of China is most impressive as an adequately heavyweight potential adversary of the United States. What is more, China is India's enemy number one for more than forty years now. Don't you agree that, in the circumstances, it is India's holy duty to accumulate a nuclear stockpile which could cramp Beijing's style? The Americans would surely not mind. After all, the wretched Chinese are sworn ideological enemies of the United States as well.

India's official spokesman evidently chose to slur over the developments in recent decades. India no longer belongs to the same league as China, period. It would, in fact, be convincingly argued by many that had India shed her China complex and restructured her defence budget accordingly, her rate of growth would have accelerated considerably, thereby reducing the size of the predicament the country is currently experiencing. The more the country spends on defence, the less are the prospects of rapid economic growth. The inevitable outcome is the persistence of social and economic instability in the country.

Raising the spectre of China to explain the reluctance of the Indian authorities to sign the CTBT will not, it is hoped, fail to impress the United States of America. Disappointment, disappointment. The Americans have other instrumentalities to cope with the Chinese problem; they do not therefore, thank you, need India's helping hand.

The initiative exhibited by India's official spokesman could spoil some other broth though. The gist of the confidential conversation will be duly reported to the Chinese authorities. They will be peeved no end at India's pretensions, there is however a little bit more in the matter which should cause anxiety. Trade liberalization is now much more than a mere catchword; the free marketeers want instant decisions to be taken on a number of issues which would make India's external trade liberated from restrictions of all kinds. The local zealots for globalization, who are prepared to die for the cause, are getting impatient. Withdrawal of trade restrictions, they know for certain, promotes economic efficiency. Inefficient domestic units will go to the wall following the formal announcement to do away with tariff and non-tariff barriers to imports. The output of the domestic units, adversely affected by the official decision, will disappear. So what? Cheaper, better-quality substitutes will arrive from foreign lands. There will be heavy loss of employment as the domestic units close, with considerable suffering on the part of the nation's working class. But those who are inefficient must face the consequence of their inefficiency. That is what free market economics is about.

The transition from inefficiency to efficiency is never smooth; as is well known, vested interests often play a nefarious, interfering role. This year's union budget intended import restrictions on sugar to be lifted forthwith. This was done, but there has since been a setback. A bunch of worthless politicians got into the act; they persuaded the Prime Minister to drop the proposal to liberalize sugar imports. Something went wrong, the Prime Minister has actually ordered the reimposition of import duty on sugar at 50 per cent c.i.f. This is, to say the least, scandalous, in the view of the pro-liberalization crowd; they cannot hide their impatience with the politicians who worry over the prospective loss of livelihood for half-a-million farm workers as a result of the withdrawal of import restrictions on sugar. As if employment is of greater national priority than the pursuit of economic efficiency.

An academic economist has one great advantage, he is free to tender his advice to the government without bothering about social correlates. While tendering his advice, he does not have to take into account the ground realities governing the polity. The academic economist does not consider it a part of his concerns if half-a-million workers have to be laid off because of the withdrawal of the import duty on sugar. He is shocked no end by the official decision to return to the status quo.

The economist we have in mind has perhaps done some undergraduate work in this or that Indian university, then proceeded to the United States to get a Ph.D. in liberal economics; he was perhaps offered an assignment in the World Bank, the International Monetary Fund (IMF) or the WTO. He has been an emigré since then. He is therefore conceivably not at all aware of the social implications of 5,00,000 farm workers suddenly losing their jobs in Bihar and Uttar Pradesh in the wake of the abolition of the import duty on sugar. Had the amateur economist his or her way, he or she may complain about this crass act of indecisiveness on the part of the Indian authorities to the powers-that-be in the United States administration, or within the portals of international financial institutions. Why, it is a question of efficiency; the economist will expect the western bosses to pay heed to him or her, and tick off the worthless bunch of Indian decision-makers. It will not occur to him or her that what is involved is not just an issue of efficiency, even though a question can be genuinely raised whether non-optimal use of labour is reconcilable with efficiency. But the other issue, that of the country's suzerainty over economic decision-making, may not at all appear to be relevant in the judgment of the young economist. He or she is a post-midnight child; whether the dignity of the nation is duly protected is no part of his or her agenda.

This also lays bare the dilemma of survival the subalterns in a colonial ambience have to experience. The Indian authorities need to continue breathing in a democratic climate and win elections at regular intervals. If they allow the 5,00,000 workers to slide into starvation, there could be big trouble in the election season. On the other hand, flouting the wishes of the masters from across the seas would be an equally unpalatable proposition.

It is confusion abounding, and we might return to the theme introduced earlier. The Chinese will, in due course, get to learn about the recent whisperings into American ears indulged in by responsible Indian officials: the real reason for insistence on the part of Indians to remain on the nuclear course (what do you know) is because they want to give China a bloody nose. Till now, it was possible to nurture the hope that China's selective patronage in the WTO would help India protect some of her export lines, and, at the same time, ensure an orderly dismantling of import restrictions. Once China is peeved by the nuclear story, that prospect might fall through.

A postscript to the comments above may not be altogether out of order. Actually, even in terms of the Marrakesh Treaty, India need not have opened up imports in all sectors with immediate effect. For example, according to Article XVIII-B of the Treaty, a developing country has the right to continue with barriers on agricultural imports for balance of payments reasons. Whether the balance of payments position is genuinely uncomfortable is to be decided upon by the WTO on the advice of the IMF; the Fund, in its turn, will seek the views of the Ministry of Finance of the country concerned. In other words, if only the country's own Ministry of Finance would argue vigorously for the continuance of the trade restrictions on farm imports, on balance of payments grounds, the Fund and the WTO are likely to accept that position. Thereby hangs a most interesting story, though. If market gossip is to be believed, a couple of years ago, the Indian Ministry of Finance, consisting of theologians who are great believers in trade globalization, did not even wait for the referral from the Fund. It, so to say, jumped the gun, and on its own wrote to the IMF and the WTO that India's balance of payments position was fine and excellent, meaning thereby that the WTO should now order India to withdraw all restrictions on imports, including on farm imports.

Please do not blame the foreign financial and trade regulatory organizations, they have checked with the Ministry of Finance in New Delhi and followed its cue. This is what, in essence, the liberal spirit amounts to; global interests must precede the country's own self-interest. The Ministry of Finance is a proud and dispassionate taskmaster. Honour it, it knows its duty; it knows that in a global framework, the will of the external parties will always prevail.

Calculations, calculations ...

13–19 May 2000

Not to take notice of the incident will be to play false to contemporary history. The furore over betting and payments on the outcome of international cricket fixtures was giving India a bad name. But simmer down; where there is a will, there is a way. The Union Minister for Sports himself, no less, has suggested an easy way out of the predicament. Let us be realists, the nation must catch up with the times. Most of the hullabaloo has been occasioned by an arcane law which fails to take into account the datum that our country is now an integral part of a complex global system. The central point at issue is the invocation, against this background, of economic efficiency as the be all and end all of human existence. The notion of efficiency is defined in terms of a single criterion: whatever maximizes money-making from a particular line of activity reflects the hallmark of efficiency, and let not anyone try to tell you something that is different. Consider, for instance, the situation obtaining in the arena of international cricket. In addition to the fees a cricketer is entitled to for participating in international fixtures, provided he has already established a reputation for himself through his performance in the field, he is a major candidate for endorsing luxury consumer goods, durable as well as non-durable. It is not an even playing field, though. You may represent a country where the domestic market for luxury commodities is of a restricted size, perhaps because of its sparse population; endorsement money is therefore unlikely to flow at a fast pace towards your direction. Never mind, just give in to temptation; you will receive thorough-going technical advice in the matter from the subcontinent's bookmakers and the mafia crowd they belong to. Betting is easy money, you don't have to even append your signature on a piece of paper; an oral commitment will do: a tradition has developed whereby your word of mouth is worth its weight in gold or whatever other coveted precious metals you can conceive. The scope for personal embarrassment, you have been assured, is as good as negligible these days: trade and payment devices have been dematerialized to such an extent that it is not at all easy to trace the source of origin of a commitment or a pledge entered into in the name of x, y or z. The individual concerned remains invisible, but the havoc he can create both to the social process and the moral foundation on which the economy is supposed to stand is of frightening proportions.

The matter is worth pursuing further. The Indian bookmaker operates at different levels. The ongoing commotion, the medley of accusations and counter-accusations, does not deter him. He makes a pragmatic assessment of the ingredients of ground reality. What however poses a challenge of a different nature is the fact that, under Indian law, betting in cricket is a criminal offence. The cricketers and cricket administrators from different countries who have, wittingly or unwittingly, openly or surreptitiously, taken bets on the possible outcome of this or that match, can be taken care of without much difficulty. The way out is very simple. Why not amend the piece of legislation and inform the world that betting in cricket is no longer a culpable offence in India? The solution suggested is indeed of a breathtaking calibre. In case it receives social approval, it could be applied with equal felicity to tackle other outstanding national problems as well. We could take out rape and murder from the roster of criminal offences; what a relief, all murderers and rapists would immediately be declared as belonging to the lily-white species; once the law is changed, murders and rapes would cease to be anti-social acts.

This, then, appears to be India's principal contribution in the arena of moral philosophy in the post-globalization era. The mind and heart of the Minister who sponsored the proposal to make betting in cricket a non-culpable transaction, there is no question, was very much in it. If silly senior politicians had chosen not to intervene, he would have chalked up a coup of a sort, India's number one contribution to the *ethics nouvelle*. We are going to be hemmed in for some while by such unfortunate setbacks, but, in the long run, nothing succeeds like success. This time, the attempt to usher in formally the code of the new civilization failed. But do not be despondent, it will not fail the next time. There is impatient waiting for this piece of legislation; once it is enacted, that will be the cue for mafia groups to move into the Indian economy. The Government of India has meanwhile been most helpful in other directions. It has set up a new Ministry of Disinvestment, and has also announced the schedule for selling off precious public property at throwaway prices. The monetary system has been liberalized as well. It is therefore a pity that the cheer-filled official prognoses are not yet coming true. Confident extrapolation notwithstanding, direct foreign investment continues to be on a declining track. The country's stock exchanges, already taken over by the foreigners, are the only stable source of foreign exchange acquisition. It is the anticipated generosity on the part of the market operators which has persuaded the government to withdraw all worthwhile restrictions on international trade and financial transactions. Like it or not, these foreigners who have come to corner our stock exchanges have a reputation, whether well or ill-founded, one is in no position to infer, of symbiotic relationships with mafia and other goon groups who operate on a global scale. It is not a bad model per se. Every now and then, investors like Namasq will open their fangs and leave the share markets in the developing countries exhausted. The frequency of such bearish activities will intensify in course of time. Every now and then, there could be a run on foreign exchange resources. The cumulative effect, it is possible to speculate, would be an accentuation of the downward trend in the external value of the national currency. The international financial institutions too would by now have been reduced to the state of a bunch of nervous Nellys. Seattle has been a nightmare. The commotion at the Fund–Bank meeting in Washington DC was a shade less vociferous. But it will henceforth be difficult for these institutions to envisage a horizon not replete with risk and uncertainty. Don't you remember those dog-worn textbooks dealing with themes like the ones the early Frank Knight, for instance, tried to expiate upon: the occurrence of an unexpected event as an aspect of economic dynamics, and the non-occurrence of an expected event equally qualified as an aspect of economic dynamics?

The notion of dynamics, back in harness, is inspiring globalization across the seven seas too. Perhaps our relatively narrow domestic system is going to be increasingly dependent upon the whims and fancies of determining variables from outside. Politics and economics have succeeded in obliterating their operational distinctions. The outstanding concern of the US administration at this particular juncture is somehow to ensure that Russia's nuclear stockpile remains outside the orbit of control by mafia gangs. That, presumably, is also a major objective of the foreign policy of the Chinese authorities. Taking advantage of the confusion, India and Pakistan have played their private game by attaining minimal nuclear capability. But the difference between possessing 500 bombs and just one bomb, the wise ones say, is purely metaphysical. The theory of countervailing terror leaves no impression on the sensitivity of mafia groups; they do not particularly care whether the world explodes in their face or not. It is to them a precarious world, and they practise a precarious polity of their own.

Perhaps, to be more precise, even they do not operate the polity at all, it functions on its own and has created its own mess. Globalization is free-for-all, foreign governments do not feel the least compunction to team up with shady elements within the system. Morality has departed from the international framework of things; domestic calculations point towards the direction of an enveloping anarchy. Our Union Cabinet sanctions more and more funds for defence spending; it is thereby left with less and less for development of outlying regions and for classes and communities that lag behind.

New class alignments will meanwhile begin to take shape within the existing system. On one side will be the swelling army of millions who are deprived, or threatened to be deprived: thousands and thousands of insurance and bank employees, many more thousands who are victims of 'reforms' in the public sector, meaning large-scale disinvestment, and those others in the cottage and farm sectors felled by the decision to proceed with 100 per cent liberalization of trade. It is going to be a tough scenario. The very, very rich enjoyed high indolent living even in the epoch of the regulated economy; they had the money, which they spent nonchalantly, to acquire the accoutrements of luxury consumption, and they devised ways and means to play around foreign exchange restrictions. The stakes are, however, much greater for the new middle class. For decades on end, they had been held back from the comforts of foreign goods; now the barriers are gone, and the paradise gained will not be easily given up. The confrontation between those who have formally written off the system and those who have entered the orbit of foreign goods-based high consumption will turn increasingly bitter. The world's only superpower will be tempted to take sides; the temptation will be equally great for goons and tricksters. It will be a no-holds-barred battle, and with no moral qualms. The conscience of hardened criminals will preside over the polity, here and everywhere. The days of romantic poetry will finally be over. The website crowd, in any case, detests poetry.

The left-behind parents

26 August–2 September 2000

The phenomenon is widespread in the metropolitan cities; and not just in the metropolitan cities, the contamination has affected the small towns too in most states. In a large number of middle-class homes, the children have gone away. They have departed for foreign shores, a fair majority to the United States. These boys and girls were outstandingly meritorious students, and have earned a piping first class either from one of the Indian Institutes of Technology or one of the Indian Institutes of Management. Perhaps some of them have top degrees in physics and chemistry. It is even possible to come across young people who, after graduating from an IIT, have undergone a course at one of the accredited IIMs so as to further strengthen their academic credentials. They are excellent professional material for transnational companies and such like. A market for their talent exists particularly in the United States, and also in West Europe and Japan. No sooner than they offer themselves to a foreign firm, they are snapped up. It often happens that, even before they receive their degrees, they engage in correspondence with foreign companies, who wait anxiously for them to complete their course and then fly away to their assignments in Europe or America.

The allure is easily understandable. A corporate unit in the United States will perhaps offer a salary that is ten, fifteen or twenty times higher than what the young boys and girls could hope to obtain in the Indian market. There is, in addition, a large array of perquisites. The young flock, therefore, go away. A generation or two ago, young people would grow up in a milieu where ideology and patriotic emotions weighed a great deal. These attributes are now safely dead. The youngsters fly away and enjoy high living in the United States or elsewhere.

They rapidly fall into a groove. They slog in their firms or offices for five days in the week, from eight or eight-thirty in the morning till six or six-thirty in the evening. Commuting between home and place of work takes as much as another two to three hours. During the weekdays, they are therefore robots who move about mechanically, soulless creatures. Only the Saturdays and Sundays they can set aside for their families. But even the weekends follow a specific pattern. During the day on Saturdays, they take out the car and shop like mad downtown. The society they have chosen to settle in flaunts a luxurious style of living, and can afford to do so. Goods of all varieties and descriptions are available in the downtown stores, and, of late, in the neighbourhood market plazas as well. The migrant young folk are paid a fabulous sum according to Indian standards; they load their house with goodies, durable as well as non-durable, essential as well as non-essential. The Saturday evening is given to partying, where food, drinks, music and dance are common features. Sunday mornings, they sleep late, do some more of cursory social visits during the afternoon, and in the evening possibly go to watch a baseball match or an ice-skating competition.

The parents are left behind. The nuclear family, a pucca western concept, has invaded the Indian psyche. There is no question of the parents joining their offspring in the foreign country. They stay home and fend for themselves; the boys and girls satisfy their conscience by arranging a monthly or quarterly remittance. And perhaps they condescend to visit their parents once every two years or thereabouts. Meanwhile, the grandchildren would have arrived; they too accompany their parents to visit the desiccated, worn-out grandparents. Since most of the time the grandchildren do not know the language the grandparents are accustomed to speak, there is a communication problem, so that the parents of the grandchildren, half-amusingly, act as interpreters. The ordeal, however, does not last long. The leave expires, or it is time for the grandchildren to return to school. The sons and daughters and sons-in-law and daughters-in-law depart with their families. The old parents are left to their fate.

Back home, prices rise every week and every month. The pension of the father shrinks in real value; the same rule applies to the remittances sent by sons and daughters. Old people grow infirm and suffer from diverse illnesses. The household chores also multiply as the years roll by. To obtain help is increasingly difficult these days at the wages the old people are able to offer. There are also such daily headaches as shopping for vegetables, fish, meat and eggs, paying instalments of dues to, for instance, insurance companies or the house owner, going to banks to draw or deposit money, worrying about payment of electricity and water bills on scheduled dates, filling income-tax returns, and so on. Kindly neighbours might occasionally help out, but the neighbours too will have their own mounting household problems to take care of. In the natural process, their chores of doing a good turn to the left-behind parents of those who have flown away, thin out.

To be fair, the sons and daughters offer to buy, every five or ten years, concessional air tickets, so that their parents could visit them in the United States or wherever they are. But these foreign trips are no fun for the old people. The sons – and these days the daughters-in-law too – leave for work at seven in the morning and return only at seven or eight in the evening. The children too leave for their schools. The old couple are therefore left stranded in a strange house in a strange neighbourhood in a strange country. They soon have enough of it and pine to go back home. They cannot be easily persuaded to revisit the children and grandchildren in the States or Europe.

There is however a rider to this reportage. In case the daughter or the daughter-in-law is a working woman and there are infant babies to be looked after, the mother or mother-in-law is detained by the son, the daughter or the daughter-in-law so as to make her act as a live-in maid. There is a certain advantage in this arrangement: the mother or mother-in-law will not need to be paid any wages.

Even if this last-mentioned aspect is underemphasized, the tragedy of old people left to fend for themselves is indescribable. The children have gone away. They, the parents, had devoted the best years of their lives and the bulk of their resources to turn the children into finished products. They, the children, are, really and truly, the intellectual property of the parents and the country they emigrate from. But, for this intellectual property, neither the United States nor any of the West European countries are prepared to pay the proper price to the parents and the nation.

Many such parents, helpless beyond endurance, silently move to old people's homes, where they have to pay through the nose. Mercifully, they die soon after. Sometimes, the sons and daughters fly home to attend the last rites. Sometimes, the children do not bother.

Is there not such a thing as nature's revenge? It is conceivable that a generation or two later, the children and grandchildren of the migrant men and women would receive their comeuppance: they would be victims of crass racial discrimination in the country they have adopted as their own. But you never know, even when they are hounded and harassed by the whites, they would boast of their Aryan ancestry and shudder to think that, in the society their parents have condemned them to be members of, they are bracketed with the Venus and Serena Williamses. The latter may be world champions in tennis; to the migrant Indians, they are nonetheless untouchable specimens.

The town cynic could here pipe in. It is an ill wind that blows nobody any good. One positive outcome of liberalization is the influx of foreign companies into the country who offer their local recruits compensation at international rates, forcing domestic corporate units too to offer vastly improved wage packets. The exodus of young talents to the United States and elsewhere should therefore slow down, which would be a boon to old parents. The cynic, however, tends to overlook the fact that the number of technically competent young professionals greatly exceeds domestic demand. The flow of emigration, therefore, is bound to continue.

Cricket, the spitting image

16 September 2000

There is no escape from the basic fact: the crisis in Indian cricket encapsulates the problems the Indian economy and, for that matter, the Indian polity as a whole are facing. The free market ambience has overwhelmed the sphere of cricket too. It has translated itself into a free-for-all. As is the rule with so-called perfect competition, those with talent and efficiency in performance outdo others in this *mêlée*. In no time, they come up on top. Glamour attaches to these few, and glamour in turn paves the way for lush earnings via endorsement of adver-tisements. The rush of endorsements in turn creates even further glamour for the select group of players. It is therefore a two-way pattern: glamour is the magnet which crowds in advertisements, advertisements in their turn pile up more glam-our upon the initial base. This process can continue indefinitely and the talented players soon come to accumulate fabulous wealth.

This is the dilemma of the free market. It does not remain 'free' for long; the inexorable logic of market operations soon ushers in a monopoly, or at least a duopoly or a polipoly. The less-talented players are crushed in competition and are rendered into non-entities. Some of them still manage to scrape a living, but nothing much beyond.

The developments do not entirely stop here. The *crème de la crème* amongst the players are pampered and lionized. They, inevitably, come to bel-ieve that they are next to God. In other words, they assume they can do no wrong. The stockpile of money induces in them greater avarice for money. They have also continuously dinned into their ears, the central message of the free market: it is no sin to maximize your income, whether by hook or by crook. These players soon succumb to the lure and pursue the slippery path of non-integrity. Match-fixing and betting come in the wake. The name of cricket be-comes mud.

Is the situation in the Indian economy any different? Since 1991, restric-tions and regulations are off. Make your pile, make your pile, the state will not stand in the way, it will look the other way were you to adopt even the dirtiest means to attain material success. Here too, the efficient units put in superior performance and, despite the legend of the free market, are able to outperform units with lesser efficiency. In the different sectors of the Indian economy, we therefore once more witness the spectacle of abler units edging out the less-com-petent ones. The phenomenon that emerges is very close to monopoly. The deg-ree of monopoly determines prices and costs and, accordingly, overall profits. Since a contraction of output from the hypothetical point of perfect competition equilibrium pushes up revenue, the objective of profit optimization coincides with the policy of restrictive output. The handful of producers left in the field are still not satisfied. Society has been transformed, old concepts of fairness, honesty and frugality are blasé. The neighbourhood is full of stories of how x, y or z has made tonnes and tonnes of money through recourse to unconventional proce-dures. Since ethics have been banished, the few at the top of business or produc-tion do not have the least compunction to indulge in the shadiest of means. They fleece the consumers, they fleece the workers, they cheat on taxes, they overinvoice imports and underinvoice exports, they get involved in insider trading and for-gery. In case their severely personal code of conduct justifies it, they do not flinch from organizing murder and mayhem either.

This is, then, the internal contradiction of free market economics so dependent on the premise of efficiency. Beyond the weekend, the free market does not stay free, it becomes the servile underling of the monopolist or the duopolists or the polipolists. And all the evils associated with a monopoly situation come to visit the economy. Once you come to establish total command over production and distribution, you say boo to the notion of efficiency.

The polity, alas, does not behave any better. It can commence its day under the umbrella of multi-party parliamentary democracy. But power corrupts, and absolute power corrupts absolutely. A political party which, through some honest pyrotechnics, initially captures the imagination of the people, wrests government power; within a short while, the other parties are reduced to minor entities. This tendency is specially acute in newly emerging societies where there is a large incidence of poverty and illiteracy. A party which transforms itself into the indubitable cock of the road attracts attention and gains in glamour. Funds easily accrue to it; the accrual of funds makes it easy to subsidize, and thereby seduce, large masses of the electorate, who are woefully lacking even in a modicum of social awareness. Come the next election, the party in power thereby becomes even more successful and therefore even more corrupt and more powerful. The heightened power facilitates access to even greater funds, and renders the party blind to the codes of scruples and fair play. What began as free competition between equally situated political parties is converted into a near-monopoly of a single political party. Temptation is great in these circumstances. Instead of waiting for the natural marginalization of the other parties, the party in power plunges into designs such as were brought into vogue in India in the name of 'the Emergency'. Multi-party parliamentary democracy is rendered into crass authoritarianism. There can, of course, be variants of this process. The monopolist political party, ensconced in the *hauteur* of power, unleashes such repression on the people that there are overt signs of a general uprising. The opposition parties, which had been reduced to helplessness and futility, start regaining strength, which makes the government party commit silly mistakes, provoking an insurrectionary situation, leading to chaos; the chaos leads, at the next stage, to a military takeover.

The game of cricket – and the organizing of it – is still part of the entire polity. Therefore it is possible for the country's government, taking into cognizance the large-scale public revulsion towards the shenanigans going on in the name of cricket, to propose to step in and enforce punitive measures. This has raised the ire of the largely capitalist-owned Indian press: how dare the authorities intervene in cricket, do they not know that we are in a free market environment, and that cricketers have the freedom to indulge in whatever activities they prefer, including theft, robbery and plunder?

It is yet not altogether certain whether the government will finally be able to clamp some discipline on Indian cricket and cricketers. The pressure mounted by the free market-wallas is intense. Perhaps this pressure might even have some foreign sponsorships, much in the manner the economy has slipped under foreign sponsorship. The symptoms suggest that it is only a matter of time, the polity too will go under. It will be no surprise if, even as the Indian polity proceeds to its doom, it drags along Indian cricket.

Some will agree to disagree and say that the malaise started with the polity itself. It is the crooked Indian politicians who have debauched the economy and, in turn, provided the principal inspiration for the downfall of cricketers. Who knows, it could once more be a two-way traffic. And if no politician of any stature has gone to prison convicted of a criminal offence in the course of the five decades and odd since independence, it would be somewhat lacking in natural justice to pack off a cricketer of note to serve a term of imprisonment. Come to think of it, no politician has even ever been fined for transgressing the law. So why should a fine be imposed on any cricketer either? Please do not forget we have a written Constitution, and Article 14 of it is emphatic that all citizens are equal before the law.

The mourning reformers

4–10 November 2000

In all epochs, the cliché patronized by the ruling classes is the dominating cliché in society as a whole, towering over the rest. Tariff reforms, a euphemism for raising prices across the board, is currently the dominating cliché around here. Ruling classes love the thought that inspires the cliché. To raise prices is in effect to add to the profit margin, or the rentier income, of producers, businessmen and landowners. A subsidiary argument for tariff reforms has, by now, also emerged as a major rationale for pushing up prices: such a measure is expected to boost the prospect of what is described as direct foreign investment.

We should remind ourselves that tariff reforms are an integral part of the economic reforms introduced in 1991: come June, it will be anniversary time, marking the completion of a decade of 'reforms'. Never mind if the Prime Minister who had set the reforms ball rolling has meanwhile been convicted for proven acts of corruption. Accidents of this nature should not deter pioneers of the Mayflower vintage; the voyage across hitherto uncharted high seas in quest of lush new lands which spell bliss and prosperity must continue unhampered, stormy or no stormy weather.

Unfortunately, there has been, of late, turbulence *en route*. This should not have happened, the tryst with destiny ought to have been featured by tranquillity and triumphs. Conspirators are however at work. Brigands and sea bandits are labouring overtime to stall reforms, disinvestment and structural transformation in, for instance, telecommunications operations and services. The enemies of reforms – who, in the view of dreamers of the new society, are, shades of Ibsen here, enemies of the people as well – are hatching dark plots. The conspirators are being led, predictably, by good-for-nothing trade union leaders. These species are demanding protection of existing pension benefits of the departmental employees, – how unreasonable – even after the departments have been turned into corporations; their demands also include job security of the employees, notwithstanding the corporatization of the government departments. Most outrageous of all, the trade union bosses are insisting that the authorities must underwrite the financial viability of the newly set up corporate unit which is supposed to replace the departments. The obtuseness of the trade unions does not quite stop here. At their instigation, a National Action Committee has reared its head; it has pledged to fight tooth and nail, the policy of transmutation of government departments into corporations, thereby challenging the 'mother principle' of the reforms itself.

A strike by departmental employees to register their protest against official moves to implement what the votaries of liberalization consider as basic reforms, had immobilized the telecommunications network in the country for the best part of a fortnight. The Minister in charge, after some preliminary bravado threatening dire action against the employees absenting themselves from duty, suddenly cooled down. Secret negotiations were on, the strike was withdrawn and the employees returned to work. The Minister, the new frontier persons suspect, is planning to play the role of Judas Escariot. Although no open statements have been forthcoming on behalf of either the Minister or the trade unions, perhaps a deal has already been struck endorsing practically most of the atrocious demands pitched by the employees.

The lament of the reforms lobby is reverberating all over: what can be more shameful than ministers buckling under pressure and sabotaging the holy mission of globalization and liberalization? Those who have embarked on this tough mission are, however, lion-hearted enough, they will not be easily daunted. They have sworn to regroup their forces and relaunch their crusade against obscurantism and anti-modernism. Ministers can no longer be relied upon, the government's commitment to see through the reforms appears to be wobbling. So what, the crusades will not flinch from their destiny-ordained obligation. They will resume the war, and, this time, they hope to have the people of this country on their side. The perfidy of the trade unions and the feeble-mindedness of the authorities, just you see, will be of no avail, for the people, deeply appreciative of the boons corporatization and privatization have already ushered in – and likely to further usher in, in the coming years – will mobilize massively and give a most vigorous impetus to the great adventure to complete the exciting telecommunications revolution. It will be a people's uprising in support of the economic reforms.

Pray, who are these people, distinguished members of the honest public, who have been bowled over by the portrayal of the immense potential embedded in the privatization, among others, of the country's communications industry? Consider the entire range of communications services and the trend of prices at which these services have been offered over the past decade. Since 1991, that is to say, with effect from the year the reforms, marked by upward adjustments, in tariffs and large-scale privatization, were introduced, the prices of postcards, inland-letter cards and postal envelopes have more than doubled. The same has been the case with respect to charges for money orders, postal orders and registration of postal articles. The tariff for sending telegrams too has increased several-fold in the course of the past decade. To complete the story, rentals for telephone connections as well as charges for calls have also gone up by more than 100 per cent during the heraldic decade of liberalization.

Would it be impertinent to append a few comments on the quality of service in the communications industry during this period? An ordinary letter or postcard posted at any location, urban or rural, in the country would, thirty or forty years ago, reach the destination in a couple of days, or at most in a week; now, despite the skyrocketing of tariffs, it would be quite normal for a postal article to take a fortnight or more to travel to its destination. In the 1960s, a letter with a twenty-five-paise postage stamp affixed to it would be lifted from one metropolitan city and delivered to another such metropolitan area within a span of twenty-four hours. Now, in a semi-privatized regime, for the same service you will pay tariff at the rate of thirty or forty or fifty rupees, and yet you will not be quite sure whether the letter would reach the addressee even after a lapse of two days.

To be fair, a slight amendment needs to be introduced in this sombre chronicle of upwardly mobile tariff charges and steadily downward slide in the quality of service in the communications sector. In the very recent period, while rentals and charges for domestic telephone calls have continued to be raised, tariffs for intra-country trunk calls and overseas calls have been brought down by official order. And, of course, cellular telephones have made their advent, enabling the very rich to talk to other very rich persons, and crooks to talk to other crooks, here, there and everywhere in the country.

It will nonetheless be a truly formidable task to identify, in this concatenation of events, the people who will determinedly mobilize themselves in support of the ongoing communications revolution, and against the reactionary parasites that infest the trade unions as well as the dismal crowd of opportunist politicians. Whatever the weakness in the country's national income estimates and estimates of the incidence of poverty, to claim that a doubling of income has taken place over the past decade in the earnings of the overwhelming section of the Indian population, so that no resentment would be felt by this section at unbridled increases in the charges for communications services, will be quite extravagant. Citizens subsisting below the level of poverty, most statisticians agree, constitute roughly one-third of the national population; a World Bank assessment places their number at approximately 400 million. Add to this another 400 to 500 million belonging to the fixed income groups and such others, including those who have lost their employment because of the inexorable march of liberalization policies. These groups will have little love for a structure of continuously rising tariffs which puts communications with relatives, friends and well-wishers beyond the pale of feasibility. It strains the imagination that they will act as zealous cheerleaders for a revolution which promises greater and greater affliction on their cost of survival.

A bunch of Luddites would be the sneer of the technology revolution buffs. These antediluvian elements are, it will be maintained, totally unaware of the transformation that has already occurred, and continues to occur, in the quality of service made available to users of communications services, such as in the shape of improved technology from the marrying of dot.com and satellite transmissions, and new facilities exemplified by the expansion of mobile phones at reduced unit costs, for instance, the recent decision to lower trunk call and international call charges. Attention will also be drawn to the mind-boggling agrarian revolution that is bound to come in the wake of the opening up of the countryside through widespread tele-linkages, a process that has happily already begun.

The latest tidings from authoritative sources are however likely to be a damper on such enthusiastic claims. None of the six private entities granted licences to extend telecommunications services in different parts of the country have been able to deliver the goods. At the time the licences were given to them, these entities had entered into a pledge to install telephone connections to as many as 1,00,000 villages. They have been able to arrange connections to not even one-quarter of the stipulated number. The reason for the slippage is uncomplicated. In the poor country, few people in the villages can afford telephones and pay the tariffs that can ensure profit for the installers of the lines. It is only telephones installed within the precincts of the office of a village panchayat – or some public functionary – which makes 'economic' sense, since the payment of tariffs is underwritten by official agencies. The infrastructure called for establishing telephone links with a remote rural location is, in any case, highly capital-intensive. Having hogged the licences, the private companies are therefore no longer interested in fulfilling the commitments they had entered into. A so-called telecommunications revolution cannot obviously spark off an agrarian transformation; the sequence has to be in the reverse order. If this sounds like vapid politics, such politics is the hard reality of native conditions.

In the circumstances, who are the people who will forgather to frustrate the alleged conspiracy of the intransigent Luddites, bent on blocking the telecommunications revolution in the country? Such people cannot come from the 400 million subsisting below the level of poverty, they cannot come from the fixed income earning groups, small artisans, humble workers, the labouring classes and such like, who easily number another 400 to 500 million. One has to define 'people' in a very special manner so as to satisfy the revolutionary claims of the anti-Luddites. Massive popular support, according to the lexicon of the anti-Luddites, means the assembly of the handful of themselves, to wit, the top wealthy layer of the community, for whose sake charges for trunk telephone calls and overseas calls have been lowered; such lowering has been rendered possible by raising the tariffs for all other communications services, including the prices of postcards, inland-letter cards, ordinary and registered covers, and money orders. Delve into classical literature, the dispensation thus arranged fits the description of Plato's Republic.

But, then, the revolutionaries pledged to ensure the stability and security of an unequal state of affairs have no particular regard for symmetry, logic or compassion. They are jubilant beyond measure that the querulous administration has finally been persuaded to raise the prices of petroleum and petroleum products. Given the prevailing level of international prices for crude oil, it was insane, in their opinion, not to raise the domestic prices of petroleum products; hesitancy in the matter was every day contributing to accentuation of the deficit in the oil pool account. None amongst this tribe of impeccably correct economists and other distinguished citizens appears to have even a nodding acquaintance with not-so-ancient history. Barely a couple of decades ago, the oil pool account was lush with surplus; surplus that, year after year, kept adding to its corpus. A sensible contra-cyclical policy would suggest that surpluses accumulated during a favourable spell of years – when international prices of oil and oil products were lower compared to domestic prices – should be utilized to cover the deficit in the oil pool account when the situation turned adverse for the country. No reform-monger has bothered to enquire where and how the surplus in the oil pool account built in the 'good' years has disappeared. It has disappeared because of forced contributions from the account for augmenting the union government's budgetary resources. There is therefore every justification for the demand that the government forks out the sums it once stole from the oil pool account, and thereby avert a rise in domestic prices in the current season.

The 'reformers', habitual non-readers of history, will no doubt be scandalized beyond measure by this suggestion.

Sovereignty and the WTO

16 December 2000

The climate changes. New ideas and thoughts litter the concourse. Activists latch on to some of these ideas and transform them into material for political battles.

In the course of the past quarter of a century, an agenda that has captured the imagination of both regional and at least some national parties is the necessity of restructuring centre–state relations in the country. As social awareness has kept spreading amongst the populace in different parts and regions, demand has been voiced for the transfer, to a relatively greater extent, of effective administrative, legal and financial powers from the centre to the states. An adjunct of this demand is the clamour for further decentralization of functions and responsibilities from the state to the district, the block and the village panchayat levels; the old Leninist dictum, power to the people, has thus had an echo along these distant shores.

The inspiration behind this demand for greater devolution is a pre-independence heritage. A federal structure for liberated India was an integral part of the dream and pledges of the freedom movement. Even the Quit India resolution of 1942 had promised a Constitution for free India which would be distinctly federal in character, with the federal government assigned delegatory powers in the spheres of foreign affairs, defence, monetary policy and foreign trade, and the rest of the powers left to the care of the federating states. The Constitution, as it was drafted immediately following independence, makes much noise over the nation's supposed federal persona. India, the very first Article of the Constitution says, is a Union of States. The states, the logic of this statement suggests, precede the union, for without the existence of the states there could be no collective entity to be described as the union government. The details of the constitutional arrangements, however, demarcate the reality to be altogether different from the décor of the illusion: the substance of the powers of the republic rests with the centre, the states are only residuary recipients of functions and responsibilities. In fact, the very presence of Article 356 which permits the union government to despatch to the gallows a state government, on practically any pretext or even without a pretext, belies the claim of the preamble; the centre is overwhelmingly powerful, the states are weak servitors.

The campaign for realigning centre–state relations is intended to change this regimen: there must be, in the view of the joiners in this campaign, greater devolution of effective administrative powers from the centre to the states; greater prerogatives must also be granted to the states in the formulation and implementation of law; and, finally, the states must be allowed a much larger share of financial powers, including in the arenas of taxation and public borrowing; in addition, they must be permitted to exercise a certain measure of control over the banking sector, and, in special situations, to create credit as well.

This campaign for greater devolution has had its ebbs and high tides over the recent decades. The conjunction of political circumstances and strategic considerations has determined the course of such ups and downs. What is nonetheless remarkable is that even the most radical and vociferous campaigners favouring the rebuilding of the relationship between the centre and the states have taken care not to breach one specific '*Lakshmana rekha*': the union government, it has been implicitly admitted by even the most enthusiastic lobbyists for state rights, must have exclusive charge of defence, foreign affairs, foreign trade and monetary management. Demands for the abolition of the Concurrent List in the Seventh Schedule of the Constitution have also been aired from time to time. Amendments have been urged in the Constitution so that state legislations pertaining to land reforms are not subject to the veto of the union government. Controversy has arisen over the role of governors and whether the prerogative of appointing the Finance Commission, and deciding its terms of reference, should be shared by the centre with the states. Even the advisability of according blanket approval of Article 74 has been questioned: it has been maintained that where such delicate matters as recourse to Article 355 or 356 for either issuing directives to or disciplining a state administration is concerned, the centre should invariably seek the counsel of the inter-state council, on which the states are represented. But, apart from a few mavericks, none has raised any queries over the exclusive jurisdiction of the union government with respect to defence, foreign trade, monetary policy – and, of course, foreign affairs.

In the matter of external affairs, the constitutional provisions are unambiguous. The Union List in the Seventh Schedule, which lays down the items subject to the exclusive jurisdiction of the centre, has, among others, the following entries. Entry 10: 'Foreign affairs, all matters which bring the union into relation with any foreign country'; Entry 13: 'Participation in international conferences, associations and other bodies and implementing decisions made thereat'; and Entry 14: 'Entering into treaties and agreements with foreign countries, and implementing of treaties, agreements and conventions with foreign countries'. The script could not be more categorical. Entering into treaties with foreign countries and implementing decisions taken in international organizations come within the ambit of foreign policy. Till now, no occasion has ever arisen to contest the legitimacy of the union government's prerogative in this area. New Delhi offers credentials to representatives of foreign nations and sends ambassadors to these countries. New Delhi also enters into treaties with foreign trade, taxation of foreign nationals, external credit and such like. Here and there, state governments may or may not like aspects of the union government's foreign policy. They may, on occasions, express unhappiness over particular tilts in the centre's foreign policy. The *Lakshmana rekha*, it has however been tacitly agreed, is the *Lakshmana rekha*: the states have no right to interfere on foreign policy issues; the centre is the final decision-maker in this sphere.

But the climate changes, so do situations. Consider the Marrakesh Treaty, the blueprint of the World Trade Organization, which India signed in 1994. It is an international treaty which the Government of India has signed along with a 100-odd other country governments. New Delhi did not think it at all necessary to consult the state governments before signing the Treaty: it was its beat and why should it bother to solicit the opinion of the states. Most state governments too, at that particular moment, did not worry the least about the implications of this international Treaty. What belonged to the centre, they primly concluded, belonged to the centre; they have no business to poke their nose in the centre's affairs.

The past half-a-dozen years have witnessed unprecedented expansion in the frontiers of knowledge. Leave aside all other sections of the Marrakesh Treaty, concentrate only on those Articles which have relevance for agriculture and allied activities. The World Trade Organization has been set up to homogenize trade regulations as between various member-countries and render foreign trade free of impediments: at least such was the initial claim proffered on its behalf. That claim was only a façade though. Trade relations, the WTO has asserted in no time, are determined by production and distribution relations within the countries; there can be, in its view, no free trade unless production and distribution arrangements are also liberated. Therefore, the provisions of the Marrakesh Treaty enjoin that the structure of all domestic activities, not only in the arena of industry and services but also in agriculture, must be subject to its surveillance. Its provisions will, for instance, set the tone of how agricultural production is to be organized within a country, how farm prices and prices of inputs are to be fixed, how production and technology modalities are to be determined, and what will be the conditions governing the distribution of agricultural outputs. In other words, as per the Marrakesh Treaty, even Indian agriculture is now subject to the discipline laid down by the WTO.

This is where the dilemma arises. For, under our Constitution, agriculture is the absolute prerogative of the states. Here too, provisions of the Constitution do not lend any scope for ambiguity. The State List in the Seventh Schedule incorporates, *inter alia*, the following entries. Entry 14: 'Agriculture, including agricultural education and research, protection against pests and prevention of plant diseases'; and Entry 18: 'Land, that is to say, rights in and over land, land tenure, including the relation of landlord and the tenants, and the collection of rents, transfer, and alienation of agricultural land; land improvement and agricultural loans; colonization'. Land, land use, land tenures, land settlements, or, for that matter, whether farm inputs are to be supplied to the producers at subsidized prices, or farm output, including foodgrains, are to be supplied to the consumers, including consumers below the line of poverty, through the public distribution system at prices below production costs, are, by virtue of the provisions of our Constitution, the sole privilege of the state governments.

The Government of India, however, signed the Marrakesh Treaty, and Indian agriculture is therefore supposed to be under the total discipline of the World Trade Organization. The Treaty has transferred, without the leave of the states, prerogatives pertaining to agriculture which belong to them.

This is a piquant situation. The WTO is already on the move. Its Articles question the right of the states to subsidize the cost of inputs for the farm sector. They also cut athwart the decision of the state governments to sell foodgrains and other farm products to poverty-ridden citizens. The stretches over which the WTO is entitled to extend its dominion over Indian agriculture are much too numerous, given the fact that the Government of India has signed the Marrakesh Treaty.

Sign in haste and repent at leisure. Those in New Delhi who signed the Treaty had their focus on being on the right side of the US and other western governments, whose neo-imperial baby the WTO is. New Delhi has also reached the judgment that, considering its clout, it will always be able to browbeat the state governments to fall in line with the conditionalities of the Marrakesh Treaty. The internal situation can however change very rapidly. In the wake of the resentment provoked by the contradictions between state rights and WTO prescriptions pertaining to agriculture, at the next round of debates over centre–state relations, some states, it is distinctly possible, would demand that, even in some matters of foreign policy such as the signing of treaties, the states must have concurrent rights. At the other end, those who cannot wait even a fraction of a second for the completion of the globalization of the Indian system would, no doubt, ask for the abolition of the states as well as the scrapping of the existing Constitution, and its replacement by a no-nonsense unitary framework.

It is total war, and battles will be joined in different sectors, even over treaty rights.

The raison d'être

30 December 2000

Privatization, it almost seems, is for the sake of privatization alone, disinvestment for the sake of disinvestment. In the beginning, the pretext was there that the unloading of government shares will be confined to loss-making public sector units. That pretext has now gone the way of all flesh. Even public undertakings enjoying massive profits, such as the oil corporations, are to be denuded of government equity. The comparison with impoverished feudal princelings who start with selling plots by lots, and end up by disposing of pots and pans, inevitably comes to mind. The government in New Delhi is now even prepared to lease out airports.

The significance underlying such apparent madness is easily comprehended. Privatization and disinvestment are to assure foreign investors that we have moved away from the shibboleths of socialism; henceforth we mean business, henceforth it is the private sector which will rule the roost in *Mahaan Bharat*. Unfortunately, would-be foreign investors are not impressed by such gestures, nor are international credit agencies. The magnitude of direct foreign investment has dipped in recent times; the credit rating for India, already low, has gone further down. Even short-term capital flows, in the garb of portfolio investments, have been behaving temperamentally in the current year. As a result, the country's foreign balances fell continuously for five to six weeks. That trend has been halted because of renewed interest of speculators in the Indian share markets and the dubious sale of so-called millennium bonds. Such renewal of ardour for picking investment already on the ground is not echoed in the case of fresh investments though. Not surprisingly, overall employment in the economy has shrunk during the 'reform' years, even as growth has slowed down. Imports have supplanted growth; industrial units, bereft of the state's protective cover, have closed their shutters one after another. Enlarged imports have depressed agriculture as well, and the impact on output and employment in the small-scale sector has been most severe. As happens in any recessionary period, as employment contracts, the bargaining power of the working class and the poorer sections weakens as well. But a time comes when even the worm turns, witness the spate of industrial unrest in the last few weeks.

The defenders of the official stance, of course, have what they consider a clinching argument for selling off public property, although they are chary to articulate it too openly. The deficit in the government budget is at this moment exceeding Rs 50,000 crore. The World Bank and the International Monetary

Fund frown upon such profligacy, as do the multinational corporations: deficits imply preempting the market for the government, thereby reducing the space for the private sector. The deficit accordingly has to be, for dear life, brought down to a tolerable level. The only way out of the dilemma is to sell off public shares in corporate bodies, and to privatize banks, insurance companies, the oil industry, transport systems, airports, the whole lot. Given the circumstances, we are not, the vocalizers of this point of view say it plainly, the arbiters of our destiny; we go by whatever the foreigners advise; we will otherwise be in a jam. Even if the foreigners do not shower us with bounty in the form of direct foreign investment all the time, we cannot extricate ourselves from the habit of obsequiousness. It is a way of life which dies hard. It dies hard even when subservience to external forces in the near-decade since June 1991 does not bear evidence of any positive impact on the rate of either industrial or agricultural growth. Our rate of growth of food output has, available data suggest, fallen behind the rate of population growth over this period. Capital formation has levelled off. Public investment is, in any case, frowned upon, and private investment has not played any supplementing role. Capitalism, in the formal sense, has emerged triumphant in the country. We have, however, chosen to be hewers of wood and drawers of water on behalf of foreigners under this dispensation. Such submissiveness is not yielding any perceptible dividends. Even the crisis that has overwhelmed the American polity in the wake of the debacle over the result of the presidential election has failed to rattle our decision-makers, and, along with them, the comfortably placed upper strata of society. Faith, the latter continue to tell themselves, does move mountains: faith in the positive role of capitalism will see us through the tunnel; beyond the tunnel is paradise, and paradise is going to bless us with ambrosia.

But why target your barbs at the direction of the hoity-toity bourgeoisie alone? They can list several reasons for their persistence with optimism. Emissaries from God's own country have been trying hard to convince them that the imbroglio over the choice of the forty-third president will not affect either global American policy or American munificence. So, for the present, leave them ensconced in their class dreams. What about the defeatists swelling the ranks of the ideologues of the Left? Consider, for instance, the by now most respectable crowd of so-called post-modernists. Most of them started their romantic sojourn as Marxists of some hue, but passion soon got spent. The long, arduous, time-consuming trek along the route of ideological adherence was too much for them. They migrated, bit by bit, towards other destinations. Such migration, no doubt, satisfied their individual egos; it also, after a time-lag, ensured, at least for some of them, cushy chairs in American universities. There is no surprise in this kind of development. The deep calls to the deep; the shilly-shalliers too call to other shilly-shalliers. The formula of deconstruction, after all, bears a family resemblance to the process of splitting macro-organisms into micro ones. In both cases, society and collective aspirations give way to individual, self-centred propensities. The enemy of my enemy is my friend. In no time, therefore, the former ideologues, now flaunting deconstructionist credentials, are hugged and kissed by descendants of citizens of the Congress for Cultural Freedom vintage. The frustration-mongers in their midst are much more interested in the collapse of Soviet socialism than in data concerning the failure of capitalism to sponsor meaningful growth and equity in the poor countries, the inhabitants of which constitute the predominant majority of the human race. It is an aspect of the phenomenon of self-destruction; besides, is not the Soviet collapse itself another manifestation of self-destruction? Birds of the same feather flock together.

Why concentrate, however, exclusively on the post-modernists? Take into account the recent perambulations of those describing themselves as the New Left, who were, a quarter of a century ago, supposedly the beacon of the refurbished socialist millennium. These star-gazers too have thrown in the towel, like the Audens and the Spenders of the late 1940s; they too are not a disillusioned lot. Their plainspeaking could not be more revealing. Capitalism has won on all fronts, the socialists should better surrender in sackcloth and ashes. The only prospect for a qualitatively superior civilization lies in pathbreaking scientific and technological revolutions, which are also the gift of capitalism: there will consequently be, it is hinted, so much of material goods and services that exploitation will lose its relevance. It is a throwback, but perhaps with a difference, to the Schumpeterian theory of capitalist development; capitalism will rectify itself not on account of assaults and uprisings from the nether ranks, but because of the evolution of rational thought, which will teach one and all to detest social inequality; have rational thought, will travel. Scientific breakthroughs, the new version claims, will transform society. The comrades of the New Left do not explain how a breakthrough in science will automatically ensure a turnaround in social organization. Conceivably, they are banking upon the onset of euthanasia amongst the capitalist class because of a surfeit of lovely, lovely goodies that revolutionary achievements of science and technology will bring about. Hope springs eternal in the human breast, even in the breast of deformed deconstructionists and their acolytes.

To be fair, one must not be too hard on the votaries of defeatism. The fatalist view is influenced by class attitudes. The ambivalence of the intermediate classes is a crucial datum determining the shape of human affairs. Some belonging to this genus are moderately successful in declassing themselves; a few others try and fail. Those amongst the residue suffer from the affliction of a fractured mind. An archetypal instance, much quoted in twentieth-century annals, is that of Alexander Blok. Blok, the romantic idealist, was passionately in love with the October Revolution which transformed society and, he was convinced, ushered in a new civilization. At the same time, he could not hide his mortification because, in the wake of the Revolution, quite a few mansions owned by the aristocracy were pulled down. The libraries located in these mansions were set on fire; some of Blok's volumes of poetry were also consumed in flame. Blok was inconsolable.

The narration of this episode formed a part of Vladimir Mayakovsky's valedictory remarks at the grave-site of Blok. Mayakovsky himself was yet another specimen of the dichotomy in the intermediate class mind. Society succeeds in transforming itself because a handful from within it are able to transgress this duality and set themselves firmly along the path of progress. Since they are against the prevailing grain, it is their fate to be ridiculed in the beginning, to be called antediluvians, terradactyls, hopeless romantics. Such is the irony of the situation; because they dare to dare, think and act differently, and are for change, they are dubbed as reactionaries. It is for history to judge who are the realists and who are hopelessly out-of-date. Are those who refuse to face the fact of recession in the Indian economy over the past decade, and the growing suffering of the people on account of the ongoing 'reforms', going haywire, realists or otherwise? Should they be accused of depending on faith alone, or do we admit that they have the grit which allows them to separate the wheat of truth from the chaff of illusion?

It is, nevertheless, faith which enables the mobilization of courage without which the goal will remain as distant as ever. Even in the current Indian milieu, faith will continue to be at work despite the unfriendliness around. The Mayakovsky oration cited above is from a magnificently produced publication, *People's Art in the Twentieth Century: Theory and Practice,* put together by Jana Natya Manch, Delhi. It has excerpts, in Hindi and English, from the works of George Plekhanov, Romain Rolland, Maxim Gorky, V.I. Lenin, Lu Xun, Antonio Gramsci, Mao Zedong, Ervin Piscator, Bertolt Brecht, Haans Eisler, Dario Fo and Amilcar Cabral. Amongst Indian authors and activists who find a place in the volume are Prem Chand, E.M.S. Namboodiripad, Ramvilas Sharma, Utpal Dutt, Ritwik Ghatak, Safdar Hashmi. Never mind the hostile milieu, the Jana Natya Manch obviously still believes that people's faith can move mountains. The conventional economists – yes, even economists, for is not economics too basically people's art – who are in raptures because the second phase of the 'reforms' has commenced, should go through some of the pieces assembled here, maybe as rapid reading. Who knows, those who come to scoff might yet stay to applaud.

Trade and hypocrisy

12 May 2001

Continuity, the union Commerce Minister has gone on record to say, is the hallmark of sensible policy-making, particularly where agreements entered into with external agencies are concerned. The floodgate of imports last year's and this year's export–import policy has opened is the outcome of the Marrakesh Treaty signed in 1994 by the then Congress government. The present government, he maintains, has no alternative but to implement the conditions spelled out in the Treaty.

The Minister is absolutely right. Of course the export–import policy currently pursued, which promises to push Indian industry as well as agriculture to the wall, is the direct consequence of the country's admission to the World Trade Organization (WTO) pursuant to the signing of the Marrakesh Treaty. The BJP-led government can legitimately claim that, with continuity the supreme consideration, it is merely fulfilling the conditions membership of the WTO entails. In fact, the implications of this continuity in policy were already manifest in the concordat between the country's two leading political parties in regard to changes necessitated in the provisions of the Indian Patents Act 1970 for allowing the sovereignty of foreign patents in the Indian economy, an obligatory condition of WTO membership. When the BJP was in opposition, it was a great champion of anti-globalization tenets, and joined other groups and parties to stall the statute change proposed by the ruling Congress Party. The government had no problem in the Lok Sabha, but it lacked a majority in the Rajya Sabha. The legislation the foreign manufacturers had expectantly looked forward to, was aborted. That was however in 1995. By 1998, the Bharatiya Janata Party had switched places with the Congress; it now constituted the government, and the party of the Nehru–Gandhis was the main opposition. The Congress is a party which believes in ethics and morality; it also, at that point at least, believed in the continuity of official policy. Just because it was not in the government, it could not forsake its responsibility for ensuring that amendments to the patents legislation demanded by the WTO and the multinational companies got passed. In December 1998, therefore, the two major parties in the country joined hands in parliament and performed the last rites for the Indian Patents Act. The same alliance resurfaced when the issue arose of denationalizing the insurance industry and allowing American insurance concerns to come in and mulct the people.

But one should not be narrow-minded. It is not only with respect to legislative matters that continuity in official policy needs to be, and has been, rigorously observed in the polity. Consider, for instance, the scandals that sustain the share markets in our country. These are for ever. The 1992–93 scam, once it was revealed, created a lot of furore. A Joint Parliamentary Committee sat in judgement, produced a fat tome, and parliamentarians thought they had done their duty by their countrymen. Nothing of the sort. Since the nation had embraced the cult of liberalization, the markets, including the share markets, had to be freed. The Securities and Exchange Board of India (SEBI) may, every now and then, take the press into confidence with respect to the surveillance it is exercising over the stock exchanges. That is a pretence much like the other hypocrisies abounding in the system. A principal factor underlying the 1992–93 scam was the active role played by the banks, including a number of foreign banks, to prop up the shady activities of the eminent rogues who dominated, surreptitiously or otherwise, the share markets. Much in the manner of the SEBI, the Reserve Bank of India too has, over the past decade, been dishing out long rigmaroles about how it is ceaselessly mounting guard, like Rembrandt's *Nachtwacht*, to protect the interests of the people. No bank accommodation, it has asserted from time to time, is provided to evil-doers. All this is for the consumption of the gullible: the stable door has always remained ajar and the horses have continued to bolt. Neither the SEBI nor the RBI can be blamed too much; their political masters, they know, are sold out on the notion of the free market; they are committed to do the bidding of their masters. Nor, for the matter, is the Unit Trust of India in a position to behave any differently. The free market is basically a crook's market presided over by share-forgers, past masters in insider trading and similar types with whom bank chairmen and managing directors are in eternal cohort. That suits the ruling politicians. Therefore these scandals will continue to recur in our bourses till as long as the liberalization philosophy holds sway. Enough evidence is already available to suggest that the manipulators in the share markets have links with the tribe who control the ICE stocks, that is to say, outfits which deal with information, communications and entertainment scrips. Many of these characters, in turn, have a symbiotic relationship with the enemies of the country operating from the safe havens offered by the Gulf countries. But such things cannot be helped; to disturb the free market is sin.

An element, in fact a crucial element, is still missing from the picture depicted above. In a milieu where these blue-chip ICE stocks are expected to yield, and actually yield, a rate of return of 100, 200 or 300 per cent per annum, investors of any description would be fools not to divert their minds from genuine productive ventures to the miracles being enacted in the bourses. The recession in Indian industry can be accounted for by other factors as well, but one reason for it must be the fatal attraction to moneyed people of the urge to stray away from productive activities, where profit is either moderate or extremely low, and cross over to speculation. The lead given by such investors–speculators is faithfully followed by thousands of men and women belonging to the middle class who want to fatten their income, more so in view of the crisis they face in their daily living because of ever-spiralling commodity prices. The good government and the equally good Reserve Bank of India do not want to play false to the cause of the free market. They have lowered the rate of interest to encourage industrialists to borrow more from the banks and engage in productive activities. Rich men are no fools; they have taken advantage of the cheap credit, handed to them on a platter, to speculate merrily in the stock exchanges. Innumerable members of the bourgeoisie, petty and not so petty, have followed suit, withdrawn their bank deposits, now offering a derisively low rate of return, and made a beeline to the bourses with the objective of swelling their portfolio of ICE shares.

The bull masters are always ready for such a situation. They avail of this opportunity to inflate the prices of their favoured stocks. Sometimes they too take accommodation from the banks against shares so that the prices of the same shares could be further boosted through bull operations. A few brokers, who have been in league with these characters, have supported them with *badla* operations and short sales, thereby raining ruin on both the Mumbai and the Calcutta stock exchanges. This is all in the game; how does it matter if, because of their nefarious doings, thousands of households come to grief.

Whatever the Finance Minister may say in his umpteen statements on the floor of parliament, and whatever alibi the RBI and the SEBI may trot out for their lotus-eaters' indolence, nothing much is likely to change in the existing circumstances. Both the RBI and the SEBI may go through the motion of framing a new set of rules to discipline the banks and share markets in order to bring the rogues to book. All this will be for the birds. As long as the fascination for the free market does not dissipate, things will be much the same in the years to come; homage to continuity.

Let us face the facts. The number one culprit universally mentioned as responsible for the blow-up – or is it meltdown? – in 1992–93 remains very much out of prison. He goes about as an uncrowned *maharaja*. Books have been written by budding journalists hailing him as the foremost star in the Indian firmament, the champion of champions. One or two newspapers have invited him to write a regular financial column for them. The latest bunch of villains – sorry, heroes – have no apprehension, will be similarly honoured, give or take the interregnum of a few weeks. Not only is public memory short, the slide from old-style ethics is also along a steep gradient.

What has been discussed in the foregoing paragraphs is however an unfinished story. It has missed out the role of foreign institutional investors. Stray allegations have been lodged, not without basis, against some family-based industrial concerns: they are presumed to manipulate through their agents the share prices of their own companies, thereby chalking up huge gains. There is still a lacuna in this reportage. In all the inferences made by official and semi-

71

official quarters on the ills that visit the share markets, there is not one mention of what foreign institutional investors have been up to. Can we be sure that they are not the real artists behind the ongoing marionette dance, pulling the strings which determine the behaviour as much of the sneaky bears as of the big bulls? Is there not ground for suspecting that many of these foreign institutional investors have connived at lowering prices of chosen scrips to rock-bottom, acquired shares at throwaway prices, then conspired with the bulls to raise prices sky-high, sell their stocks at these prices and despatched post-haste their windfall profit to foreign shores, made possible by the most convenient mechanism of the convertible rupee? The Reserve Bank of India furnishes data on net invisibles on the current account from year to year; it does not inform us, though, what have been the gross takings of foreign institutional investors from their operations in Indian bourses and the remittances therefrom every year. It is not that the Reserve Bank of India will be unable to collate and present this information. Who knows, it has perhaps been instructed not to do so. Our masters have their masters too.

Dump food in the sea

23 June 2001

A parliamentary committee is a weighty proposition. Such a committee has seriously considered a suggestion that a part of the stockpile of foodgrains, of the order of close to 50 million tonnes, lying with the Food Corporation of India (FCI), should be dumped into the sea. The world is too much for the FCI, its storage costs are going up and up, the burden is impossible to bear any more for either it or the Government of India. In any case, the international financial agencies are breathing down the neck, public expenditure must be pared down to the minimum so as to create space for private activities. And it is not just external advice which the New Delhi regime has to heed to. The party heading the ruling coalition is heavily indebted, ideologically or otherwise, to the domestic trade lobby. If only the FCI, and, along with it, the entire business of public procurement and public distribution, could be done away with, it would open up the road of golden opportunity for private traders. A couple of years ago, the government had tried the stratagem of a recommendation from a similar parliamentary committee to dismantle the provisions of the Essential Commodities

Act. That recommendation was subsequently discovered to be a fake; a large number of the members of the committee were not even informed of the recommendations its chairman had submitted to the government. Whatever that bit of history, the façade of a parliamentary committee has tremendous advantage for implantation of dissimulation. Should an official committee of this nature decide that it is high time to dump foodgrains into the sea, the government's secretly nurtured desire receives the respectability of a parliamentary *dhobi*-mark.

The committee did not bother to ask itself whether, even in case the foodgrains in question were in the final stage of decay, these could not be used as fertilizers, instead of being thrown into the sea. Nor did it enquire whether, at an earlier stage, despite not being fit for human consumption, these grains could not be allocated for animal consumption. Another impolite query seems logical: could not the grains be distributed, at a stage when no decline in quality had in fact started, among the millions and millions of the hungry and the starving in the country, at a nominal price? It is taken as understood that it was beyond the means of these wretched people to pay the so-called economic price.

The government and the majority of the parliamentary committee would conceivably manage a riposte; the rules of the World Trade Organization (WTO), of which we constitute a loyal member, do not permit the government and the FCI to sell food at subsidized rates to consumers, even if they happen to be hungry and starving. The price charged must cover full cost, otherwise private traders would complain of being discriminated against. Still, should the WTO provisions induce us to abdicate common sense? The government has, in any case, spent crores and crores of rupees to procure and stock the foodgrains. Even if the grains, the whole lot of 50 million tonnes, were sold at one rupee or two rupees per kilogramme, at least Rs 5,000 crore, or Rs 10,000 crore, could have been recovered. There is also an Article in our Constitution, Article 282, which says that the government can make any grant for any public purpose with no questions asked from any quarters. It is not even necessary, therefore, to refer to the charter of international human rights: free distribution of foodgrains to famine-stricken people is a constitutional obligation. In case the mandarins ensconced in New Delhi would argue that the sovereign rights of the WTO abrogate the provisions of the Constitution, what about at least launching food-for-work programmes? Hungry men and women could be asked to build roads and dams, irrigation channels and primary schools, drains and land reclamation works, and so on, in exchange for food; no subsidy would be involved.

Fifteen or twenty years ago, no official committee would have dared to suggest that this country, where roughly one-third of the population is without the minimum calories necessary for subsistence, should nonetheless dump food into the sea rather than feed the deprived. The change of values that has taken place is of a staggering magnitude; this is what global acculturization has brought about. After all, surplus foodgrains have been dumped in the ocean by the US administration in the past. Is not the hallmark of civilization to do what the Americans do, or did?

An *anna* panchayat was organized in the nation's capital late in May. It was an unusual congregation. Poor, dishevelled people – men, women and children, gathered from all over the country, from almost every state, from villages and towns, mostly from villages. The heartland was largely represented by peasants and workers from Rajasthan, Madhya Pradesh, Chhattisgarh, Uttar Pradesh, Bihar and elsewhere. The humble spice and oilseeds growers from Karnataka were there; so too were cotton pickers, growers and weavers from Andhra Pradesh; farmers – middle and small, from Punjab and Haryana; and a procession of famished humble folk from the fringes of Orissa. Even as a team of jurors sat and listened, this stark assemblage of the Indian nation came up and narrated their woes, narrated tales of falling farm prices, lowered wages, distress sales of both crops and land, forced land alienation, shrinkage – or disappearance – of public procurement, abysmal failure of government agencies to buy crops at the assured minimum support prices, and rapidly dwindling supplies from the public distribution system. Rustic specimens from Rajasthan districts had harrowing tales to narrate of scarcity of water, both potable and for wetting the land, of government promises remaining unfulfilled years after years; of taps which are non-existent, wells which have dried up and irrigation channels, a joke. There was a frail woman from Orissa, with a tiny tot in her arms and a slightly older one in tow, who broke down as she recounted the horrendous story of how her tiny piece of land was taken away and just Rs 5 thrust in her hand as exchange value.

It was not a sequence of weeping and whimpering alone, though. Evidence, sharp and overt, was manifest of the anger seething, in state after state, among those who have received the lowest possible deal not only from the government, but also from the big farmers and the *mahajans*. A considerable part of the proceedings consisted of descriptions about how poor tenants and sharecroppers were goaded by their big brothers into switching from food crops to cash crops over the years. Now that the market for cash crops has collapsed, their income has been more than halved. They have no home-grown food to fall back upon, the wherewithal forthcoming from the sale of cash crops cannot cover the cost of the minimum of foodgrains they need to keep body and soul together. The other emerging phenomenon, widely commented upon, is equally noteworthy. Since the 1960s, following the government's adoption of a class-based farm price policy, acreage has shifted away from coarse grains such as jowar and bajra, to alluringly high-priced crops like wheat and paddy. As a result, the supply of coarse grains intended for consumption of the poor has continued to dwindle. It is superfluous to point out, so it was said, that in the course of more than half a century since independence, the production of pulses, on which the poor exclusively depend for their supply of protein, has remained more or less stagnant in absolute terms. Continuous reference was made to the havoc the likes of Monsanto was doing to our seed farms, and how the proposed planters' right legislation was intended to protect not Indian planters but breeders and planters from elsewhere.

Rude voices were raised at the *anna* panchayat. Determination was expressed not to allow the centre to run away from its responsibility to ensure food security on the plea of lack of resources. Food security, it was asserted, is no less important for the nation's survival than the defence of the country's territorial integrity. Will the government dare to hand over the country's defence to the private sector, or, for that matter, to foreign agencies, on the ground of dearth of resources? If the nation withers away because of the government's decision that it was much too expensive to maintain the public procurement-cum-distribution system, or since foreigners would not approve the luxury of such expenditure, it would be altogether purposeless to boost defence outlay, including investment for the upkeep of the nuclear arsenal. The *anna* panchayat took cognizance, with sarcasm, of the centre's airy-fairy proposal to transfer the onus of public procurement on the state governments. Will the centre agree, the caustic enquiry was posted on the floor, to transfer full control over banks and public financial institutions too to the states, so that they are not starved of funds to buy grains and are able to maintain the public distribution system in good order? Also, since the centre is in such an apparently desperate hurry to transfer functions to the states, what about permitting the states to renegotiate on their own terms entered into with the WTO, and, in case felt necessary, to opt out of this neo-imperialist body? The wrathfulness of the question could hardly be mistaken: what sort of mind has this international community which does not bat an eye when the Americans spend one billion dollars every day for subsidizing their agriculture, while our government is forbidden to follow the same practice? The panchayat was unanimously of the view that the WTO's insistence on the withdrawal of quantitative restrictions on imports was the source of most of the sorrow that has descended upon the poor millions in the country. Quantitative restrictions, the panchayat thundered, should be immediately reimposed. An equally vociferous demand was for extensive resumption, straightaway, of the food-for-work programmes everywhere, to begin with in the most distressed areas.

To listen to the heartrending descriptions of immiserization and starvation was an instructive and chastening experience. Should not a government and its agencies, as well as parliamentary committees, cultivate the sensibility to come down to earth, sit at the feet of such panchayats and learn about the unfolding ground realities in the country? Let there be no mistaking, if they fail to do so, big trouble lies ahead, not only for the ruling politicians and civil servants who take snap decisions at the top, but also for the entire nation.

But, as Ezra Pound once said, maybe in a different context: all this is folly to the world.

What the love-lorns talk these days

4 August 2001

Fifty years ago, double-decker buses were a common sight in Calcutta streets. They would ply from the northern fringes of the city to Ballygunge and back; the up and down journeys would take roughly 50 minutes apiece. Occasionally, a pleasing sight would catch the eye. A boy and a girl, both in their early twenties, would climb to the upper deck of the double-decker and occupy a front seat nestling against each other. During the span of 50 minutes, they would perhaps pour sweet nothings into each other's ears. Or they would recite some poetry in unison. Or, in case they had a fascination for politics, they would discuss the prospects of their favoured candidate in the ensuing assembly by-election in a Calcutta constituency. Or they would have a whispered dispute over the ins and outs of existential philosophy, and spout quotes from Kierkegaard, Heidegger and Sartre.

Double-deckers are now almost extinct in Calcutta but a few can still be seen to crawl along the old north–south route, although the time to cover the distance takes today at least half an hour more than it did half a century ago. It is no surprise if, every now and then, as in the days of yore, a young couple ventures to go up and occupy a double seat on the upper deck. But, eavesdrop with care, they do not exchange any more romantic sayings or lines of poetry or discourses on politics or philosophy. The hour and the mutual company are used for what they consider a more worthwhile purpose; they talk, incessantly, about share market prices and how they could make a killing in case they invested in this lot of shares rather than that lot.

This is the cultural revolution that has overwhelmed the country's middle class; Calcutta is no exception. The great transformation initiated in 1991 has, of course, altered the contours of the national economy. Much more than that, it has affected, wholesale, people's mores, ethics, cultural pattern and general attitude to life. Poetry is blasé, words of endearment are *passé*, politics is a bygone fad, philosophy is for the birds. The nation – or that portion of the nation which matters – has forsaken all worn-out apparel. It has embraced an altogether new garb and a refurbished system of values. Maximizing the rate of return is the be-all and end-all of existence, to wit, maximizing the wealth of oneself; the rest of the society can go to dogs. In this milieu, the stock exchanges have their special charm. Speculation, the youngsters have been told, is the turnpike to material success. The syllabi in universities and other supposedly academic institutions are undergoing a sea-change. Science graduates shun basic research in physics or chemistry; they migrate to institutes of technology. That first-order migration is however not enough. After graduating from a technology course, the collies spend another two years in a management institute to round off their skills and aptitude. Arts baccalaureates make a beeline for finance and accountancy; their next port of call is information and computer technology; and the subsequent halt is a business management college.

True, only the more meritorious students can travel along this route and land cushy jobs. They splash money on luxury living. A major part of their savings they set aside for the purchase of shares. They, or at least some of them, soon acquire the art of making the right connections, which even ensure their access to insider trading.

Young people with less smart academic record and lower intellectual capability try to do the best of a bad job. Computer courses are life-saving devices for them; so too are coaching classes for managerial training. Quite a few amongst these youngsters fail to secure good, steady assignment. Some do, but of the mediocre sort. They nonetheless do not allow their vaulting ambition to die down. The stock exchanges beckon to them. They cultivate the proximity of professional brokers. If luck holds, they themselves manage to slink into the profession, provided they have, once more, the proper connections.

Like it or not, it is a new society. The Fund–Bank–WTO complex has taken over the economy. This has not spurred growth, barring in a small segment of the services sector, which is not however terribly labour-absorptive. The crisis in industry and the continuing phenomenon of lock-outs and shut-downs have swelled substantially the volume of unemployed. The withdrawal of quantitative restrictions on imports has worsened the situation. At the other end, there is an upward surge in people's urges and expectations. The satellite television channels have been, if not a great civilizer, at least a great globalizer. Even the unemployed and the unemployable now know what the contents of a good life are. They are a sullen and angry lot. They had been misled by yesterday's leaders and politicians who talked gibberish about the virtues of self-abnegation and frugal living. The new generation is determined not to repeat the blunder. They will beg, borrow or steal in order to reach wealth and affluence. They will smuggle heroin or run guns so as to grab a package of money. And a considerable number amongst them will, as a matter of course, patronize the share market.

Cross-section as well as historical studies have revealed an interesting datum. An inverse relationship exists between industrial prosperity and bullishness in the share market: slow industrial growth induces investible funds to seek solace and a good return elsewhere, in speculation on stocks and shares; a fast rate of industrial production, on the other hand, decelerates such away flows of funds to the bourses, so much so that bears take over the share market. A section of the Indian middle and upper classes had not till now overly worried over the ongoing industrial recession and employment slack. The stock exchanges had served as a lifebuoy. The members of the middle class knew their mind, they crossed over to the share market. After all, this is also the advice offered by the international financial agencies. The secret of modernization and efficient economic performance, those sage institutions have dinned into the ears of our politicians and administrators, is to start a state-of-the-art stock exchange system. The goal has been attained in India, to the satisfaction of the Fund–Bank apparatchik, over the past decade. True, the rate of overall economic growth has slumped to near-zero; the rate of growth of industrial production is not in much better shape either. Never mind, the children of rich families have been getting absorbed in services, such as in foreign banks and insurance companies, and in information technology outlets. Constituents of the middle class, ensconced in their joblessness, have not been totally unhappy either; they had the share market to fall back upon.

Now there is a spanner in the works. The Unit Trust of India has let down the middle class. There can be no forgiving of this sin. As many as twenty million citizens have invested, over the years, in the UTI's prize-ship of a scrip, the US-64. They represent a populace of easily one hundred million. There are yet others who have invested, separately or concurrently, in monthly income schemes and such like. In the aggregate, they make up a significant segment of the total electorate. The UTI's perfidy is threatening to set the river of panic on fire amid these sections.

Confidence is a funny attribute. While one is brimming over with it, nothing can go wrong with the universe. The economy may go to the dogs, so what? Unemployment may swell from month to month, so what? Income inequalities may widen, but citizens could not care less for the emerging crisis. But once confidence gets eroded and the elasticity of expectations turns negative, none can escape the fate of being hurtled into a state of chaos. The UTI fiasco is a politically sensitive issue and the government is more than likely to launch into a number of firefighting operations. But, once befuddled, twice shy. And, besides, a collapse in the share market is no guarantee for a revival of industry and manufacturing: the results of cross-section and historical studies are apparently a one-way street.

Large elements of the middle class are rattled. Their discontent is bound to express itself appropriately. A hundred reasons exist for the travail infesting Indian society, not excluding caste and communal schisms and linguistic bravados and counter-bravados. The danger the revolt of the middle class is likely to pose is however of a completely different genre. Paul Sweezy had, once upon a time, composed some notes on the dichotomy in the middle-class psyche. This class is an amorphous substance located between the ruling class and the proletariat. A considerable body of the Indian middle class had, during the phase of the freedom movement and in the early post-independence decades, lent its sympathy to the toiling masses. That was the long-standing national ethos, the ethos which dominated the middle-class mind. It is no longer so, not since 1991. The instrumentality of information technology and the share market is a concrete reality; the middle class is now aspiring to be an inseparable part of the ruling class. Upmarket mobility is the key word; let the working class be damned, the breed of the middle class would not be caught dead in the company of society's wretched ones. They – middle-class men, women and children – have begun to cultivate a taste for the good things in life, alongside a genuine hatred for the working classes. Their devoutly wished ascent to the upper stratosphere has experienced a hitch following the holocaust caused by the UTI's maladroit handling of things. The constituents of the middle class are gripped by fear; would they lose their shirt and be pushed once more to the fringes of the working class? That eventuality would, no doubt, be a bad omen for the ruling class and the international financial agencies as well. Conversely, it could lift the morale of those who have not lost their faith in cynicism.

The level of awareness

16 February 2002

Suffering and tolerance of suffering are different kettles of fish, just as destitution and tolerance of destitution are. Indians, by and large, are in a much more desperately destitute state of living than the people of Argentina. The skewness in income distribution is horrendously more here than there; the rate of unemployment, if one counts in the workless in the countryside, is worse in our case than for the Argentinians; the per capita income is much higher in the Latin American country. The standard indicators, however, signify little. The people in Buenos Aires and other towns and cities in the Argentine Republic have rolled into the streets with their pots and pans and sticks and umbrellas, and faced police batons and teargas shells and flying bullets, because they have a tolerance level which is different from ours. We are hungrier than they, more emaciated, with less health care and with perceptively less clothing and other protection against the elements. Even the level of literacy is lower for the Indian populace. The relative level of suffering is however irrelevant, for, compared to that of the Argentinians, the level of tolerance in our case is pronouncedly on a higher plateau. At the risk of being dubbed a Lukacs copycat, one could even sneak in the concept of level of consciousness. The wretched categories in India have a level of consciousness, or of awareness, of a low order. They have been trained over the centuries to assume their state of being as Almighty-ordained; you can cheat them, beat them, flog them, crush them under the boot, they will not fight back. Some of them will even take their persecution as benediction. The deprivation one is not aware of cannot constitute the powder keg for revolt. The Indian tolerance level is exceedingly high.

Not so with the people of Argentina. Their patience has snapped fairly early because, some would say, their tolerance level is relatively low. As is obvious, the relationship between the level of consciousness and the level of tolerance is obverse: as one rises, the other falls; as one falls, the other rises. But, the complaint will be posted, this is tautology. A tautology does not extend the frontiers of knowledge; it cannot, for instance, offer us a plan of action for remedying the ills of society. Are we so sure? Suppose, looking at the Argentine landscape, we conclude that the pragmatic need of the hour in India is to reduce the level of our tolerance, it should not necessarily be considered as a dumb statement. The level of tolerance drops even as the level of consciousness rises. To alleviate the situation in our backyard, we need, therefore, a course in awakening and enlightenment which could push up the level of awareness. Even knowledge of what is taking place elsewhere in the world can assist in reducing the period of waiting for what Left radicals excitingly describe as the emancipation of the Indian people.

The Left radicals are, however, no longer the determinants of the fate of humanity in any corner of the globe. Even as they reeled under the impact of unwholesome experiences, major new combatants have crowded the field. History, these fresh entrants assert, is no longer a process in time; it is a dead full stop. At a meeting of the National Development Council some years ago, a state chief minister was heard pontificating on one beatific aspect of Indian existence: we had the poor sections in our society way back during the Aryan civilization; we had the poor during the heyday of Buddhism; the poor were around at the time of the temporary Hindu revival in the Gupta era. Once the Pathans came in, the wheel of fortune did not change for the poor. The same situation obtained during the later Muslim incursions. Malign emperors succeeded benign ones, the poor were there for ever. The Mughal empire disintegrated, India was sliced up into local fiefdoms and anarchies; poverty-stricken Indian masses remained steadfastly poverty-stricken, dying in millions at the first hint of crop failure in stray years. The British period did not offer any relief either. India continued to be divided between the microscopic minority of lords, barons and *maharajas* nestling the superstructure, and the countless famished plebians at the base. What a relief, the chief minister attending the meeting of the NDC gloated, the conflation of class forces has been invariant in the post-British calm waters of the nearly half-a-century-long Indian National Congress reign. Why should then the Council waste time discussing the details of silly anti-poverty programmes; are these not for the birds?

For this species of believers in stagnation, the level of tolerance is extra-ordinarily low. They hate to be described as fundamentalists. There are, they honestly feel, a number of eternal verities which are not susceptible to the buffet-ing of time: in our beginning is our end, in our end is our beginning. Science and progress are, they allege, superstitious notions each sane citizen must stay away from. Supersonic planes used to pierce the sky in the days of the *Ramayana,* all the medication that one needs is already crammed in Ayurveda, and astrology is going to inform the rulers whether they are going to win the impending elections hands down, or whether a *yagna* has to be performed to correct the kinks along the fortune line; why, it will also predict the country's victory in the coming war with Pakistan. Should you demur, they will explode; they have a low tolerance level.

We thus land into an environment where several levels of tolerance con-front one another, each propped up by assorted levels of consciousness. A humble citizen of the country may be resident in a habitat barely a hundred miles from Mumbai or New Delhi or Chennai or Kolkata, but he or she may in effect live in a milieu three or four or five thousand years old: social and economic exploita-tion is acute; literacy is zero; food, as in every epoch, is awfully short in supply for the poor. For this individual and similar down-and-out ones, the level of tolerance is very high. In contrast, for those few at the top who are determined to proselytize the rest of the population into the belief of the impossibility of alter-ing the human condition, the level of tolerance is extremely low; they operate, in other words, on a very short fuse. They look for their guns at the first sign of a meek, not protest, but question, emitting from the lips of one of the millions and millions of the dumb multitude. In one sense, the so-called fundamentalists are right. They realize that in this tussle between the level of their tolerance and that of those whom they oppress, they hold the advantage. They have the advantage because they have monopolized the nation's wealth which entitles them to the weaponry of intolerance. The other side, the masses, of course, do not have any such entitlement.

The issue is actually even more complicated. Even amongst those who had once pledged to fight for the cause of the masses and challenge the congeni-tal non-believers in progress and history, occasional lapses of concentration are a common occurrence. It is the shadow of the Marxian cloud: the ideas of the rul-ing class tend to have an opiate influence on the psyche of others in society; those aspiring to guard the ramparts of resistance on behalf of the persecuted also succumb, every now and then, to the wiles of ideas beamed from the pinnacle of the superstructure. Because the non-believers in science and rationality see a spy in every bush, those who in other seasons want to resist the enemies of the histori-cal process feel shaky; they too begin to play the reactionary pastime of spy-hunting, here, there, everywhere.

The issue is further complicated by the globe suddenly turning into an

integrated village. It now becomes important to include in the matrix of calculations not only the parallel and competing conglomeration of levels of tolerance
within the home precincts; we need to generalize our system after taking cognizance of the external variables. We can no longer pretend blissfully that our
internal quarrels and squabbles are our own business, foreigners must keep out.
The superpower cannot be kept out. As everybody knows, the more powerful you
are, the less is your level of tolerance. It is perhaps legitimate to profess doubt
about the level of consciousness or awareness of the superpower; that has, however, nothing to do with the level of temperature at which its blood boils in the
context of a particular episode or event. Once the superpower takes a dislike to
Osama bin Laden, he has to be captured, dead or alive. The record, as of now,
shows that he is yet to be captured either dead or alive. This is datum the superpower finds it impossible to get reconciled to; its level of tolerance, to repeat, is
low. Therefore the change of regime in Kabul has not mattered; the Americans
must persist with their carpet-bombing of Afghanistan, and its intelligence network must spread to every nook and corner of the world. Barely six years ago,
an Indian prime minister pledged on the floor of parliament that the US Federal
Bureau of Intelligence would not be allowed to open offices in India under any
circumstances. That was half-a-dozen years ago, and it was a different prime
minister; the old order has changed, yielding place to new. What is interesting,
though, is that an FBI officer, or maybe a couple of them, could find their way
even into the citadel of the Left in the country. The pretext was almost readymade:
an attack on the local American Centre which killed only four Indians, and,
serendipity is as serendipity does, not a scratch on any American. Since the so-
called terrorists had come to Calcutta, President Bush's men could not be far
behind. The local fellows could not object: their level of tolerance is high even as
that of the American president's men is low. Some non-worthy ones will even
ascribe the difference to the difference in the content of bone-marrow.

The hand of the super-bosses

16 March 2002

The time-horizon for expectations has shrunk to the limit. It is now a
wobbly still-point. Disinvestment is not even for the luxurious sake of disinvestment per se; it is for the desperate reason of somehow temporarily narrowing the

fiscal gap, otherwise the Fund–Bank superiors will turn grumpy, never mind tomorrow's state of stocklessness. Translated into vernacular, the argument proffered is nearly as follows: we will cross the bridge when we come to it, meanwhile let us go ahead and dismantle it; if a great chasm of fierce water awaits us, well, tomorrow is another day. And, perhaps it is also added, *sotto voce*: who knows, some of us will have stashed enough money by then in Swiss accounts, thereby saving the bother to be around tomorrow.

There is cause for jollity elsewhere too. The foreign exchange holdings have crossed the 50-billion-dollar landmark. The polity may be in dire straits, the economy is sinking with every day; the creamy layer will however be spared sleepless nights, they will not be inconvenienced in any manner. In case the flow of incoming speculative dollars continues uninterrupted, why should the privileged set to worry about the plight of the poor and down-and-outs? The government is well-seized of the matter. With 50 billion dollars of foreign moolah in the kitty, the rupee should have been considerably strengthened in the exchange market. It has been otherwise, courtesy the Reserve Bank of India, which has nudged the commercial banks to sell rupees and buy dollars, thus ensuring that the rupee keeps reaching record low levels. A depreciating rupee, it is being hoped, will guarantee the tranquil flow of short-term speculative funds: the movers of such funds will make their killing and repatriate a larger amount in dollars than they had brought in. The other, more explicitly stated, apologia – maintaining the export competitiveness of Indian goods and services – is bogus: the illiteracy of the policy of competitive depreciation of the currency in order to boost exports had been discredited as far back as 70 years ago. No, other explanations are without relevance: in the roster of dos and don'ts engraved in the structural adjustment programme, currency devaluation occupies the pride of place. Masters order, we obey, for theirs is the kingdom.

History marches on. Consider the colourless budget the union Finance Minister presented on the last day of last month. Even he could not but admit the sorry reality of the economy having come to a screeching halt. The alibi he has provided is a photocopy of the Washington Consensus line; 11 September is the villain of the piece as if Osama bin Laden's spell had operated retroactively. This is tedious nonsense. To pick one stray instance: the country's exports had actually begun to dip several months ahead of the ides of September. There is no need to read the budget between the lines; it is an open book. Orders are orders, the union government does not dare propose public investment in the industrial sector. The private sector, the hint has gone out, will henceforth be on its own; no pandering to the thesis that public outlay does not draw out, but in fact draws in, private investment. The much-touted allocation in the plan for the agricultural sector is mostly fluff. Such cosmetics have been the feature in the preceding years as well; this time the exercise in pretension will only be more wide-bodied. That is not the case, though, with outlays proposed for infrastructure sectors like telecommunications, civil aviation, and roads and harbours. Outlays of this nature have an inordinately high import propensity, and will therefore gladden the heart of foreigners.

The budget travels much farther to emphasize the sovereignty of policies, decisions and measures which toe the line laid down by the Washington super-bosses. The chronicle of the past decade has exposed the harsh truth: direct foreign investment is incentive-neutral; howsoever we cringe, long-term investment will not come hither but will go thither, to the Middle Kingdom. That knowledge has not prevented the New Delhi mandarins from continuing to offer additional bonanza to potential investors from overseas. The noble NRI species should feel proud: they will, from now on, be allowed to repatriate their profits in full. No complaints can be lodged anymore that India's capital accounts are a *cul-de-sac*. Generosities abound in the budget. *Hawala* has, in effect, been legalized. Not just mutual funds outfits, but corporate bodies too, will now be permitted to take money out of the country, and utilize it for whatever benevolent or malevolent purposes they have in mind. This decision will however put to some disadvantage our intelligence personnel: they will no longer be able to claim that the kidnapping of a minor industrialist in Calcutta or the burning down of the Sabarmati Express in Gujarat has been financed by the Inter-Services Intelligence of Pakistan through *hawala* transactions. It is a sacrifice one wing of the government will have to bear so that another wing could present a budget which is pleasing to the Washington Consensus.

The budget is a path-breaking exercise in another sense too. Investment in the country may have dried up, foreign investment too may be playing hooky, the rate of industrial growth is down, agriculture is unable to expand because of the non-expansion of irrigation and drainage in new areas. Nonetheless, a substantial part of the nation's savings is to be pushed out of the country. This is where the nobility of the country's moral philosophy shows up: just ask the Minister for Human Resources Development; ever since the Vedic days, Indians have been taught the art of self-abnegation, the world has invariably been regarded as belonging to a higher order of priority than the home.

Time must not have a stop. After a decade of non-success with the structural adjustment programme reforms, the government has chosen to go the whole hog. Admonitions were arriving thick and fast: you have come a cropper with your reforms because you have been cowardly nervous Nellys; you have done things in half, whether in the financial sector or elsewhere. The season has come, the Washington walrus has ordained, to be extravagantly bold. The budget has now initiated, drastically, the second generation of reforms; no half-measures from now on, it will be a full-fledged comprador regime.

Do consult any dictionary of good credibility, the expression 'comprador' has respectable Latin roots; the meaning provided is 'a native servant employed as a head of the native staff and as agent by European houses'. The compradors, in other words, exist not for the sake of themselves or their native country, but for foreigners in whose employment they happen to be.

What the Indian National Congress commenced eleven years ago is currently being rounded off by the NDA alliance. The budget has led to resentment across the broad spectrum of native sons and daughters. The prices of gas, fertilizer, kerosene, postal articles and such like are up, steeply so; the rate of the dividend tax has been raised; the interest rate has been lowered. While this has infuriated the middle and lower middle classes, the big bourgeoisie do not consider the interest rate cut enough of an incentive. On the other hand, the decline by at least 2 per cent in the interest rate over the past couple of years has had no positive effect on private investment activity. Even consumption has not been boosted by the availability of cheap credit. The elasticity of expectations has remained unmoved. If there are no land reforms and no extensive restructuring of the distribution of income and assets all over, demand will continue to be sluggish, and the economy will go to seed. The supply-side exponents of economic theory will not buy this proposition; it cuts across their theology. The purpose of existence is linearly related to the protection of exotic theology as well as of buccaneers of foreign lineage. Therefore, rejoice that retrenchment is the order of the day, and legislation permitting snap hiring and firing will soon be on the anvil.

The dilemma is the same as that faced by the US General in Vietnam. Vietnam, he confessed, had to be destroyed in order to save the free world. The Indian economy has to be destroyed in order to reform it appropriately. Jobs must shrink, prices must rise, factories must close, investment must come down, output must wither, in order that the reforms might emerge triumphant. To bring up the old cliché, the operation was successful, but the patient died.

There is one hitch though. Compradors constitute a minuscule minority of the nation. They will, no doubt, prosper, and will receive the protection of the foreign masters. The overwhelming majority will, sooner or later, begin to get angry; deprivation provokes anger. And anger can seek several outlets. A possible solution of the problem of accumulated anger is however worth experimenting. If the hungry ones can be taught to embrace a fundamentalist faith of this or that genre, the outcome could be lovely. The symptoms in contemporary society are promising. Nobody has yet alleged that the *Ramsevaks* have been instigated by the ISI; they are an autonomous entity, springing from the heartland of Lord Rama. Every action induces an opposite, and often equal, reaction. This reaction too can be native-born, with conceivably some help from the ISI, just as the Pakistanis allege that the MQM in Sind is the handiwork of India's Research and Analysis Wing.

In any event, civil strife and more civil strife are going to take over. The comprador crowd will never say die; they will worship the foreign masters till the glorious, frightening end of the festival of blood-letting. Be proud, it is the epoch of the comprador.

A layman asks

22 June 2002

Lay persons are a public menace. They ask silly, often exasperating, questions. One such layman has shot off a letter, the main text of which runs as follows:

> May I, Sir, request you to explain to me why we are not utilizing our seemingly large foreign exchange reserves to finance our pressing and priority projects, so as to accelerate our short- or long-term development programmes, particularly those which are likely to provide assured returns by way of direct or indirect revenue to the national exchequer? In asking this question, I am assuming that the published amount of foreign exchange, as at date, is not merely a notional figure but that the funds are actually lying with the commercial banks or the Reserve Bank of India. I appreciate that there may be stringent rules or guiding criteria governing the usage of foreign exchange reserves. But when I read that the government of India proposes to release large sums of foreign exchange to deserving (?) entrepreneurs for setting up or acquiring industries abroad, I can only assume that such allocations would be funded from our foreign exchange reserves, keeping in view that our imports are of a higher order in terms of foreign exchange expenditure than the value of our exports. Would it not be more prudent to utilize temporarily the foreign exchange funds, if lying idle, to develop our infrastructure, modernize our steel and other core sector industries, tasks which would uplift our GNP, generate employment and enhance the potential for export earnings?

The quotation is unedited and unexpurgated. It is of the same genre as the query why millions and millions of tonnes of foodgrains are kept stacked in government storages, and are deployed neither to feed the one-third of the national population who go to bed every night with hunger in their belly, nor to give a push to development projects through food-for-work programmes. Resolving questions of this nature obviously belongs to the higher stratosphere of economic wisdom. Our learned economists and equally learned politicians and public administrators know the proper answers. The problem lies elsewhere: how to put them across for the benefit of lay people who sadly lack common sense of both the ordinary and extraordinary variety.

The gentleman scribbling the letter can of course be doled out, in a couple of sentences, a simplified version of rarefied truth. He could be reminded of the adage that they too serve who stand and wait. Idle foreign exchange reserves serve a crucial social purpose. The bulk of these reserves is made up of two components: (a) short-term speculative funds sent in by so-called foreign institutional investors in search of quick profits in our stock exchanges; and (b) deposits parked with domestic banks by venerable non-resident Indians so as to fetch high interest, both the principal and the interest earnings repatriable overseas on demand. These reserves should be displayed, but not used, in normal circumstances. Assets, after all, create liabilities. The foreign exchange assets are a sort of security blanket for the external investors. Their existence tells the foreign parties that their investments and deposits in this country are fully assured. Should, for some reason, things tend to turn bad in the country and foreigners suffer from a spell of nervousness, they might be tempted to take their money out. Were such a situation to arise, our respectable-looking kitty of foreign exchange reserves would becalm them; they would know that should they decide to pull out their money, the foreign exchange reserves would come in handy to satisfy them.

In that sense, foreign exchange reserves are built strictly not for benefiting the country and its people; these reserves are for the sake of ensuring the august presence of foreigners, NRIs including, in our midst. The latter are our honoured guests; so that they are enabled to disabuse themselves of any unwholesome worry, the reserves will act as ultimate guarantor.

It is a near-parallel with the theory underlying the holding of foodgrain stocks. These stocks provide an assurance to big landholders and rich peasants, particularly those concentrated in the north-western parts of the country: they should entertain no doubts in their mind, whatever grains they produce will be duly purchased by state agencies and kept in public godowns. Such an arrangement strengthens the faith of the big shots in the farm sector in the system; irrespective of the size of output or its quality, the public agencies will be there to buy up the whole lot that is offered. Strides in agricultural production and productivity are for the edification of the affluent sections swelling their profits. Let us cut out the nonsense and call a spade a spade: the government is of the rich, by the rich, for the rich. Foodgrain stocks are not supposed to be released either free or at low prices to the hungry and the needy. The purpose of foodstock-building is to provide the fullest insurance to rich peasants. As for the poor, they are expected to fend for themselves; they should not be greedy and hanker after a portion of the huge stockpile of grains – just as those others who want to speed up the country's economic development must perish the thought of drawing on the foreign exchange reserves to finance industrial, agricultural or infrastructural projects.

A slight elaboration of what has been said above is perhaps called for. The foreign exchange holdings, regular bulletins on the day-to-day movement of which are issued by the Reserve Bank of India, are what can be described as primary foreign exchange accretion. The piling up of these holdings has a public relations objective: to let the world know that India is always deferential to the interests of external parties. The accretion of exchange assets will, it is hoped, induce a process of secondary foreign exchange intrusion, such as in the form of direct foreign investment, precursor of milk and honey flooding the country. Here is the rub though. The phenomenon of massive direct foreign investment has failed to manifest itself despite our very impressive foreign exchange holdings. Again, the parallel with foodstock holdings is quite comforting. Now that agriculture is flourishing and foodgrains are available in abandon, those who suffer from foodlessness are expected to empower themselves with enough purchasing power, and buy the grains directly from the trader or the producer. If, for some reason, the market mechanism does not function properly and the consumers are unable to spare the money to buy grains at prices the producers and traders insist upon, and, as a result, several thousand deaths take place, the government must not be blamed for the failure of the market mechanism. Providing for the famished should be only a secondary objective, and will come into the picture only as a last resort. Meanwhile, poor people are not supposed to grumble. They should take advantage of the opportunities thrown up openly by the liberalization rules set by the World Trade Organization, and endeavour to reach a level of earnings in consonance with the price of foodgrains offered by the producer or the trader. To release hastily government stocks of grains so as to feed the poor, who have proved themselves to be nincompoops in the marketplace, will be committing a sin against the WTO.

Surplus foodgrains constitute a prestige item. They allow us to inform the rest of the universe about our attainment of food self-sufficiency. Whether such sufficiency helps to feed the nation's poor millions is beside the point. Foreign exchange reserves, it is possible to argue, also belong to the prestigious category. They are intended to improve our international credit rating. Once more, we face a conundrum. Our foreign exchange holdings continue to soar while the credit rating we receive from Standard & Poor's or Moody's keeps dropping from B plus to B and further to B minus minus. The rating institutions are obviously not impressed by the size of our foreign exchange kitty. They reach their own judgment; what we hold, they have concluded, is a brittle corpus and could disintegrate overnight, in the manner the reserves did in the East Asian countries during the 1997–98 crisis.

Between the two world wars, literature buffs were wont to spend an enormous amount of energy and talent to discuss the pros and cons of art for art's sake in creative pursuits. That debate, several others thought, was a drip. We appear to have run into a similar situation with the controversy on the role of foreign exchange holdings in accelerating national development. A theology is threatening to take over: foreign exchange holdings are for the sake of holding foreign exchange, and we better desist from exploring other façades of the phenomenon.

Imagining parallel situations, however, has its limits, much in the manner the endeavour to discover parallel passages in literature has. Foreign exchange and foodgrain stocks possess one major dissimilarity. You can never tire of foreign exchange holdings; on the other hand, piling foodgrain stocks can land you into an embarrassment of riches. Inventory-building is expensive. The process, therefore, must have a surcease. And, in that event, peeved rich peasants will have to be pacified by offer of hush money through the intermediary of state governments in kulak-dominated regions. Middle and small peasants will be thrown to the wolves.

It is all very clear and satisfying. The problem, nonetheless, does not go away. How to put all this across to the letter writer innocent of high-grade economics? The theory of art for art's sake met its Waterloo once the Spanish Civil War commenced. Those were days before the arrival of the Congress for Cultural Freedom; artists, poets and writers, altogether a dim set, chose humanity before art. The context is a shade different with the theology of foreign exchange holdings for the sake of foreign exchange holdings alone. International financial institutions have been long at work to educate citizens in the poor countries on the virtues of flush foreign exchange reserves: certainly no equivalent of the Spanish Civil War is visible in the international money and financial markets. Even so, the frequency distribution of intelligence is rather kinky in the underdeveloped countries. These people may, one of these days, refuse to buy any more the thesis of foreign exchange holdings for the sake of foreign exchange holdings. A naïve letter a day could actually keep the voodoo doctor away. Practitioners of the art from downtown Washington DC, you never know, could then discover themselves to be without a profession. After Argentina and Venezuela, sceptics are proliferating, here, there, everywhere. It is like atmospherics.

The political transiting

12 October 2002

Worrying over transitional economies is, shall we say, the current pastime. Look up any of the publications by the hoary international financial institutions located in downtown Washington DC: this or that transitional economy is the cynosure of attention, with prescriptions piled up on prescriptions for alleviating the problems of transition. Such prescriptions nevertheless miss out on the principal issue. There can be no transitional economy without a transitional polity. The transition alluded to is obviously from a regime of market regulation to a free market milieu. The problems underlying a cross-over of this kind will be impossible to solve without bringing in the context of the state. After all, it is the state which regulates an economy; it is also the state which engineers its so-called unshackling. The state constitutes the centrepiece of transition. The nature of the state is, however, determined by the political system. To discuss separately the problems of economic transition without referring to those of political transition, is on all scores, a futile exercise.

This juxtaposition of politics and economics is the real-life story of contemporary India too. Consider some of the most recent developments. That wretched New York-based rating agency, Standard & Poor's, has the cheek to lower its rating on India's local currency denominated debt to 'junk'. Such a rating is the bluntest possible warning to external investors: they could get involved with Indian affairs only at their own risk. The Government of India's credibility, as per this rating, is just worthless; please abandon all hope, those who propose to enter that country's portals. Standard & Poor's has not flinched from elaborating the rationale behind its assessment. The growing local currency debt of the national government, in the view of the rating agency, affects the country's macro-economic stability and vastly diminishes the prospects of domestic economic growth, which in turn reduces the government's ability to raise sufficient tax revenue to service both its local and foreign currency debt, now as well as in the future. In addition, Standard & Poor's has drawn attention to what it describes as the limpid pace of economic reforms. All told, the verdict is categorical and unequivocal: India is a burnt-out case.

Official Indian reaction, one would have thought, would be explosive: patriotic sentiments would be aroused and prim civil servants, after consultation with their ministers, would have told the world that this great country stands on its own dignity and cares two hoots for aspersions cast by pompous foreigners. No such thing: apart from one or two minor regretful squeaks, the Indian response has been extraordinarily low-key.

This is no enigma, though. What is involved is the nitty-gritty of political transiting. We simply cannot afford to alienate Americans, any Americans, at any level. The US Department of State has told the Indian Prime Minister and his entourage that they better make themselves familiar with the basics of realpolitik. The United States has the right to ignore the combined, considered judgement of the United Nations, that it should not, must not, launch another unilateral attack against Iraq. But who cares for the UN? Not the USA. The United States may be just another member of the UN, so what; it writes its own law. It will, on its own, teach Saddam Hussein the facts of life. It does not however follow that, inspired by the example set by the United States, India too should think of mounting a unilateral cross-border attack on Pakistan for ensuring the safe custody of Jammu and Kashmir. The subcontinental country could not be more wrong: India could not, does not, enjoy the freedom the United States enjoys. That is the harsh, hard reality. India must come to peace with Pakistan. It must do so, for, otherwise, the US President would not admit India into the charmed circle of his favourite lapdogs.

Who lives if the United States dies, and who dies if the United States lives? At least India does not then die. Don't you know, George W. Bush has gone on record: the US administration perceives India's potential to become one of the great democratic powers in the twenty-first century. Differences remain, the President is candid enough to admit, between the two countries, including over the development of India's nuclear and missile programmes, and over the assessed tardiness of India's economic reforms. But while in the past, these concerns might have dominated American thinking about India, things are now different; the US administration now recognizes India as a growing world power with which the United States of America shares certain strategic common interests. The reasons for this developing communion are not far to seek. In the remote past, India was a snarling dachshund who presented the visage of the late unlamented V.K. Krishna Menon; today, it is a lapdog. The occasional pranks of a lapdog are to be ignored. The lapdog too has to lump it, in case specimens such as Standard & Poor's pass an occasional uncharitable comment.

Such, then, is the modality of master–comprador relationship the United States and India have reached. Symptoms of compradorism are, at the moment, breaking all over like a rash. The case of Coca Cola India is a lovely instance of how bilateral relations have undergone a magnificent transition. It is indeed an absorbing tale. As per the agreement signed between Coca Cola and the Government of India in 1997, the company was committed to the public listing of its shares and to divestment of 49 per cent of equity within a specified period. This was to ensure that the fantastic wealth the soft-drink corporate entity would realize in India was shared with the Indian public. Besides, it was not a directive issued to Coca Cola alone; it was a part of the mandatory prescriptions imposed on all foreign companies intending to invest in India. The Department of Industrial Policy and Promotion under the Indian Ministry of Commerce and Industry sent repeated reminders to Coca Cola India to honour its commitment and divest the agreed-to proportion of its equity. To no avail. The reminders gathered dust. Another gentle reminder from the Ministry of Commerce and Industry led to the American ambassador in New Delhi writing directly to the principal secretary of the Indian Prime Minister. The ambassador went directly to the point: 'It seems to me that in view of India's ongoing economic reforms and considerable efforts to attract and maintain greater levels of foreign direct investment, there should be some flexibility possible in resolving this (that is, the Coca Cola) issue in a way that is acceptable to both sides.' Never mind your standard rules and prescriptions; we, the United States of America, are special: Coca Cola is special. Therefore the Government of India better do something about it. What the American ambassador was hinting at was, of course, the master–comprador relationship between the two countries.

Grass was not allowed to grow under the feet. The communication from the ambassador was followed by a letter from the assistant secretary in the US Department of Commerce to the Indian Ministry of Commerce and Industry. The text of this letter read, *inter alia*, as follows:

> . . . another issue has been brought to my attention that I would ask receive your immediate attention. Recent Indian press reports indicate that the Minister of Commerce and Industry, Mr Murasoli Maran, has turned down Coca Cola's request for a waiver for a requirement to divest 49 per cent of its India holdings by July 2002. I understand that this is the second time that Coca Cola's waiver request has been denied. I find this to be very unfortunate not just for the company but also for India's investment climate.

The hardly suppressed anger of the US assistant secretary of state is easily explicable. For two times running Coca Cola had requested the waiver of the clause for compulsory divestment; how dare the Government of India deny its request twice over? This time, the US assistant secretary of state therefore does not convey a polite request; he asks that the matter be immediately resolved to the satisfaction of the master power. The assistant secretary of state does not fail to insert a pinprick either: 'When the Indian government approved Coca Cola's Indian investment plan in 1997, the divestment condition was part of the agreement. But I believe it is fair to say the India of 2002 is different from the India of 1997.'

How true! The American official has hit the nail on the head. India 2002 is qualitatively different from India 1997. The transitional phase has advanced, and to a remarkable degree. What was once an independent republic had been in the process of progressing to a state of comprador existence. The year 1997, barely half-a-dozen years from the initiation of the great economic reforms, was sort of a mid-point of the transitional phase. Another five years have now elapsed; the picture of a comprador state is very nearly complete. In such a circumstance, it is simply unthinkable that American officials will continue to submit requests to Government of India officials; no, they will not. They will ask and order the Indians to do the needful. Should the Indians fail to comply, nemesis no doubt would be set to work.

Politics is always in command. Politics commands economics. India, once a proud nation with a sense of self-respect and moral integrity, has been reduced into a territory populated by servile politicians and timid civil servants. The international financial institutions in downtown Washington DC should better stop worrying over conditions prevailing in transitional economies. In countries such as India, the political transition is almost over. That will also take care of the problems of economic transition. Very soon, Foggy Bottom will send another communication to the principal secretary of the Prime Minister of India asking that, no further dilly-dallying, the Union Cabinet must at its very next meeting agree to 100 per cent foreign equity in the oil, mining and civil aviation sectors.

The Minister for Justice in Germany can compare George W. Bush with Adolf Hitler, irrespective of the consequences. We cannot tell off even a mere assistant secretary of the US government when he pitches a peremptory demand. We capitulate meekly. That is what defines compradordom.

The hokum of economics

2–9 November 2002

Newspaper headlines blare in the boldest types: Disinvestment at the Top of the Planning Commission's Agenda. The irony is devastating. The Planning Commission is supposed to take care of such holy tasks as promoting growth in national income and employment, even if other obscenities like reduction in income inequalities are left out of consideration. To ensure growth in income and employment, investment, one would have thought, and not disinvestment, should be the Commission's primary concern. It is, however, a topsy-turvy universe: syllogisms are being made to stand on their head. From Cabinet meetings down to corner tea shops, the chant is for disinvestment, disinvestment and yet more disinvestment. In the early phase of the new era, disinvestment, it was explained, was intended to target only the loss-making public sector units. That salad phase is over. Discriminating between one public undertaking and another is, according to the latest communiqué, a vice to be averted under all circumstances and in all concourses. The dividing line between profit- and loss-making enterprises has been got rid of. The market for profit-making units is, in any event, much brisker; a long queue of fortune-hunters wait impatiently, they have to gobble up public undertakings prone to netting comfortable profits. They and their protagonists in government belong almost to a religious order.

A self-perpetuating process is thereby set in motion. For, whatever the abstract theorization – or the pretence of such theorization – the disinvestment programme in our neighbourhood is essentially because of the International Monetary Fund breathing down the neck of North Block mandarins, the pedigreed mandarins as well as those parading as politicians. The year-end deficit in the union budget must not exceed a stipulated percentage of the gross national product. Since growth in all its aspects has gone on a sabbatical, both tax and non-tax revenues are rising at an extremely sluggish rate. Expenditure, on the other hand, knows no bounds, the more so as you are bloodily nuclear-and-delivery-systems-minded and Pakistan remains an inveterate enemy. On top of all that, Kashmir has to be established as an inalienable part of the country. The milieu of competitive democracy also rules out the termination of subsidies and handouts for near and dear ones. There is further trouble ahead. The moment one proceeds beyond sales transactions involving only loss-making public enterprises and embraces the divestment of profit-making entities as well, the causal effect immediately is an even greater enlargement of the budgetary deficit. So much so that the government is driven to sell off even more profit-making units. This can be a near-interminable process. Or perhaps the terminal point will be reached once the government has disposed of not only all its immovable assets, including real estate of the genre of the Red Fort and the Rashtrapati Bhavan, but fighter planes, cruise missiles, and other similar oddments too. That is to say, the business of defending the nation too will need to be privatized at that stage. This development will gladden the hearts as much of non-resident economists as of doctrinaire anarchists, heralding as it will the surcease of the state.

Vacuous rhetoric of this nature, the protest is bound to be posted, is altogether unnecessary. Is not the purpose of disinvestment to create additional space for private initiative? Sensitive people, it will be urged, must discard old notions such as that public investment draws in private investment; the history of the advanced industrial countries has proved beyond a speck of doubt that the state has little business to step out of infrastructural activities. In the matter of infrastructure too, if certain activities like building airports or turnpikes happen to be profit-inducing, the government should jolly well keep out; it is only in special instances where the private sector fails to achieve a satisfactory rate of return that public agencies should step in and offer handouts to private entrepreneurs. Not otherwise. For, let there be no misapprehension on the issue, once the animal spirit is released, private persons can perform miracles. Leave the supply side to the exclusive care of private entities; magnificent rates of growth of output, income and employment will be the irresistible sequel. Here is the rub though. In the course of the past dozen years or thereabouts, despite space being increasingly allotted to the private sector, growth in the system has been of an extraordinarily paltry order. The only exception is the services sector, which, however, does not contribute to the cause of employment, and, what is worse, aggravates social and economic inequalities. True, the counter-argument will be forthcoming; it is not disinvestment, but actually the limpid pace of it, which has frustrated growth; if you therefore want prosperity, overwhelming prosperity, in this land, just accelerate disinvestment, and, please, do not be a stickler for orthodoxy, disinvest profit-making units too. For, it is a sin for the government to get diverted from its main concerns: it must concentrate on the maintenance of law and order so that the environment is congenial for the private sector to make profits; it will be sheer poaching if it itself makes profits.

Cross over from the old orthodoxy to the new one: disinvestment in the public sector will promote corresponding new investments in the private sphere, enabling each and everyone to live like a lord. Unfortunately, some second-order complications enter the picture. The manner of public disinvestment casts a shadow on private investment incentive. This is easily seen. Take the recent instance of the outright sale of the Centaur Hotel in Mumbai. The individual to whom the government-owned hotel was handed over, in exchange for 82 crore of rupees, is a smart cookie. Within four months of purchasing it, he resold the hotel to another private party at 115 crore of rupees, thereby registering a clear profit of 33 crore of rupees. This has been a remarkable *tour de force* and works out to an annual rate of return of close to 117 per cent. But does this not set an uncomfortable example for citizens at large? An ordinary householder, if he keeps his money in the bank, is currently offered barely 7 per cent interest per annum. The householder, it is naively assumed, will take the bait of this 7 per cent interest and opt for a savings account. The savings deposited thus with the bank, it is hoped, will be made use of by private entrepreneurs to expand productive activities in the economy. We are however in the midst of a tricky situation. Everybody becomes aware that at least some individuals in society are being allowed by the government to rake up a return of 117 per cent on their money, while the wretched banks are offering to ordinary householders a laughable rate of return of only 7 per cent on their deposits. Those possessing a sophisticated mind might be pained at the clear lack of aesthetics in an arrangement which allows 117 per cent return for one set of citizens, and just 7 per cent for another. Such symmetry-seekers may be peremptorily asked to stew in their own juice. The basic problem, nonetheless, does not disappear. Given the datum that some individuals are, in the counting house, counting the bonanza yielded by a 117 per cent of return, those being offered a teeny-weeny 7 per cent rate will feel mighty disenchanted. They will stay away from putting their savings in the banks and search for alternative parking lots which could give them 10 or 20 times more profit. Not only individual householders, even would-be entrepreneurs in industry and agriculture will begin to have second or third thoughts: why take the trouble of borrowing from the banks and investing in activities which will at most yield a rate of return of 10 or 15 per cent, when, should you join the fly-by-night adventurers, you might make as much as 100 per cent or more: all you need are friends at the right places.

The implications are obvious. If disinvestment boils down to a network of arrangements which enables those close to the centre of power to make mind-boggling profit on their money with the bottom line at 100 per cent, while the rest of the species are condemned to a paltry profit, none amongst the latter will be agreeable to graze in the village common any more; about everyone who has the animal instinct implanted in him or her will try to cultivate the appropriate contacts. They will convert themselves into cronies of ministers, or cronies of cronies, or cronies of cronies of cronies, and entertain the not-unreasonable hope of achieving a 100 per cent rate of return, or even higher. A quick mental calculation will follow: of the 100 per cent or more of the takings, conceivably 10 or 15 per cent will have to be offered as commission, by whatever name it is called; the rest will be entirely one's own. Not even a moron will, in such circumstances, drag himself into productive pursuits in industry or agriculture. The dream area to concentrate on will be where the returns are not less than 100 per cent. Purchasing ministerial favours will be one modality to reach paradise, but there are others equally available. One can borrow from the banks and not return the money, as our patriotic tycoons have made a habit of. The return here is infinity. Or one can steal; all one needs is the procurement of some implements for the conduct of the profession of thievery; the rate of return will then be calculated with reference to the capital outlay on the procurement of the necessary equipment. Or one can commit a murder, or a spate of murders; the investment called for will perhaps be what has to be spent on the acquisition of an AK-27 or an AK-47 rifle. The rate of return from such operations can be astronomically high, provided the right victims are chosen.

Economics, let us then agree, is sheer hokum. Those pronouncing the disinvestment of the kind taking place in this country at this moment to be economics of the most excellent order are welcome to their thoughts. The country's Constitution guarantees them that right. But they better be eased out of governance. No point in choosing words carefully, what is going on in the name of disinvestment is highway banditry. Bertold Brecht was, thank goodness, no economist, but he had a good hang of capitalist economics. Not for nothing did he let drop the remark: what is raiding a bank to owning one? His sympathies lay with the bank raiders; Mac-the-Knife any day rather than the crooks who refuse to repay to a bank what they had borrowed from it and later use that money to buy up the bank itself. It is somewhat unjust that the owners of the banks make the Forbes list, but not Mac-the-Knife. But, then, that is the capitalist moral order.

No right to live

23 November 2002

At long last, the full blast of light at the end of the tunnel. For almost a century and a half, the world has suffered on account of the woolly thoughts and miscalculations of welfare state lobbyists. Early capitalism had placed maximum emphasis on the virtue of efficiency: those who are efficient, it had stated outspokenly, will prosper; the inefficient and nincompoops have no business to survive. Spurred on by the excruciating beauty of this doctrine, the animal spirit in human beings had set to work at a furious pace; wealth was amassed by a narrow band of people who happened to be efficient, paving thereby the road to capital accumulation and industrial and commercial growth, which percolated, with a slight time-lag, into the farm sector as well. It was a quirkless, straightforward universe, where the competent enjoyed life and living, and the laggards were sent to coventry. Everything was proceeding exceedingly swimmingly. Suddenly disaster arrived in the form of so-called social do-gooders. They had the milk of human kindness of the most dubious kind oozing from their pores. At their insistence, such asinine legislations as workmen's compensation act, minimum wages act, housing act, etc., were put on the statute book. Worse things followed. A few cranks, who passed as economists, thought up the concept of progressive taxation, which propagated the view that the state is justified to take away an increasing proportion of income as income rises. This was in sharp contrast to the practice of regressive taxation that prevailed in the Middle Ages, ordaining that the state could only take a decreasing proportion of income as income rose. The cognoscenti are now agreed that human civilization would have prospered much more speedily had the system of regressive taxation been persisted with, ensuring a continuous fillip to accumulation and growth.

Humanity has been cheated for a long while, spanning a period of at least 150 years. But now, with the booming globalization process, a major turnaround in thinking is taking place. India has always been in the forefront where the supply of revolutionary ideas in the realm of philosophy, including economic philosophy, is concerned. It is therefore not at all surprising that, even in the matter of taxation, a historic departure has been heralded by a report recently submitted by a committee set up by the Government of India. The committee has dared to dare. It has recommended raising the level of minimum taxable annual income from Rs 50,000 to Rs 1,00,000. What is even more path-breaking, it has suggested only two layers of tax: 20 per cent for those having an income between Rs 1,00,000 and Rs 4,00,000, and 30 per cent for those earning more than

Rs 4,00,000. Even this proposal of two levels of taxation, almost everybody knows, is purely tentative. Once the initial reverberations die out and the implications of the revolutionary proposal sink in, the authorities will no doubt opt for a uniform rate of taxation all along the line; that is to say, we will enter a regime of uniformly proportional taxation. This form of proportional taxation will, in effect, be no different from the medieval institution of regressive taxation, since the committee's major recommendations are complemented by a number of equally breathtaking additional suggestions: abolition of dividend tax, abandonment of long-term capital gains tax and wholesale scrapping of wealth tax. The rate of corporate taxation too has been proposed to be brought down from the present high levels to a uniform 30 per cent. In other words, where the issue is taxation, no discrimination will henceforth be made between personal income and corporate income. All told, the unabashed regressivity of the suggested new arrangements is bound to create retrospective envy in the diehard souls of medieval barons and suchlike specimens.

This is where the Indian imagination shows up so magnificently. Likeminded Europeans and Americans have conceivably been toying with similar ideas. But they were afraid of being seen to be too outrageously pro-rich. Such an inhibition does not detain the liberated Indian. He or she does not mind going the whole hog. One or two neighbourhood cynics may point out that the proposed fiscal changes are old hat, and an integral adjunct of the paradigm of the Republic envisaged by Plato. That may be so. The free-market Indians, it has still to be admitted, have beaten the ancient Greeks in the game. Even Plato was in search of one or two fig leaves. Indians in the new millennium, on the other hand, believe in calling a spade a spade. They abhor the idea of taxing efficiency at discriminatory penal rates; higher incomes, after all, are the hallmark of ability and excellence in performance.

Render, though, unto Caesar what belongs to Caesar. Advances in economic theorization have helped too. The concept of diminishing marginal utility has been exposed as bunkum. What is even more encouraging, indifference surfaces of different individuals, it has been mathematically established, are not comparable with one another. India's revolutionary practitioners have taken heart from these developments.

The discussion till now refers, however, to only one aspect of the revolutionary turbulence currently sweeping India. One must consider the proposal for a uniform rate of taxation along with the Reserve Bank of India's decision to bring down the bank rate to almost a negligible magnitude. Members of the mean-minded middle and lower middle classes are desolate; some of them have the temerity to refer to the cut-rate monetary policy as a cut-throat policy. They, of course, have their private reasons to feel disequilibrated. Several amongst them depend on interest earnings from bank deposits for their survival; as the deposit rates shrink, their earnings shrink, making it increasingly more difficult for them to make ends meet. They are however myopic. What is lost on the swings is likely to be more than made up on the roundabouts. There is an income distribution aspect of a continuously lowering bank rate; the income the middle and lower classes lose provides an additional incentive to the upper-income groups, including big industrialists, businessmen and capitalist farmers, so much so that the latter feel encouraged to expand their activities and raise the level of their incomes. The relatively poor are being denied in order that, alongside burgeoning national prosperity, the rich are enabled to further enrich themselves. Such enrichment is the engine of growth. Please be understanding; some groups in society have to experience a few privations if the nation has to advance.

There is, besides, a third strand of thought endeavouring to activize itself. This is in that other area of functional finance, buying and selling. The ongoing disinvestment programme fits in snugly into the frame of fiscal and monetary policies that are on the anvil. The reduction of taxes and the consequent shrinkage of government income cannot but reduce the space for public sector activities, and increase, *pari passu*, space for private activities. The cut-back in the bank rate has the same effect on the supply side of investment decisions; private entrepreneurs are buoyed up, it cuts their cost. Come to think of it, disinvestment will have the same consequence. True, the sale of public sector units will create some extra liquidity for the government, but this is only an ephemeral phenomenon. Especially the divestment of profit-making public enterprises will yield large-scale benefits over the long run; it will diminish the propensity of those in government to indulge in activities that encroach on the quintessential domain of private affairs. Disinvestment of profit-making public undertakings will ultimately lower the receipts of the government, which will therefore be forced to curb its expansionary ambitions.

Impulses set in motion in three different areas, but all of them converging towards the fulfilment of a single-minded objective: the creation of ample breathing space for the private sector. There is an exciting parallel here with the general equilibrium theory Leon Walras had innovated for the market system. Prices prevailing in the different segments of the market, whatever their initial chaotic levels, ultimately come to rest; that is, they reach equilibrium levels, through a process of trial and error, *par tatonnements*. In the sphere of economic policy too, we are witnessing in India a similar *tatonnement* at work: once the early hiccups are over, fiscal and monetary instruments cease to operate at cross-purposes; the disinvestment programme also falls in line. They converge, they are determined to establish an economic regime where only the rich will exist, the rest will be swept away by the tide of well-deserved misfortune.

It should therefore cause no surprise that the country's foreign exchange reserves should be threatening to cross 65 billion dollars. India is, at the moment, the safest haven for global fly-by-night operators. The rich and those who have a philosophical aversion to paying taxes, or paying for money they borrowed from others, are safe in this country. The general lowering of the bank rate does not affect the earnings from repatriable overseas deposits; speculative gains reaped in the stock exchanges are also freely exportable. It is a different matter if the wealth that is being brought in or realized right here is not being put to productive use. One cannot have everything in life. The plethora of foreign exchange assets is now providing the opportunity to Indian citizens to open dollar accounts on home turf itself. The avarice of the top layer of Indian society – to satisfy their craze for foreign goodies and foreign climates – can now be satisfied with the least fuss. Some lucky Indians will even be able to book advance seats for the first commercial flight to the moon, or, for that matter, to Mars. Starvation deaths will however continue; those who are inefficient have no business to claim the fundamental right to live, casually mentioned in the Constitution.

Aha, securitization

4 January 2003

'Securitization' is a word no lexicon will yet carry. So what! A world which puts up with, and is actually petrified by, George W. Bush, cannot afford to be finicky; it has to get reconciled to 'securitization' as well. It does not still follow that one must go into raptures over the curiosity described as the Securitization and Reconstruction of Financial Assets and Enforcement of Security Rights Act – or is it still Ordinance? Much ballyhoo is being expended on the twin virtues supposed to flow from it. It will, so goes the confident prediction, protect and expand lenders' rights. At the same time, it will usher in a milieu where accountability of borrowers will be enforced without the encumbrance of constant judicial intervention. Will it though? A statute can be ordained and rules can be framed to dot its i's and cross its t's. On paper, everything will look perfect, with recovery of loans guaranteed and the waywardness of corporate entities in their handling of borrowed funds disciplined, once and for all.

Most of all this is, alas, building castles in the air. Politics has been in command, and will remain so, in all spheres, including in the country's financial system. The message has already gone round: the big sharks infesting the corporate waters, aka India Incorporated, need not worry too much; the rules will be so arranged that they will continue to be outside the purview of the punitive provisions of the new statute. The stratagem is simple. In order to attract the rigours of the Security Interest (Enforcement) Rules, a sick account must first be declared as a non-performing asset. In order to declare an account to be a NPA, the authorities, however, will have to make bulk provisioning for it. The shoal of reality will be hit here. The total amount outstanding in the books for the so-called sick accounts of the nation's commercial banks is likely to reach, or even exceed, Rs 2,00,000 crore. It boggles the imagination how the banks will go about making full provisioning for this huge amount. Please relax, they will not try to do so. They will plead financial inadequacy for their inability to clamp the 'securitization' rules upon the fat sick accounts run up by the filthy rich. The tycoons have walked away with money from the banks over years and decades, and never cared to return a penny. The new legislation will not affect them, for the banks will not touch them; the tycoons, in other words, will stay secure. That is what 'securitization' is about.

The pretence of breathtaking reforms will nonetheless be kept up. The government and the banks will chase the small fry. A young man who borrowed Rs 10,000 from a bank to start a small business, and defaulted after making only three payments, will have his assets seized. The proprietor of a cinema house, with a seating capacity of barely 500, who had taken a couple of lakhs of rupees from his neighbourhood bank to introduce a cooling system, and had failed to pay up, will be dispossessed of the cinema house and therefore of his profession. A father who borrowed money from his bank to cover the expenses for his daughter's marriage, including the payment of dowry, and has not a clue how to repay, will have his miserable little house attached by the bank; if the bank is venture-some enough, it might even organize a raid and forfeit the sparse jewels the daughter was bedecked with at the time of the wedding, or seize the Hero Honda motorcycle the son-in-law had insisted upon as a marriage gift. One should be thankful for little mercies: the 'securitization' statute could indeed be a shot in the arm for the anti-dowry movement.

The criminal lot of big defaulters will continue to have a luscious time. They have walked away with 2,00,000 crore of rupees, or more. They have not returned even a minuscule fraction of the borrowed money. But the authorities cannot afford to declare their accounts as NPAs. The tycoons are therefore safe. The penalties the new legislative measure proposes to impose will not be imposed upon them. They will remain free, in the manner of Matthew Arnold's Shakespeare.

It is all a matter of technicality. The rules can be changed at a moment's notice, leaving out the clause regarding compulsory provisioning. That will not be done. One should learn the facts of life. Politicians are in command, and the tycoons command the politicians. Maybe the rules have been formulated in consultation with the tycoons, so that they could go scot-free.

Those who steal money from public accounts will slip away from the catchment area. That other proposed objective of the new statute – to compel creditors to learn the grammar of competition and cost-effectiveness – will be equally unfulfilled. With politics in command, it is a joke to talk of efficiency and optimum use of financial resources. By now everybody realizes that the nationalization of banks, one-third of a century ago, did not hamper the tycoons in the least. Indira Gandhi's intentions were altogether different. She national-ized the banks for two reasons: (a) nationalization would help her to swing the mood of the electorate, or the vast majority of it, in her favour; (b) it would force the capitalists to come to her parlour: only if they pleased her, the banks would please the tycoons. That state of affairs remains undisturbed. The balance of conditions is always tilted all the way towards the direction of bigger, richer borrowers. Nationalization merely made some rearrangements in the cultural pattern. In the past, money put in by thousands of depositors in the outfit known as the Birla bank would be used to facilitate advances mostly to the Birlas. What was reputed to be the Thackersey bank would see to it that credit advanced by it overwhelmingly benefited the Thackerseys. Similarly, the Jaipurias would be the monarch of all the money going into the coffers of a Jaipuria bank. The politi-cians are constantly in need of money; they also love to acquire money on their private account. In the pre-nationalization era, in case they wanted a part of the resources lying with the banks, they would have to cultivate the friendship of the Birlas, the Thackerseys and the Jaipurias. Indira Gandhi reversed that indignity. Since, following the take-over, she as Prime Minister was in total command of the banks, the Birlas, the Thackerseys and the Jaipurias had to run after her, instead of her running after them. They learnt quickly the new rules of game. The lady disappeared from the scene nearly two decades ago. But the new struc-ture she set up has continued to thrive. The tycoons pay their tributes to the politicians and manage to walk away with bank funds. Bank executives are not necessarily in league with the defaulting big borrowers. True, they get their occa-sional *bucksheesh*. What is much more relevant, they do the bidding of their political masters. As long as the tycoons keep on the right side of the politicians, the latter will see to it that the provisions of the 'securitization' rules do not apply in their case. So what is new, pussy cat?

The securitization *mantra* will not increase the efficient use of borrowed capital either, even if accompanied by divestment. All that could happen is a shift of the centre of gravity of the control over bank funds, once again from the politicians to industrial and business tycoons, as in the days of yore. In the emerging scenario, private owners of banks would come to an appropriate deal with ruling politicians and obtain, from time to time, government accommodation under this or that pretext to cover the financial damage inflicted by some crazy lending to parties near-and-dear to politicians or recommended by them. Those bank owners whose linkage with the government is imperfect would encounter a few difficulties. Their banks could even fail. Still, they themselves would be un-harmed and could perhaps start another bank. The good Finance Minister has, after all, clarified the point on the floor of parliament: bank defaulters are entitled to compete for the purchase of banks under indiction to divest, so even the near-and-dear ones of politicians could end up as proprietors of banking institutions. The proposition that a regime of free competition will inject efficiency into the financial system is sheer hokum: in a milieu of uneven opportunities, competition, even a school kid knows, is the progenitor of monopoly, private monopoly.

Much of the buffoonery could have been cut out. All you need is a simple piece of legislation which says that any person defaulting on a bank loan will not be allowed another loan from the same bank, or from any other bank operating under the dispensation of the Reserve Bank of India. A further provision could be that the near-relatives – as defined by law – of the person concerned are to be denied further loans from the Indian banking system. Third, such a defaulting person or any of his near-relatives will be excluded from assuming the directorship or any other executive position in any bank in India. A final condition: no exceptions are to be permitted in the enforcement of these rules.

You will be a fool to get excited over the prospect of such a set of rules descending upon the Indian financial system. Such 'securitization' will hurt the class interests of politicians and tycoons. The regime of obfuscation will therefore proceed uninterruptedly. Every now and then, fresh legislations will crowd the arena; rules and sub-rules will also dazzle by the reality of their illusion. Ponderous articles in scholarly and non-scholarly journals will hail such rules as epoch-making events. Ring out the old, ring in the new; the new is the same cliché as the old one – but with a different coating.

Cross-subsidies, out, out

15 February 2003

John Rawls has passed on, but disputations over the concept of justice and its optimality persist. It was always a cauldron of confusion, and things have worsened of late. Ever since the wise ones made the ponderous discovery of non-comparability of the state of being of persons, or sets of persons, or communities, or sets of communities, chaos has taken over, justice is threatening to become increasingly non-definable and therefore non-enforceable.

Consider the philosophical point of view expressed by India's highest judiciary. It is altogether impermissible, they have told the nation in a recent judgment, to cross-subsidize electricity duties; that is to say, it is against natural justice to tax one set of consumers of power with the specific purpose of reducing below cost what is charged from another set of consumers. As the same product is being supplied to both sets of consumers, the same price, the judgment implies, must be charged to both; to do otherwise will be unjust, period.

The verdict is of immense significance. Ever since the dawn of the so-called liberal conscience and awareness on the part of some social categories of the miserable plight of certain other categories, public measures, operating on the principle that the rich and the affluent should give up something in order to increase the well-being of the poor and deprived sections, have been vogue in country after country. Rob-Peter-to-pay-Paul has been the approved community custom. The dictum became the foundation of the principle of progressive taxation. The indifference surfaces replaced the concept of diminishing marginal utility, but the escape route provided by the twosome of ordinality and cardinality could still offer a breather to those who would tax the rich at higher rates so that the poor could be provided with the barest means of survival.

The end of that tranquil world, it now seems, is really near. Liberalization has given way to liberalism. The substitution has assumed the form of a whirlwind, particularly following the collapse of the Soviet system, and is now claiming more victims every day. The judgement of the Supreme Court of India is a clincher. To charge the rich at higher rates than what you charge the poor or to set a relatively stiff price from industry so as to cover the loss caused by the fixation of a lower price for householders, is, it almost implies, a sin, and if not a sin, an illegality. The official task force set up to restructure public finances has also endeavoured to proceed along the same lines. It has not exactly suggested a uniform rate of taxation on all income earners; it has just stopped short of taking that ultimate position. It has, however, recommended only two rates of income tax instead of the myriad ones society has been accustomed to, since the mid-point of the nineteenth century.

The new regime established for electricity rates regulation across the country does not intend to gather any moss. It is pressing hard on all state governments to fall in line and immediately enforce the doctrine underlying the Supreme Court judgement. Should any state or a number of states be reluctant to join in, pressures can be, and are being, applied upon it or them in different ways. The signs are clear. The country is moving inexorably towards assuming a unitary structure of administration, including fiscal administration. In the circumstances, the number of hold-outs among the states against a uniform structure of tax-cum-pricing is unlikely to be large, and the time-frame of their resistance is also going to be extremely brief. We can therefore soon envisage a situation where the rich and the poor, the big industrialists and small-scale industrial entrepreneurs, the rich capitalist farmers and the indifferently doing sharecroppers, are all made to pay the same price per watt for the supply of power. It boils down to a matter of how the views of society, as filtered through the prism of thinking of the nation's highest judiciary, impinge on the concept of justness: no discrimination please, we belong to the same society, and it is the state's bounden duty to charge the same price for the same service or product, irrespective to whom it is sold.

So far so good; this is the new liberal hour and, besides, defying the verdict of the country's highest legal authority is out of the question. The problem, however, lies elsewhere. What is sauce for the goose should be sauce for the gander as well. If you charge everybody the same price for electricity, you should, it would appear most logical, charge the same price for rendering telephone services too; if cross-subsidy is to be ruled out for electricity duty, it should be prohibited in the case of telephone charges too. Complications have however arisen. It is an interesting story and deserves to be recounted at moderate length. The erstwhile state monopoly over the nation's telephone system has been discontinued with the advent of liberalization. The 'fixed' telephones are still, by and large, in the government sector, while cellular telephones have been taken over, almost wholesale, by private entities, who are free to reap the advantage of a telecommunications infrastructure assiduously built with tax-payers' money. There is a Telecom Regulatory Authority of India in place to enforce a central discipline, but till now its role has been somewhat restrained. It has allowed competition to bloom in the mobile phone sector. By no stretch is it, however, a competitive milieu where an infinite number of buyers confront an infinite number of sellers. The milieu is very much of an imperfect market and the consumers of cellular services are at the mercy of, at most, half-a-dozen suppliers. To corner as large a slice of the market as is possible, the latter initially engage in some cut-throat competition amongst themselves. Charges for cellular phone calls, outgoing as well as incoming, have therefore come down dramatically in recent weeks. The slashing of rates has covered both domestic and international calls. The practice of charging pro rata according to distance is also being given a decent burial: it does not matter whether from Calcutta you dial Murshidabad or Mumbai, you will be charged more or less at the same rate.

This is bonanza. But, let us take a wager, this will be only a temporary bonanza. Once the field has been narrowed to just three or four providers, they can be depended upon to form a concordat. Call it by your favourite nomenclature, duopoly or polypoly or whatever, once the suppliers have united in a tight-fighting cartel, charges and rentals are more than likely to be gradually revised upwards. This has been the general experience all over the capitalist world. It will not be very different in India as long as the global glut in supplies does not assume an overwhelming scale.

Meanwhile, though, there are problems. As cellular charges tumble, those availing of trunk services – national and international – from 'fixed' telephones have the worst of the bargain. They cannot be prevented from entering into some fresh, quick calculations: it will make sense for them to cross over from fixed phones to cellular phones; they can thereby save a lot of money. The bottom will therefore fall out of the system of fixed telephone connections.

The Telecom Regulatory Authority of India went into a huddle. It is sort of a crisis; customers are threatening to desert the fixed telephone arrangements in a drove; some desperate efforts are needed to stem the exodus. The TRAI has acted swiftly; it has scaled down the trunk charges, both domestic and international, for calls from 'fixed' telephones, in the process making them competitive with cellular phones on all routes.

But that was not the end of the trouble. With a substantial reduction in operational and other charges for trunk routes, the 'fixed' telephone system now faces the prospect of a severe revenue loss. The TRAI has been agile enough once more. It has decided to raise, from April onwards, rental and operational charges on local calls from 'fixed' telephones all over the country. The calculations must have been done more or less meticulously, and the authorities have obviously satisfied themselves that the extra money collected by hiking charges for local calls will adequately compensate for the loss resulting from lowered trunk call charges, including for international calls, from 'fixed' telephones.

The position is getting clarified. The revolution in telecommunications that the country is going through has a unique feature. Those having relatives, friends or business connections in foreign lands or in distant locations in the country will have their calls to and from such parties subsidized by those who use their 'fixed' telephones mostly for local calls. In other words, relatively affluent people are to be subsidized by people not so well-off; the new arrangements, it will be fair to say, amount to compelling the poor and the middle classes to cough up extra money for the calls they make, so that the relatively affluent sections of the community might enjoy cheaper rates for holding animated conversations with their business partners, or boy or girl friends overseas or in different metropolitan centres of the country.

This raises a basic issue. Electricity charges are being made uniform for the rich and the poor; the advantages some of the poor have been enjoying till now are being revoked in pursuance of the Supreme Court's frowning upon cross-subsidies. How come, then, the TRAI has embarked on a different course and decided to charge the poorer and less well-placed classes at higher rates, in order to subsidize the indulgence of affluent sections in society?

Since the government itself is a party to this proposed arrangement, it will not do anything on its own to correct the anomaly. What about a public interest litigation, though, on the basis of a writ petition filed by some humble owners of 'fixed' telephones who can afford to make only local calls? And even without a public interest litigation, cannot the nation's highest judiciary on its own take cognizance of the matter and rap the TRAI on the knuckles? That indeed would seem to be the rational course to adopt, in case it is accepted that cross-subsidy deserves to be forbidden under all circumstances. But one never knows. Under the present dispensation in India, perhaps the operational doctrine is heads-I-win-tails-you-lose; where the rich will gain an advantage, you apply the principle of fixing uniform rates; where the application of such a principle will disadvantage the rich, you will wink at discriminatory practices, and, further, purposely set up a structure of rates which takes from the poor and gives it to the rich.

The great harlotland

5 July 2003

The news item is reproduced, verbatim, from a leading English language newspaper in the country:

London: Office flings have become quite a normal story since people spend most of their time at their workplace.

A new survey of more than 1,000 workers has found that one in two workers have an affair with a colleague at the office.

And the most popular methods of getting promotion these days include having sex with the boss, blackmail and sabotaging other people's work.

One-fifth of them acknowledged sleeping with the boss just to get a promotion. It also showed that employees are prepared to cheat, lie and stab work-mates in the back to get on in their jobs.

Researchers found that one in five people regularly claim credit for work done by a colleague. A staggering one in three had attempted to get a work-mate sacked while two-thirds admitted to flirting to get their own way, according to a report in *The Sun.*

Seven in ten said they were willing to cover up for a colleague's extramarital activities by lying to that person's partner.

But, despite their own faults, four in five were worried about the ethics of their company.

Careers consultant Anjula Mutanda said: 'The pressure to demonstrate value to your employer is intense. It is encouraging people to cheat and lie.'

The survey was ordered by Paramount Home Entertainment to coincide with video of 'Changing Lanes', which stars Ben Affleck as a worker who marries his boss's daughter to get on. – *ANI*

It will be puerile to question the findings of the survey. Social Darwinism has reached its climacteric. Applied business management, as reflected in the annals quoted above, needs to be practised during all hours of existence. That is, in case you want to survive. Survival, Darwinism says, depends on efficiency. Efficiency is, in turn, coterminous with maximization of money-making – in the jargon, the rate of return. If you are efficient, you will earn recognition and money; if you are not, you will disappear into oblivion.

Therefore, in a society where return maximization is the only desideratum of success, you must be prepared to shed all your inhibitions. Morals have no place in this version of economics, neither scruples of any genre. If, for an office girl, promotion depends upon the frequency of her going to bed with the boss, then obviously she has no choice, she has to do what the criterion of efficiency demands. Suppose, in a *mêlée* of twenty office girls, everyone will, with alacrity or otherwise, be willing to sleep with the boss, that state of affairs would be ordinariness and harlots would be in no position to seek Alfred Marshall's quasi-rent. It is only where one girl is 'forward' enough while the others are not, that that girl would be termed as efficient and rewarded the quasi-rent. Should the structure of society be rigid to such a degree that the other nineteen girls never agree to perform what their one colleague has been performing, the latter would be enjoying no longer a quasi-rent, but rent – compensation for her scarcity value.

Good for the office boss and good for neoclassical economics, prurience is no longer the inheritance of the world, certainly not of the western world. The news item refers to a British situation, but it is no different from the prevailing culture in the rest of West Europe or, what is more relevant, the United States. The ethos of permissiveness has entered the soul; one's survival is functionally related to the inhibitions one is willing to get rid of. One must not flinch from committing murder or adultery or from running over one's own grandmother, in case one aspires for rapid rise along the office totem pole. The quicker one assimilates the new culture, the faster is one's prospect of going farther in life.

Since survival and money-making have become synonymous, society is fast learning to be tolerant. Take the case of the office girl who has to go to bed regularly with her boss. In case she is married, she has either to take her husband into confidence or to cheat him. The husband is however a contemporary person too; he knows the lie of the land and perhaps the young lady will, beyond a point, not find it necessary to shield her secret – or quasi-secret – he will be understanding and himself take a leaf out of the wife's book. Or, if no husband is around and only loving parents are in the vicinity, they too are unlikely to stand in the way, they too know the way of the neo-classicalized world and will be adequately understanding.

That is to say, the problem is now more or less defunct in the western hemisphere. Matter has triumphed over everything else and society has adjusted itself enough to meet the challenge of or, rather, get reconciled to, the new civilization. Actually, the code is not very new; it was anticipated 70-odd years ago in Aldous Huxley's *Brave New World*. Life has imitated fiction. As a natural follow-up, western society has attained an equilibrium of easy-goingness. Harlotry is no longer a deviant occupation, it is part of the accepted civil code. Since everybody is in the pursuit of money and everybody grasps the reality that, in the race for money-making, no holds are barred, the exchanges that take place in the great marketplace are between individuals or communities who understand. appreciate and endorse one another's norms. No possibility, accordingly, exists of any queering of the pitch in any direction. US presidents such as John F. Kennedy and Bill Clinton went awhoring even when they were in the White House. Their wives were in the know, and had to put up with the philandering on the part of their husbands. They put up with it because they were appropriately compensated for the humiliation they suffered. After all, were they not the nation's First Ladies on account of their husbands' presidency, so why should they carp about their plight? Their husbands' infidelity was the price Jacqueline Kennedy and Hillary Clinton had to pay for the classiness of the position they occupied; the postulates of the market were satisfied. And the American public too are not overly concerned over the fact that, from time to time, they elect presidents who are congenitally polygamous. The popularity ranking of neither John Kennedy nor Bill Clinton was affected even marginally because of their voracious sexual proclivities.

True, a problem arises when this code of civilization is transported across the oceans, such as the phenomenon now taking place in the post-globalized world. The ruling philosophy, the western establishment insists, is short and sweet: money talks, money talks in all situations and circumstances. You can buy the favours of an office employee, you can buy the favours of accountants and engineers and revenue officials, you can bribe the president or military chief of this or that African or Latin American country; where necessary, you can arrange to assassinate him. Everything and everybody has a price; just pay the price and forget your pains and qualms. Those not agreeing with the content and format of this new morality are a nuisance. What is to be done about them? Take the post-Iraq imbroglio. The Americans have entered Baghdad and established formal control over the entire country; the active opposition has melted away. Like Osama bin Laden, Saddam Hussein too has done a Houdini. Their followers, though, are not yet discouraged. They have continued with their guerrilla operations and there are some American casualties almost every day. This is embarrassing on the domestic front. George W. Bush had promised, or at least gave the impression of promising, a swift, short invasion, and the return of the boys (and girls) home well before Christmas, well before Thanksgiving Day and even well before Labour Day. But such a denouement is not the ground reality. The United States bosses therefore want to subcontract the travails of their occupation of Iraq. Let the dirty Indians do the surveilling job there, for Americans want to go home. Perhaps Indian army personnel will occasionally be cut down by the equally dirty Iraqis. As far as the US establishment are aware, the Indians, particularly their leaders, are a reasonable lot. They will not find it difficult to accept as axiom the proposition that the life of a US citizen is, per se, more valuable than that of a common Indian, and that humanity will be better served if, at the margin, an Indian gets killed by the wretched Iraqis than a US citizen. Besides, it is a market economy and each one should respect the principles of such an economy. The Americans will compensate the Government of India for the troops they will deploy in Iraq by as much as 5 or 10 per cent of the total kitty of five hundred billion dollars they have set apart for the 'rehabilitation' of the recolonized country. In *sotto voce*, the Americans have also transmitted a particular message through the Deputy Prime Minister, Lal Krishna Advani: were the Government of India agreeable to the Iraq switch deal, President Bush would show a significant tilt towards India and against Pakistan on the Kashmir issue. The violation of virginity has a price, and the Americans will gladly pay that price. What more do the Indians want?

The world is a great harlotland and the Indians jolly well have to play the role of strumpets. Should they behave to the contrary, they will be guilty not only of unfriendliness towards the hyperpower, but of unfaithfulness to the tenets of neo-classical economics. In case the Indians are foolhardy enough to place themselves in such a miserable situation, maybe Pentagon will be forced to embark on another punitive expedition, this time in South Asia. Whoever does not believe in the laws of global economics – and global harlotry – does not deserve to live.

The excuse-mongers

2 August 2003

The more India changes, the more she remains the same. Even the alibis and excuses do not change. Way back in the 1960s, a bright North Block manda-rin was writing an essay to explain away the country's disappointing economic performances despite the five-year plans: true, our growth rate has fallen behind China's, but, don't you know, we have been victims of a triple trauma – two droughts, two wars and the death of two prime ministers – which has affected our economic performance. As if such happenings are altogether foreign to other nations.

That is not the issue though. Far more interesting is the explanation currently being proffered for the quasi-stagnant economic growth in the dozen years since globalization. Unchanging India, and even the World Bank, has now joined the troupe of excuse-mongers: India has been unable to reap the full advan-tages of liberalization because of natural calamities that have befallen the country.

Suppose some dull character were to ask whether the entire point of development was not to extricate the economy from the vicissitudes of nature, what answer would the mandarins, including foreign ones, provide? The central message being conveyed by the meteorology fetishists is tinged with fatalism: India's fate continues to be a gamble on the monsoon; if the rains come, India's economic growth picks up; should the rains play truant, growth sags, and liberal economics cannot do anything about it. Fiscal 2002–03 was a bad year because of large-scale drought; fiscal 2003–04 is expected to witness a reversal of for-tune, for the south-east monsoon is turning out to be normal.

This should not have been so. India, it has been regularly dinned into our ears, has taken off since July 1991. Revolutionary structural changes have taken place in the economy and, in consequence, roughly only a quarter of the gross domestic product now originates in agriculture and allied activities. The tail is not supposed to wag the dog. If the structural shift is vouched by logical positivism, the farm sector's role should already be reduced to a minor one, dips in agricultural performance should not therefore affect significantly the rate of growth in the economy, headlong progress in the industrial and services sectors would maintain the tempo of overall growth. The actuality is otherwise. While the services sector is claimed to have grown over the past decade at a rate of 7 per cent and above per annum, the industrial sector, including manufacturing, is showing a barely positive rate of growth. To stimulate industrial demand, banks are desperately organizing the wholesale distribution of credit cards and luxury consumption loans at low rates. At the same time, to buoy up industrial supply, entrepreneurs, especially if they belong to the fat cats category, are being offered alluring terms. To no effect. Unchanging India: what is primly described as recessionary conditions persist.

Official scribes shun mentioning some of the other basic facts of life. Agriculture may, at present, account for only one-fourth of the GDP; it nonetheless provides the wherewithal of survival for more than three-fifths of the nation and its working force. When farm production declines, it is this more than three-fifths of the national population who are set back. Their demand for industrial and service products too dips, contractionary forces spread their tentacles there as well. Globalization has failed to disturb the intersectoral relations with their latent inexorability. Having stepped into the technology-sodden twenty-first century, we have to admit to our near-total dependence on the moods and foibles of the rain gods.

Factors underlying the crisis in the farm sector are so obvious that only those blinded by the glamour of globalization can miss them. Beginning with the early 1990s, a moratorium has been imposed on public investment intended for agricultural infrastructure, including for major and medium irrigation projects. The private sector will fill the resulting gap, was the simplistic assumption. Entrepreneurs from the private sector have done practically nothing, though: they are reluctant to invest either because of the poor returns expected from such outlays, or because they do not have the requisite resources. We have reverted to the mercy of the natural parameters because our government has been cajoled to opt out of the task of making farming activity nature-neutral. Neither the traditional zamindars nor the East India Company were conscientious providers of public goods. Following the advent of liberalization, the country has returned to those roots.

A few additional comments are called for in regard to the morphology of the services sector. Services are claimed to contribute one-half of aggregate domestic output. The more revealing statistic, however, concerns the fact that it provides employment to only a little more than 20 per cent of the work force. This proportion has remained unaltered in the course of the past decade. In some of the most vital corners of the services sector, such as banking, employment has not increased but fallen steeply, notwithstanding the ingress of a huge number of foreign institutions. Mass retirement has dominated the proceedings in the banking industry: over a period of time, while, say, a hundred thousand jobs have been liquidated among the ranks of clerks, orderlies and messenger boys, at most 5 or 10,000 units of new employment have been created in the upper income range. The banks are back to profit-making: the damage wrought by dishonest tycoons through their creation of non-paying assets has been made good by large-scale lay-offs and dismissals of staff. The story is unlikely to be much different in such other spheres as insurance, stock exchange, entertainment, tourism, hotels, etc. The general character of the growth of the services sector in the post-liberalization phase is overwhelmingly labour-displacing. Income has expanded – in many years, exponentially – but employment has not. As a result, the structure of income distribution has been rendered further askew.

If, in spite of adverse agricultural conditions, the GDP is claimed to have risen by more than 5 per cent in quite a number of years, the arithmetic has been made possible due to steadily rising income levels in the services sector. But, even within this sector, most of the income growth has concentration on the upper stratum, while accompanied by widespread retrenchment in the lower ranges. The temptation to enquire whether such an income spurt which curtails the use of labour in a labour-abundant economy does not belong comprehensively to the socially useless category, is almost irresistible.

Yet another point is worth taking note of. Perhaps some young M.Phil. student could be invited to write a thesis on the foreign component of the income that has recently accrued to the services sector. Conceivably, as much as one-third of this income in the post-globalization period has been earnings of foreign nationals, so much so that the growth of national product in this sector has fallen substantially below the growth in domestic product. We have opened up the economy; we have thereby also opened up the opportunities of foreigners to eat into our economy. The reverse process – our obtaining a share of the global income – has been proportionately much less.

All statistics, let us admit, are, beyond a point, a bit of a tedium. Shove them aside, the best commentary on the state of the economy is the almost total lack of protest against the Tamil Nadu Chief Minister's summary dismissal of nearly five hundred thousand employees, including teachers. We are back at the phenomenon of unlimited supply of labour. There is such a huge reserve army of the unemployed and underemployed that summary dismissals are *passé*, and emptied slots can be filled within seconds even at sub-subsistence wages. No effective trade union movement is sustainable in such a situation. Madam Jayalalitha throws out, through the *modus operandi* of a single circular, her recalcitrant staff, hundreds of thousands of them; only the judiciary – or madam's late-hour mercy – can salvage the fate of those who lose their jobs; the mechanism of the economic system, as it is, cannot protect them. Even amongst the working class, the increasing tendency is to fend for their sectarian causes. Government employees fight their separate battle, so do public sector employees facing notice of discharge, so too is the plight of textile workers, mine workers, port employees, railway men and so on. The brief decades following independence presented a false dawn; India has withdrawn to the state of the primitive economy, where animals, including human beings, tear at one another for grabbing a share of the scanty victuals.

Economists are a lucky tribe. Ground realities do not disturb them.

Absorbed in their internal dialectics, they are busy imagining countries and territories where, following globalization, poverty has been abolished, inequality is crushed via definitional engineering, and growth is concentrated in the higher stratospheres. Economists themselves, it is needless to add, constitute an important segment of the last-mentioned vista.

It is a buyers' market, and, therefore, there are also other economists indulging in other kinds of pastime. One such set of fact-and-theorem churners have issued their latest communiqué: of the 175 member-countries of the United Nations, India's ranking in the human development index has slipped last year, down from 124 to 127. Either India's performance has been relatively worse over the year, or the performance of at least three other countries has been relatively better. Whatever the purport of this announcement, it is still overshadowed by Madam Jayalalitha's order forfeiting the livelihood of five hundred thousand public employees and their families, with no sense of outrage in any quarters. Welcome to the zone of primitivism.

Once more, the third market

27 December 2003

Old theories do not die, they only hibernate. Rosa Luxemburg's 'third market' has come alive again, and in an acute contemporary context. Capitalists exploit the working class to the hilt, triggering the crisis of underconsumption. The 'third market' saves the day for capitalism. Primitive economies, surviving marginally next door to the capitalist order, provide the way out: capitalists dump their goods at fancy prices on this third market and thereby solve the realization problem. As a matter of fact, the primitive economies serve a second purpose as well: they enable the capitalists to buy raw materials at cheap prices, which further expands the rate of profit and surplus value.

In retrospect, it seems somewhat strange that while Luxemburg mentioned the import of cheap raw materials from the primitive sector, she did not dwell at any length on the implications of the import of slaves and sweated labour. The massive movement across oceans and seas of indentured workers and labourers purchased outright was a major feature of international migration from the seventeenth century onwards till the end of the nineteenth century. It was a lifeline for nascent capitalism. Imperialism allowed capitalists to gorge themselves not only on cheap raw materials, but also on labour available either free or at throwaway prices.

Rosa Luxemburg wrote her tract and went to lead the people's revolution in Germany. The revolution lasted for barely three days; the theory has survived, though, through the vicissitudes of quiet and unquiet epochs. With the lapse of a quarter of a century, Michal Kalecki went back to the Luxemburg problem; his theory of income distribution dressed it in a new ensemble. Kalecki too does not explicitly mention the factor of imported labour, he talks only of the impact of basic raw material prices on the distribution process. He does not quite spell out whether such raw materials are endogenous or exogenous to the system. His model has a chiselled, simple look. The share of wages in national income, it suggests, bears an inverse relationship with the movement of basic raw material prices. It is, as snobs would say, a quintessentially static model: if raw material prices rise, the share of the earnings of domestic labour in national income declines. This decline has a second-order effect: it reduces the degree of monopoly power of the working class and so threatens a further worsening of income distribution in society.

One derivative, whether oblique or direct, from the Kalecki model is the somewhat shocking conclusion that the working class in a developed industrial nation is at least a sleeping partner of colonial imperialism. Basic raw materials are picked from the third market at low prices, which is imperialist exploitation. As such exploitation intensifies, the share of wages in national income in the imperial country registers an advance. On the other hand, a rise in payments made to the third market for raw materials purchased leads to a decline in the wage share. In any case, there is hardly any question that, in the halcyon days of colonialism and imperialism, cheap import of raw materials – and add, labour – created an additional bonanza for capitalism.

Old theories do not die, they lie in wait and suddenly jump upon us, dispensing, simultaneously, both delight and discomfiture. The explosion of new technologies, particularly of space and information technologies, is proving to be awesomely labour-saving, promoting a fresh crisis of insufficiency of demand in the capitalist system. The advanced capitalist countries have arrived at a plateau of fantastic wealth. They nonetheless have to carry a large load of unemployed workmen, including of skilled workmen. In the circumstances, unregulated import of labour from the developing countries is frowned upon, since it will aggravate the crisis of underconsumption. This explains the concern of governments of the G-7 nations – and the World Trade Organization secretariat – to set up strict ground rules for migrant workers. The organized trade union movement in the capitalist countries, already weakened by the spate of labour-displacing innovations, is currently going through a traumatic experience. Workers are struggling hard to maintain the existing structure of wage rates. The prospect of imported, relatively cheap labour from overseas poses a further peril. It is not given to the trade unions to resist the tornado of technological progress blanketing the world. They are, however, determined to oppose the ingress of both cheap finished products and cheap raw materials and labour from the poorer territories. The Luxemburg–Kalecki theories are back with a vengeance. Cheap imports, including import of cheap skilled labour, are inimical to the cause of the working class in developed capitalist countries. You have only to go back to Kalecki's opus, *Theory of Economic Dynamics*, to appreciate the mechanism of the tensions that have been set in motion.

The concatenation of events is a challenge to entrepreneurs in capitalist lands. Despite their affluence, they are a harassed lot; it might be difficult to hold on to their affluence if innovations become the precursor of underconsumption. Capitalists are facing a great menace. The persistent recession is affecting capitalist profits. One possibility to cope with the situation is to have migrant labour from poor countries who wish to work at such sub-standard wages. Workers in capitalist economies, including technologists, are fighting tooth and nail the trend of importing scientists and technologists from the poorer countries, who can be paid wages substantially lower than what needs to be paid to skilled domestic labour. The trade union movement, determined to kill this, what they call vile practice, has partly succeeded; the immigration quota is being gradually scaled down. The capitalists have started to try out yet another gambit. They will desist from importing cheap labour, including skilled technicians, from the developing countries. Instead, they will enter into contracts with firms in poor countries – or set up subsidiary units there – for supply of certain key auxiliary and ancillary items. Outsourcing of this nature permits the capitalists to cut down costs and add to the profit margin. The organized working class, including the scientific community, are livid. The Kalecki extension of the Luxemburg schematics has come to full bloom: the interests of the working class in capitalist economies are proving to be antithetical to the interests of the working class in the poorer economies. Protest against outsourcing is a-building; the American administration as well as governments in Germany, France and the United Kingdom do not quite know in which direction to turn.

It is a tricky collage of possibilities. The lurking fear that some migrants could be terrorists is also contributing its mite. The dialectics of ensuring home employment vis-à-vis outsourcing for higher profits is very much joined. All this has been the cause of a somewhat extraordinary development. To be honest, outsourcing is the same thing as use of sweated labour, albeit under a different name. If skilled workers available locally were to be engaged in response to the compulsions of technology advancing at breakneck speed, such labour has to be paid wages on a very high scale. Instead, if skilled workers in poor countries are commissioned for the job, they could be paid lesser amounts, thereby enlarging the scope of profit-taking in the capitalist countries. This will also weaken the bargaining power of home labour. For capitalists, it will therefore be sort of killing two birds with one stone.

The hassle is generating tension on an international scale. Outsourcing takes jobs away from domestic labour in capitalist countries, and offers sustenance to labour – skilled labour – in the poorer economies. In the process, it creates a crisis within the fold of the working class in the underdeveloped parts of the world as well. Global recession has affected in great measure the poorer countries with equal or even greater severity. The problem has worsened because of the economic reforms thrust by the capitalist order on territories constituting the third market. The so-called reforms have scorched fields, closed down factories, thrown out of employment millions and millions of workers, and elongated the dark era of underdevelopment in country after poor country. The consequence is widespread discontent among the working class and their desperate attempt at mobilization against the nightmarish evil of globalization which yields only pains and no gains.

Outsourcing, subtly or otherwise, is working as a divisive force. Those skilled workers in the poor countries who benefit from outsourcing, of course, receive much less than they would have obtained had they managed to infiltrate into the labour market of the countries of capitalism. What they actually get is, however, still much higher than they would have otherwise received in their homelands. This reality is responsible for a split in the attitude of the working class in the poor countries: some of them, those – though a frightful minority – who reap the benefits of outsourcing, cross over to the side of globalizers. In the wash, the trade union movement as a whole is greatly diminished in Rosa Luxemburg's 'third market' economies too. In other words, outsourcing is bad for the working class at both ends of the spectrum – in the developed as well as in the underdeveloped countries. The interests of organized labour are adversely affected by outsourcing everywhere, either immediately or with a time-lag.

When dialectical materialism loses its verve, it becomes crass materialism. The dazzle and despair of globalization, every now and then, render radicals into former radicals. Some of them fall prey to allure and break away from their class roots. Not, however, the Indian Prime Minister. As a leader of the underdeveloped part of the world, one would have thought he would, in all seasons, rail against sweated labour which outsourcing really is. The history of imperialism is a cumulative tale of accumulation squeezed out of sweated labour and underpriced commodities. A revision of history is, however, under way. Colonialism and imperial domination are no longer non-welcome categories to at least the ruling classes in poorer societies. According to the new wisdom, unbridled capitalism, backed by unbridled colonization, succeeds in promoting growth across the entire globe, at the same time enriching the upper classes everywhere. Outsourcing has emerged as the weaponry in international class war. The Indian Prime Minister endorses it; he knows which side his bread is buttered. He would not demand equal pay for equal work across national frontiers. It does not perhaps matter to him if our people are paid by foreign parties far less for work of the same specification and quality, than what foreign workers are paid in their own countries. Outsourcing, our Prime Minister expatiated at the recent India–European Union Summit in New Delhi, is our birthright. The third market has its uses and so has the comprador class.

THREE

A single category

20–26 November 1999

The American ambassador was not naïve. He knew what he was talking about. He was blunt, as much plainspeaking as the circumstances, according to him, called for. Let your parliamentarians be good boys and pass the Insurance and FEMA bills without a murmur, thereby ensuring the effective take-over of the Indian economy by external forces. The US administration will then flood the country with mountains of investment funds. The ambassador's pledge, there should be no illusion, was in line with dreams nurtured by the leaders of the two principal political parties in the country. The two parties have an identical class base; patriotic sentiments are no part of their ethos; they are not interested in ancient history either; as long as they, as of today, experience fabulous prosperity for themselves and for their near and dear ones, why bother if the nation is again rendered into a bonded slave of this or that scion of foreigners? There is, besides, a certain snobbery savourable from the ongoing events: one has every reason to feel proud if labelled as pompadour-in-chief of the world's superpower. There is little point in ruminating over the situation that could have arisen if the American ambassador in residence had dared to offer this kind of open bribe two or three decades ago. Times change; the lesson has permeated the nation at all levels. Patriotism is the last resort of scoundrels, hence better be in a scampering hurry to discard customs and practices that are a hangover of the past. The comfort and well-being of the class fraternity is the supreme objective in the affairs of men. Once we agree to scuttle our sovereignty, the Americans have promised an uninterrupted flow of investible resources; residual pricks of conscience should therefore occupy no part of the agenda. Our leaders are aware, as much as the Americans are, that the future of one billion down-and-out people is no joke; at least three-quarters of this multitude are dead wood, garbage, richly deserving the destiny of pestilential death. The top layer of 250 million or thereabouts is an altogether different proposition though. The new millennium is a-coming, imperialism and colonialism are undergoing a grand revival! In case everything turns out well, this lot of 250 million will constitute an attractive market for western goodies. The American administration has, in fact, formalized a forward policy it is determined to implement in the course of the next couple of decades. It proposes to set up a global condominium of the comprador classes. The echo ringing round the valleys and turfs in country after underdeveloped country consequently reverberates with the inspiring note: compradors should transform themselves into a united compradordom of the whole world, they have nothing to lose but their sense of shame.

The two main political parties in India represent a single category of class interest. They have long ago divested themselves of any sense of shame, class bias is the only consideration in their system of values. The squabble over the Bofors chargesheets is a temporary occurrence; as far as roots are concerned, the two parties belong to the same genre. It is no accident that high-caste Hindus dominate the leadership of both. The parties, in effect, function as anger chambers for each other: those who fall out with the top brass of their own party cross over, on a purely short-term basis, to the other party, and vice versa. The leading lights of the two parties also intermarry; it is most normal for a daughter-in-law to function as MP for the Congress Party while the father-in-law is a member of the Union Cabinet which is BJP all the way, or for a chief minister in a BJP-administered state to have a brother-in-law who is a distinguished member of the Congress Working Committee.

To repeat, the hassle over Bofors is bound to die down; wider interests are to prevail. After all, the FEMA, the Insurance Authority of India and the Patents (Amendment) bills are one hundred per cent Congress babies. The BJP is honour-bound to introduce them in parliament, the Congress is equally honour-bound to pilot their passage in the two houses of parliament; class interests apart, the US masters, along with their underlings in the international financial institutions, expect such gestures from their trusted servitors – the bosses cannot be kept waiting.

Both the Americans and their collaborators in the poorer countries are nonetheless making a horrible mistake. Contrary to their fondly held notions, it is most unlikely to be a cakewalk for either of them. A major slice of India has no fascination for the main political parties, nor are they particularly enamoured of the prospects under a recolonized sky. Economic policies and measures which favour the foreigners and the nation's upper strata *ipso facto* put a further squeeze on the life and living of ordinary men and women comprising the nation's majority. The current hullabaloo over the increase in diesel prices illustrates the point. Shenanigans with the accounts of the Oil Pricing Committee were pioneered by Rajiv Gandhi. The BJP has merely taken a leaf out of the Congress Party's book. The lack of integrity evident in the manner the price rise was announced – waiting for the polls to close and shifting the onus on the mystifying arithmetic of movements in international oil and petroleum prices – makes one lose respect for the ruling set of politicians. But this is class war, further manifestations of this war are to follow; for instance, increase in rail and road fares and freight, across-the-board rise in indirect levies, closure and sale of public undertakings one after another thereby aggravating the problem of unemployment, and imports choking to death domestic industrial units. Black humour will not, however, be altogether dispensed with. One of the recent official statements has promised the creation of one crore of fresh employment every year for the next decade. This gem has been lifted straight out of a Congress document vintage 1980, proving once more the symbiotic relationship between the two parties.

But trouble is a-brewing. The four-fifths of the population who get nothing out of the cosy arrangement between the richer segments of society and foreign elements may refuse to be double-crossed any more. Latin America and Southeast Asia are a clincher: with all their might and arcane philosophy, the Americans have, of late, been unable to protect their native cronies; even the Argentine Republic is now out of their clutches, as is Indonesia, despite all the scheming the Americans had indulged in with the Golkars. India's vast masses, exploited beyond endurance, too could decide to have recourse to certain new initiatives. Not even 1 per cent of the people of Jammu and Kashmir, it is common knowledge, are keen to maintain their links with the Indian union; they have had enough of experience during the past 50 years; the government may now be unable even to prevent questions from being raised in public fora on the hundreds of crores of rupees wasted on the futility of Kashmir during this 50-year span. The questioning will not just stop here. How the country's economy could have been transformed if this huge sum, wasted in Kashmir, had been spent to raise the level of living of the starving masses in eastern Uttar Pradesh, Bihar, Orissa, Assam, the north-eastern states and elsewhere, will be a theme on the lips of very many persons. Year after year, millions of Indians suffer unspeakable agony on account of devastating floods bringing in their train seemingly intractable problems of water-logging, drainage, road repairs and so on. Suppose a cheeky young citizen, undaunted by frowning official eyes, demand that five thousand crores of rupees be cut back from the annual defence outlay for each of the next ten years, so that these essential nation-saving tasks could be looked after? Suppose another insolent youth follows up his introductory remark that India, one of the poorest nations on earth, has no business to spend the largest amount after Saudi Arabia, presumably the richest nation, on arms imports, with the proposal that India's defence imports be cut back by three thousand crores of rupees each year and the amount thus saved be devoted to a time-bound programme for generating universal literacy?

Just you wait, hitherto unthinkable thoughts are henceforth likely to fill the air. The American ambassador will be of little help at this juncture. On the other hand, serendipity is serendipity; now that the polity will be once more in turmoil, the Americans will have an alibi for the non-arrival of pots and pots of foreign money earlier promised.

Their own agenda

25–31 March 2000

The epochs are vastly different, or perhaps they are not. The Graeco-Roman classics are replete with narrations of how chieftains of vassal-states would quarrel with one another in order to gain an extra inch of space which helped them monopolize or near-monopolize the favours of the emperor ensconced in Rome or Athens. India and Pakistan are behaving in an almost identical manner with respect to the United States of America. Emulating the style of the Roman or Athenian supreme rulers who made a habit of touring distant conquered territories, President Clinton has announced his intention to visit this month the ramparts of his empire in South Asia. The rhetoric the electronic and the written media in India and Pakistan have opted for in this season has a single focus: the great American President is in the main visiting India; Pakistan will, at most, be a refuelling stop-over; alternatively, he has only Pakistan in mind while drawing up his travel schedule and has decided, as an afterthought, to spend a couple of nights on Indian soil to give New Delhi's politicians a spanking.

Those circulating such stories, whether in India or in Pakistan, tend to walk away from ordinary common sense. The suggestion that the presidential plane, flying the ten thousand-odd miles from Dulles International Airport to the skies of the subcontinent, will need a refuelling stop so close to its final destination, is hilarious: if the plane will have fuel enough to fly to Karachi or Islamabad, it could, thank you, land with equal ease at New Delhi; no refuelling will be called for. Those planting stories of this genre are, however, least bothered about the credibility of what they narrate.

The Pakistanis, of course, will keep spinning similar wild tales: the great US President, don't you know, is making the trip chiefly to spend time in Pakistan, a country for which he has the highest regard; he intends to talk things over with the leaders of the new regime, and, should he choose to hop over to the Indian capital, that is merely because he is driven by a single objective: he wants to admonish the Indian leaders that enough is enough, they must see reason over Kashmir and allow the people there the right of self-determination.

But it is an ill-wind that blows nobody any good. These narratives loaded with malice and hatred towards the neighbouring country which their President proposes to include in his itinerary, will make the Americans intensely happy. For, the stories illustrate precisely how an ambience of sycophancy is generated. Reports of the US administration's exasperation with Pakistan's authorities because of the domestic economic mess they have created, or Foggy Bottom's irri-

124

tation with India because of the latter's persistent unreasonableness over Kashmir, are mostly fiction. They nevertheless serve a purpose by adding to the charisma of the imperial state; the-boss-loves-me-more-than-he-loves-you kind of feeling is seemingly the ultimate vindication of one's existence: true, we have been roughly, very roughly treated by the Americans; let us nonetheless celebrate, for they have roughed up the Pakistanis to a much greater extent.

The Americans have, of course, their own agenda. They know the psychological make-up of the vassal-states and want to exploit it to the hilt. Once the US administration pretends to lean towards Pakistan, the immediate response of the Indian authorities is to concede some further demands placed upon them by Washington DC. In a similar situation, Pakistanis too will further kowtow to the Americans in the hope that such servile behaviour will induce the boss-country to shift the balance of affection in their direction and against India.

Much more than the actual Clinton trip, it is the preliminaries to it which are, therefore, proving to be far more important to the two quarrelsome countries in the subcontinent. India will hasten to cede ground on this or that issue to the Americans, for otherwise, Bill Clinton, it is feared, might lean towards Pakistan. In identical manner, the Pakistanis will be eager to make additional concessions to the Americans so as to dissuade the latter from expressing greater love for India. In the circumstances, please do not be surprised if President Clinton makes his visit to the subcontinent the occasion for a major celebration. There is scope for freewheeling speculation on the form the celebration might take. The US President, who knows, could so arrange things that both India and Pakistan are forced to sign the Comprehensive Test Ban Treaty (CTBT) during his visit. It will be rush, rush, rush – the State Department will make the announcement of the impending event to the world; a benign-looking Bill Clinton, beaming all over, will be adorning the Rose Room of the White House; the Indian Prime Minister and Pakistan's ruling General will be seated on either side of him; the affixation of signatures to the Treaty will proceed amidst great éclat; the Americans will even show the gesture of inviting, what is his name, Kofi Annan, the United Nations' Secretary General, to watch the event. Or the State Department will perhaps not go to such lengths immediately. Arranging separate signing ceremonies in New Delhi and Islamabad is therefore equally conceivable; the US President will make it a point to be present, as *loco parentis*, at both the signings. Have a heart, it is free market economics, the media have to make a living, they have to titillate the ego of their clients as well. The Indian newspapers will therefore let their imagination run riot in describing how the Americans were giving a bloody nose to the Pakistanis at our behest. The Pakistani media will not lag behind, their story-spinning faculty too will take wings: there will be vivid descriptions of how the Indians were made to eat humble pie by President Clinton who was most impressed by the genuineness of the complaints posted by Islamabad.

The cliché regarding the double enactment of a historical event, the first time as tragedy, the second time as farce, has gained acceptance as axiomatic truth in most parts of the world. One or two town cynics would want to enter a caveat; they will particularly question the sequence of the two happenings. No, the tragedy does not precede the farce; the course of events, they will maintain, actually commences with the farce and it is the accumulation of such farces which makes up the tragedy. Imperialism is, vide Lenin and Rosa Luxemburg, the final stage of capitalism. The context of that assertion may or may not be true any longer. What is however intriguing is the embarrassment of riches capitalism is currently suffering from; poor underdeveloped countries are racing against one another, they want to be recognized, pronto, as colonies once more of the west, that is what the new millennium is all about. A magnificent moral point of view has come to occupy centrestage: I am a bigger lackey than you are, the master will therefore favour me more than he will favour you, *tra la la la la*.

Since budget time in India will almost coincide with the Clinton visit, there will be no element of surprise should the Finance Minister and the Defence Minister address a joint press conference announcing, as an afterthought to the budget, that the last inhibitions are gone, the foreigners will henceforth be allowed to enter the defence sector as well. And the Prime Minister will casually inform a cluster of carefully chosen press persons about a friendly, informal arrangement whereby representatives of the US defence establishment will sit in at our confidential nuclear strategy sessions.

More surprises are likely to be in the offing. The President of the country has, of late, been providing evidence of an overarching conservatism, so much so that he has expressed a lack of warmth at the idea of revising the Constitution. Perhaps, as a suitable riposte, a full-page advertisement will be placed with the *New York Times* and the *Washington Post* inviting tenders for the leasing of the Rashtrapati Bhavan itself. Since privatization does not exclude sale to foreign parties, there will be no harm if the Federal Bureau of Investigation, for instance, buys up this lush property on top of the Raisina Hills; the President would then have to look for alternative accommodation. Surely the Pakistanis will not be able to match this feat; overwhelmed by the gesture, the US President will hopefully stop short of bullying us into internationalizing the Kashmir issue.

In this uncertain season, further folly will continue to be routinely added to folly. The latest contribution from the country's congenitally anti-Pakistan lobby is the allegation that Inter-Services Intelligence agents are the main organizers of heroin smuggling via Kashmir and Nepal. Never mind its naiveté, a hopeful syllogism is at work: the Pakistanis are a bunch of smugglers, the Americans do not like smugglers, therefore President Clinton will prefer us to our wretched neighbours. This is about as good a story as the one that since we are the world's largest democracy and Pakistan is ruled by a wretchedly authoritarian, anti-democratic regime, Bill Clinton will avoid that country like the plague and spend the entire time in India. Who will remind whom that the Americans actually have an unblemished record of coddling authoritarian military regimes in the countries they like to dominate, whether directly or indirectly.

In the given circumstances, the nation's leaders have a simple, single prayer: please, sir, permit us to be the world's champion lackey. If that is not possible for technical reasons, please certify that our lackey-like qualities are vastly superior to that of Pakistan. In this matter, the latest remarks by Madeleine Albright are a damper, but we will make one last attempt on Clinton's visit-eve: the budget will, by its breathless sycophancy, reveal the extent of our adherence to the American cause; it could have been prepared, line by line and section by section, in the US Department of Treasury.

The nightmare does not dispel though. What if, despite all these gestures of capitulation, Bill Clinton still insists that we give in to the Americans all the way and, since there is no alternative, accept the American agenda on Kashmir?

Hindu kingdom gone away

13 January 2001

The Hindutva aggression is coming home to roost. The flare-up in Nepal over the young Mumbai film star may be a happenstance, or perhaps a fall-out of squabbles between underworld goons. This kind of explosion would have occurred any time sparked by some other pretext. Nonetheless, the Vishwa Hindu Parishad and their cohorts have taken the world's only Hindu kingdom for granted. They have been responsible for several acts of overbearingness to-wards Nepal in recent months. Were the government in New Delhi sufficiently perceptive or sufficiently alert, it could have gauged the enormity of resentment swelling up in tender Nepalese minds. True, Nepal is denominationally Hindu. But its people will have no part of the boorishness characterizing the RSS crowd. In glaring contrast to a large segment of the population in Aryavarta, the Nepal-ese have no difficulty in separating the basic realities of life from crass emotions which feed on vacuous religious precepts. The youth in Nepal are, at the mom-ent, radicalized much in the manner the youth in the eastern parts of India were in the 1960s and the following decade. Some of the ignorant rabble belonging to the Hindutva fold have gone to the length of claiming Nepal to be a part of the extended Hindu empire. Nothing of the sort. By now, the brand of communists who describe themselves as Marxist–Leninists have emerged, if not as the major party, at least as one of the two major political formations in Nepal. Their concentration is not on prehistoric fables but on the hard datum of inequality in land distribution and the incomplete nature of land reforms in the country. They are aware of the economic woes of a land-locked state. They are, at the same time, deeply resentful of the ingrained superiority displayed by both resident and visitor Indians daily reflected in their inter-relations with Nepali citizens. Allegations of Indian imperialism are not just the airing of an empty rhetoric for the people of Nepal, these are perceived evil which they are determined to put an end to by their collective might. The conduct of the Indian *banias* dominating trade and industry is a particular sore point with the Nepalese, apart from their grouse over the sharing of water from rivers flowing downstream into India.

A point arrives when the perception of a phenomenon becomes indistinguishable from its actuality. The outburst of emotion would have, in any event, taken place through some means or other. The Indian matinee idol and his supposed remarks have merely provided the opportunity for unhinging the emotional doors, which is now threatening the very existence of the already wobbly Nepali Congress regime. A great passion cannot be quietened by cold logic, especially where the spelled-out logic itself has a weak foundation. It will take years and years of not just sincere contrition but scrupulously correct behaviour rooted in humility, to compensate for the great damage done to Indo-Nepalese relations. It is, however, altogether uncertain whether the present administration in New Delhi is at all capable of rising to the occasion and doing the minimum that is necessary to regain the trust of the Nepali population. The task to be accomplished calls for a total scrapping of the officious Hindu ideology and abandonment of the extravagant aspirations of its wild followers to ride roughshod over the sovereignty of neighbouring countries, the whole lot of them.

And it is not a problem specific to Indo-Nepalese relations alone. The international community, whichever manner you want to list its constituents, will be tempted to add the ugly happenings in Nepal to the interminable quarrel with Pakistan and the mess in Kashmir as question marks against India. That Kashmir is an integral and inalienable part of India is a proposition acceptable exclusively to Indians, and to none alone. Even amongst important groups of Indians, the thesis is fast losing its credentials. It would be a good thing if the leaders of the Hurriyat Conference are finally allowed to visit Pakistan. But an Indian disengagement in Kashmir is still way off. Influential sections of politicians and officials would resist any such move; so too would the military establishment. They would allude to the prospect of hostile public reaction within the country. But this demon the politicians themselves had created in the first place, and it is they who have to take the initiative to crush it. L.K. Advani notwithstanding, New Delhi has to accept as basic the hypothesis that a satisfactory solution of the Kashmir imbroglio is dependent on tripartite discussions between the governments of the two countries and a representative cross-section of the Kashmiri people, and this representation has to extend beyond the orbit of the Hurriyat and include rabid pro-Pakistani elements as well. Perhaps it would even be necessary at some juncture to induct an *amicus curiae*, the role to be filled in by a party which is not directly involved in the goings-on in the valley. The US would really love to jostle into the slot. We should, however, insist that that place is allotted to a nation belonging to the poorer parts of the world, and should not flinch if that nation happens to be a major Islamic power, such as Turkey or the United Arab Republic or Indonesia. If it comes to that, we should have the perspicacity to even accept the People's Republic of China as the mediator.

Why stop with Nepal and Pakistan, our relations are hardly healthy with Bangladesh as well. A substantial share of responsibility for this unsatisfactory state of affairs, once more, lies with us Indians. There has been, in the past, too much of a big-brotherly exuberance on our part while interacting with Bangladesh. During the first decade following the liberation of the eastern country, the proper thing for us would have been to treat that country with benign negligence. Instead, many of our officers and even citizens started assuming Bangladesh to be a territory regained by India, that is, Bharat. Apart from the communal divide, Bangladeshis harboured a not-unnatural suspicion of a neighbouring country huge in size, carrying an enormous load of population and one which had already attained a relatively more pronounced level of economic development. There were other factors too at work. New Delhi's overt reliance on Sheikh Mujibur Rahman and his Awami League provoked the anger of other groups in fractious Bangladesh. The persistent ill-will nurtured towards India is not, therefore, the sole achievement of the Jamaat-e-Islami. Whoever will be ranged against the Awami League will come, as a natural process, to develop an animosity towards India. The ULFA insurgents therefore have experienced no particular trouble to find sanctuary in Bangladesh and use that country as a conduit for the passage of arms. The persistence of the unrest in the Chittagong Hill Tracts involving the Chakma tribe has been another factor to deepen Indo-Bangladesh tension in the minds of ordinary citizens, and not just in Bangladesh alone.

We have been at the receiving end of plenty of discourses on the supposed big-brotherly attitude of the occupants of the Kremlin and which, according to some savants, contributed at least in part to the downfall of the Soviet state. We also heard during the late 1960s and the early 1970s much gossip concerning Chinese *hauteur* in their dealings with the smaller nations in Southeast Asia as well as with the People's Republic of Mongolia. It is equally moot to recognize that India's big-brotherly dominance could be an objective reality in several of her neighbouring states. This is found to act as a roadblock to the emergence of peace in the real sense with nations across our borders. Since it takes two to tango, we too will conceivably be victims of the conviction, unfounded or otherwise, that none of our neighbours appreciate our magnanimity and benevolence, and that they have launched a conspiracy, jointly or severally, against us. The Hindutva stance will strengthen this belief, the defence lobby active inside the country reinforcing it further.

The fault, though, dear countrymen, does not lie in others but in our-selves. Nepal will continue to be the only Hindu kingdom in the world. Her people will continue to be devoutly Hindu, and yet, will turn into inveterate enemies of the Hindutva-mongers whom they will soon begin to identify with the *bania* exploiters. A time will come when they will be persuaded to join the ranks of the certified enemies of this country. There was, epochs ago, a little jingle American children used to sing, and prance about in accompaniment, which went as follows: 'Lost my partner, what shall I do? I'll get another one prettier than you.' Alas, if the Hindu crowd continues to hold the reins of administration for some more while in New Delhi, not even a horrendously ugly partner will we be able to find for ourselves.

A dress rehearsal?

26 May 2001

An interregnum of about eighteen months, Seattle has been followed by Quebec. The pattern is almost identical. And Quebec has been followed on May Day by mini-uprisings in Berlin, Frankfurt, Basle, Zurich, London, Sydney, Mel-bourne. Young men and women – unemployed or university students, poets or journalists, black and non-black – congregated from all over, including the US. Agitators, individually and in groups, arrived – in fact, from different continents. None of them were organized specimens, certainly not organized on a countrywide or continental scale. Streams of young people rushed towards where the world's capitalism had chosen as its citadel. They arrived in tandem, but, despite the strides made by information technology, they remained disjointed clusters. Some of them might have carried on spasmodic correspondence via email with one another. Take the events in Quebec, for instance. Those assembled had little to show except their passion and will power, yet they did not at all hesitate to con-front the combined might of almost all the countries in North and South America. Fidel Castro, as was only to be expected, contemptuously refused to attend the gala meet primarily intended to offer obeisance to the new US President. The rest of the heads of states, almost without exception, were there, including those from

Mexico and Venezuela. For reasons of electoral expediency, the Mexican President has to wear his radicalism on his sleeves; but, let nobody forget, he was in the past a Coca Cola top executive. The Venezuelan President has other considerations in his mind, such as the gyrations in international oil prices. These reasons apart, geopolitical factors make it imperative for Latin American countries not to rub the US on the wrong side too often. Occasional expression of solidarity with Cuba is all right, but challenging the overall suzerainty of the superpower has to be ruled out.

In Quebec, the federal government of Canada behaved as if it were an extended limb of the US administration. Mobilization of police, army and other security personnel was at the highest level. Successive perimeters of defence networks were set up. The Canadian constitution accords full freedom of political activities enshrined in the Charter of Rights. The security forces, the Charter says, must display the maximum of restraint and professionalism while tackling a crowd gathered in support of a political cause. On those April days, the Canadian administration had a ready answer for its deviation from the Charter. Once the Riot Act was applied, the Charter of Rights, it maintained, stood automatically superseded. That however was the interpretation of the government, not necessarily of the judiciary. The atmosphere was surcharged or, rather, appropriate measures had been taken to ensure that the atmosphere was surcharged. The judiciary too was caught in a cleft stick: it could not quite determine whether a grey area had been reached, and reached in such a way that the situation demanded the precedence of the Riot Act over the Charter of Rights, or whether it should still be the other way round.

The few days the heads of states congregating there pontificated vociferously over the nuances of freedom, including the freedom of global trade, the capital of Canada resembled the expanse of a concentration camp, breathing the very antithesis of freedom. Troops, paramilitary personnel and policemen guarded the streets and parks, reconnoitring helicopters buzzed over, public transport was guarded as much by driver-conductors as by plainclothes men. The latter infiltrated into the crowd of wandering students and other young people, frequently acting as *agents provocateur*. They spied on the assembled groups and carried information back, post-haste, to the police command centre. Tear-gas shells, water cannons and rubber bullets were the principal instruments deployed to enforce the reign of freedom and free trade. At the slightest provocation, limbs were broken, blood was spilled and arrests took place indiscriminately. The arrested persons were carted away, put into overcrowded prison cells and supplied inedible food. The law of the land might be that those arrested are to be produced within twenty-four hours before a judge, who would not normally deny bail. This stipulation was unceremoniously infringed in several cases, confirming the arrival of a season when the accent was on lawlessness.

The episodes on May Day in countries wide apart would suggest that

Quebec was only a dress-rehearsal on the part of the capitalist system on how, and with what ferocity, to put down its perceived enemies. There was an eerie resemblance in the manner the security forces dealt with dissent in Labour Party-ruled Britain, social democratic Germany, gnome-dominated Switzerland and the darling land of the Conservatives, Australia: May Day or no May Day, trigger-happy international capitalism would brook no opposition to its holy resolve to keep in perpetual bondage the poorer people of this world and the conscientious ones who have the temerity to rise in support of the latter.

The significance of what is happening in the world nevertheless lies elsewhere. Forget for a moment Seattle and Quebec. Much more relevant is the ferment at work, either openly or, in many places, subterraneously. It is at work amongst North American and West European youth much more than, strangely, amongst the young multitude in East Europe, Asia and Africa. The impact of global economic exploitation is unquestionably much more severe in the Asian and African continents. The Russian youth too have been led up the garden path in the course of the past dozen years or thereabouts. Iron, however, has seemingly entered the soul of all young people, barring those resident in rampantly capitalist-dominated lands. Perhaps this conclusion has no hard factual basis and is an optical illusion. Is it still not odd that while the victims of applied free market philosophy are overwhelmingly in the underdeveloped parts of the world, whatever resistance, token or otherwise, offered against it is taking place in streets and university campuses in North America and West Europe?

The World Trade Organization may be poised to snuff out the life and living of their men and women, but the places which in the past were marked out as natural habitat for revolution and insurrection, remain quiescent. Even in cities such as Calcutta, with a long tradition of emotional outburst at the drop of a hat, never mind the cause, the students continue to be, by and large, extraordinarily well-behaved and chary to apply their minds to the short- and long-term implications of the doings of the international financial institutions, the WTO, the transnational corporations and the domestic compradors. The working class in these countries is no less dormant. The bargaining power of the trade unions has slumped even as plants and factories have shut down one after another and workers mercilessly ejected from their workplaces. Those occupying space in the lower echelons of the services sector are somewhat better equipped to combat the imminent threat to their livelihood; perhaps they have a reservoir of strength which enables them to try to thwart activities intended to turn into insignificance the resources they still have. They are a thinning minority. In quite a number of states in India, governments that are enamoured of revolutionary polemics are *in situ*. Similar state governments happen to exist in Brazil too. The behaviour pattern of these provincial administrations is strikingly different though. A Left-minded governor in the southern Brazilian state of Rio Grande do Sul does not mind setting aside a part of his government's limited funds to invite comrades from all over the world to assemble at Porto Alegre to join the people there in a tremendous show of united resistance to the machinations of the WTO. In contrast, state governments in India with similar ideological belief are displaying listlessness of a queer kind. Is it a lack of courage of conviction, is it inferiority complex, or is it that their supposedly revolutionary ardour is nothing much beyond oral eroticism? They have evidently other priorities. Some would go further and attribute the sloth to a backward-sloping supply curve of endeavour: the growing immiserization of the people does not induce determined action, it instead creates the urge to explore a niche of passivism.

That apart, do we at all know what the young people in China are thinking or aspiring for, at this particular moment? That country is currently enjoying the highest rate of growth in the world, and the highest rate of export growth as well. China's youth, immaculately attired in western apparel, must be beneficiaries of both these developments. From this distance of non-communication, it is not possible to know whether socialism, any branch of it, is still a compulsory text in the Chinese educational system, or whether Marx–Engels–Leninism or Mao's Ten Contributions are at all studied with awed reverence. Or take the plight of the Russian youth. In this, the first decade of the twenty-first century, in case they are taken aside and told that only about two decades ago their nation was regarded as the beacon for the underdeveloped world, that it was the second mightiest power in the world, causing sleeplessness to capitalists here, there, everywhere, while today they are a non-entity despite their fearsome nuclear capability, what would be their response? In both Russia and China, ideology, one suspects, has for the present been thrown out of the window as garbage. The great socialist thinkers in the nineteenth century, or in the first half of the twentieth century, including Proudhon, Lassalle, Marx, Engels, Plekhanov, Lenin, Stalin, Bukharin, Trotsky, Mao Ze Dong, Ho Chi Minh, Fidel Castro, Che Guevara, are perhaps judged to be contextually irrelevant in these two huge land masses. The young people there are being raised on what in the jargon is known as pragmatism; ideology is being denied space. And yet, it is the base of ideology which ensured for Russia unprecedented economic and military advance; China is in the process of going through the same experience.

The irony of it, at the other end, is that western liberalism since Adam Smith has but a handful of towering figures it can boast of. David Ricardo, Thomas Malthus, John Stuart Mill and others have at most defined economics as the subject that searches for the greatest good of the greatest number; nothing earthshaking there. Max Weber is the poor man's anti-Marx. John Maynard Keynes confessed that unrestricted competition does not solve the problems of capitalist crisis and it is necessary to have state intervention; which is to say, he, in effect, betrayed the cause of freedom. Jean-Paul Sartre really belongs to the other camp. All you are left with, then, is the species of John Rawls and Kenneth Arrow, some of whom prove with great mathematical elegance that they have

133

not a clue as to where social welfare lies. Karl Popper and Milton Friedman are consolation prizes of much lesser worth.

But maybe here is actually the answer to the riddle. The youth in the western world are left with empty ideological boxes and equally vacuous websites. They are sick of both; they are tired as much of information technology as of purposeless accumulation of wealth. They therefore read socialist tracts; conceivably, they do not even read them, they arrive at the state they have arrived at almost instinctively, after mulling over in their minds the factors underlying global inequalities, pervasive in which is capitalism's exploitative role.

Did not a sage once offer the prognostication: the road to world revolution will be routed through Calcutta and Shanghai? Should the two place names be substituted, for example, by Quebec and Frankfurt?

Into an impossible corner

5 January 2002

Let us be reasonable. We cannot expect technology to make extraordinary strides and yet order the technology of terror to remain primitive. If the will is there to chisel the artifices of terror, give or take a certain space of time, the relevant technology will answer the prayer. Fifty years ago, a weapon of the specificity of Kalashnikov 47 would have been beyond the pale of imagination; now it is *passé*. If prognosticators are to be believed, the manufacture of nuclear explosives will soon be a cottage industry and such explosives would be used by the lumpen crowd in every country, maybe to settle their private scores. Why, the lumpens alone, twenty-first century Montagues and Capulets, may not flinch, passions roused, from engaging in an atomic skirmish with each other.

As the technology of terror improves, the range of its application is also bound to expand. Practically any target will be reachable, including this or that national totem or icon. Targeting icons may even be reckoned as akin to doubling the fun. Righteous indignation that the 13 December episode within the precincts of the Indian parliament is a declaration of war on the very symbol of democracy, should therefore provoke a wry smile. If the world is globalized, terror too must be globalized. Sanctity will henceforth attach to nobody and nothing. Terror is terror. The intended victim of terror can be you, me, your neighbour, my neighbour, your enemy, my enemy, your friend, my friend.

After all, it boils down to begging the basic question: who defines terror, and in what manner? In case the demolition of the World Trade Centre was terrorism, what about the pinpoint-bombing by United States' and British planes of Iraq's schools and hospitals which obliterated the lives of hundreds of lovely, innocent children? If by surprising OPEC ministers at the conference table and holding them at ransom in Vienna way back, twenty years ago, was unmitigated terror, is the current targeting of Yasser Arafat's hearth and home by Israeli military personnel a harmless, innocuous pastime? Nearer home, was the demolition of the Babri Masjid, with the government benignly looking on, terrorism, or its opposite? If the Maoist Coordination Committee or the People's War Group is a terrorist outfit, is the Ranvir Sena any less? If the Inter-Services Intelligence (ISI) is up to no good along India's north-eastern borders and elsewhere, the Pakistan authorities could mount a counter-allegation that the Research and Analysis Wing (RAW) is behind the occasional mischiefs perpetrated in Sind and Baluchistan. It is perhaps permissible to brag that my anti-terror tenets are superior to yours; it is however awesomely difficult to prove that my tenets are nobler than yours. Value judgement is involved.

Must we not go further afield? How does one establish the hypothesis that private terrorism is condemnable while state terrorism is not? The question whether the Indian army is engaged in organizing large-scale repression in the Kashmir valley may, for the present, be kept in abeyance. But suppose some smart alecs argue that New Delhi's stonewalling of the proposal to allow the people of the valley to participate in a plebiscite, under the auspices of the United Nations, on the issue of their relationship with the Union of India, is as good as a hectoring act of terror? Ferocious rejoinders by our Ministry of External Affairs is going to be of little avail since, according to the canons of jurisprudence, an interested party can be neither a judge nor a member of the jury. In certain circumstances, terrorism does indeed even involve the cutting of corners with rudimentary norms of behaviour. For instance, when it suits them, the United States and other western governments swear by the United Nations. Where it does not suit them, the organization is bypassed, and an abstract concept, the international community, is invested with supreme over-riding authority. Or envisage a situation where the village folk, hundreds of them, drag a reluctant teenager of a wife, whose husband has just died, into the latter's funeral pyre and light a magnificent fire, while the government of the land either does nothing or quotes sanctimonious scriptures. Will that be terrorism or holiest religious practice? Definition, it follows, is all.

The state-of-the-art position of the dialectical debate can be summed up. Technology has seen to the progressive sophistication of the instruments of terror. Globalization, in its turn, has ensured that terror transgresses all boundaries and portals of sentiment. And since the definition of terror has no objectivity per se, and somebody's meat is somebody else's poison, all gestures of interpersonal or international relations are either gestures of terrorism or gestures of unadulterated innocence.

Should not the message therefore go out to the zealots: please pipe down. India may have a hundred reasons to order its troops to stay put in Kashmir, but what are reasons to India may well appear as pretexts to the local populace. Against this background, to outside parties detachment might well be the better part of valour. Otherwise, the terror lobby could proceed to ridiculously extravagant lengths, and propose the weirdest legislative and administrative measures to rein in terrorism. One should add, altogether without relevance to the purpose or purposes publicized for the initiative taken, the Prevention of Terrorism Ordinance did not stop the assault of 13 December; the conversion of the Ordinance into an Act is unlikely to do any better. The insistence on the adoption of such draconian measures itself then becomes a near-exercise in terrorism. A state government in the country is crying wolf, merely because its police have been unable to submit chargesheets against suspected criminals within the stipulated period of three months; it would like to have legislation permitting detention without trial for terrors of certain descriptions. The pretext trotted out is, however, the need to protect the land from infiltration by Pakistani agents.

This is precisely where the role of history emerges as a necessary category. Those currently in charge of the central administration in the country are a perceptive lot. They, with good reason, consider that Henry Ford's definition of history as bunk is itself just bunk. History is the crucial determinant of human destiny; it shapes the mind and forges the future. As long as prehistory can be successfully substituted for history, India and Indians, it is being hoped, will be persuaded to march back safely into the most intense regions of intellectual darkness; other genres of darkness will then become easily accessible. Those politically not on the same wavelength with the present set of rulers should, of course, also delve into history. But should not they, unless they are off their oats, concentrate more on modern history, such as the span encompassing the freedom struggle against the British and the post-independence phase of monolithic Congress overlordship? It will be, for instance, excellent liberal education to read the texts of the Rowlatt Act and the Bengal Criminal Law Amendment Act, in vogue in the earlier decades of the last century. These statutes, validating detention without trial, were supposed to target the so-called terrorists and anarchists who were making life difficult for the alien rulers. The native patriots were quick to describe these acts as lawless, and violative of the code as much of morality as of decency. The Congress Party, once it took charge of the national administration, learned fast, or, rather, unlearned fast. The Prevention Detention Act introduced in the 1950s was hardly any different from the Rowlatt Act; one or two politicians perhaps suffered from pangs of uncomfortable memory, but the Congress leadership as a whole did not mind. The new description of terrorism was subversion. In due course, the Preventive Detention Act had worthy successors, culminating in the Maintenance of Internal Security Act which filled Indira Gandhi's heart with joy.

The trauma of the Emergency put a temporary break on the ardour of the powers-that-be to legislate for detention without trial in the name of aborting terrorism, sabotage and subversion. A quarter of a century is a respectable enough interval of time. That apart, it is by now a different landscape, the nation has embraced both the technology mind-set and liberalization. The architects of national decisions that matter have actually played themselves into an impossible corner: they must eat the cake and have it too, they must cultivate democratic pretensions and yet be impatient with democratic opposition. An impasse of this nature inevitably leads to the mindless acceptance of the proposition: my anti-terrorism is superior to yours. It is then a smooth passage to the brilliant corollary that if my police are nincompoops, I must have legislation which decrees detention *sans* trial.

There is a problem though. Those who think along authoritarian lines suffer from notions of immortality. They will be, they take it for granted, in command for ever and ever. It is beyond their capability to imagine that, once in the future, they might be out of government and the opposition might be in; the detention without trial legislation could then be conveniently used against those who drafted the legislation in the first place.

He was conceivably momentarily absent-minded, but the Home Minister of the country let drop a home truth: POTO or POTA, there is no effective defence against suicide attacks. This will be more so since technology refuses to be retrogressive and globalization, as wise men suggest, is irreversible. Should not we therefore explore the roots of the basic problem: terror can have no colour, or, rather, it can assume any colour; it is therefore pointless to choose sides.

Anyway, for this country's government, the metaphysical scales do not need to be scaled. For, the Americans have taken charge.

The boss does the choosing

20 July 2002

No apocrypha but hard fact from the holy annals of the International Monetary Fund. It was the mid-1950s; a brat from an oil-rich West Asian country, with an indifferent degree in economics from a nondescript American university, was a research assistant with the Fund. A vacancy had occurred at the level of assistant chief in the division he was working, and he had expressed an interest for promotion to the slot. Not selected, he was downcast. The director of the particular department of which the division was a part called in the young man and commiserated with him: 'Please, do not take this setback to heart. Next year I will make you your country's finance minister.' And he did.

Such was the cultural pattern in international economic relations in Latin America and West Asia for more or less the past half a century. The countries were ruled either by absolute monarchs or by military dictators. They got along famously with the United States administration, that is to say, they obediently followed the American line on all substantive issues of foreign and domestic policies. Their economies were more or less in bondage to American interests; these interests were overseen, on behalf of Foggy Bottom, by the World Bank and the International Monetary Fund. It was thus quite customary for finance ministers of these countries to be named by international financial institutions based in Washington DC. No eyebrow was raised in any quarters over the quaint arrangement; quaintness was the rule. The culture spread like bonfire following the collapse of the socialist bloc, and with the United States emerging as the world's only hyperpower. The disease has since turned into an epidemic. No longer just finance ministers, even presidents and prime ministers of lesser countries are at present chosen by the powers-that-be in Washington DC – not just in Latin America and West Asia but practically all over. The last few finance ministers of Pakistan, it is generally acknowledged, have been picked by the top bosses of the Bank and the Fund. Rumours afloat in 1991 credited the two venerable Washington institutions of transmitting to New Delhi the names of two individuals, ranked ordinally, whom they wanted to be installed as India's finance minister, for implementing the structural adjustment programme on the anvil. The first nominee declined the offer for personal reasons, and the second person in the list was selected. His name is now a household word in the country. Although eleven years have passed, the substance of this gossip has not been seriously disputed by anybody.

It is therefore not any extraordinary development that the US government has, of late, decided to go public with its choice of heads of states and prime ministers of countries located in the different continents. Freedom to choose is a beautiful, liberal thought-piece. But what is freedom and what is choice depend upon how the American administration decides to define these concepts on your behalf. The Palestinians have been told in no uncertain terms that, no fooling, should they want a state of their own, they must ditch Yasser Arafat as their leader and choose another one more to the liking of the United States. There is, after all, no free lunch in life; if you want your own state, you must allow the American administration to decide who the head of the state is to be. In case you prefer to be obstreperous and fail to endorse the choice of President George W. Bush, you will be permanently denied a country of your own, and be subject to daily mauling by General Sharon and his band of outlaws. The outlaws, you see, are America's in-laws.

The no-nonsense stance on the part of the hyperpower is expected to send the appropriate signal around the globe. The Philadelphia Declaration is a dead letter; more than two centuries and a quarter have elapsed since 1776, and only morons will attempt to remind the US president of the particular nature of the foundation stone on which the great United States of America was once built. Besides, the trauma of 11 September has had a devastating impact. Osama bin Laden and Al Qaeda have transformed the American connotation of liberty; they have, in addition, redefined the ambits of friends and enemies: whoever are not with the United States are *ipso facto* against it and deserve to be deprived of their freedom of choice. The US administration perhaps wants to make an example of the Palestinians so that the message spreads not just across West Asia but also to other regions: it is the American millennium, so you better behave, otherwise. . .

Once the rationale of medieval logic is granted to them, the Americans are, no doubt, dead right. The problem lies elsewhere. The US President's focus of attention is exclusively on Al Qaeda and bin Laden. He overlooks, because none has dared or remembered to inform him about it, the other phenomenon, the rush of new ideas flooding young Arab minds. Edward Said is an exact contemporary of bin Laden; what is worse, he holds a chair at Columbia University in New York, at least held one till very recently. Said's genre of political philosophy has captured the imagination of thousands of young people from West Asia who have been, or are, students at American and European institutes of higher learning. The Arab countries are no longer the fiefdom of pashas and sheikhs. The boys and girls just referred to, certainly some of them, have emerged from the families of sheikhs and pashas. They have been victims of a fantastic alteration of identities. True, a number from amongst them have been ensnared by bin Laden's charm. But vastly larger numbers are captivated by Ed Said.

A Saidified mental process can lead to curious consequences. For example, President Bush's fiat concerning Yasser Arafat is unlikely to render the Palestinians and other Arabs into a community of obliging cowards. It will, on the contrary, steel their resolve to defy the American dictat. More ominously, it may radicalize them to an even greater extent and swell the ranks of Hamas. The American wish could then be self-fulfilling, but in a perverse sense: the Palestinians will conceivably discard Arafat, but install a Hamas stalwart as their undisputed leader. Things will then turn infinitely more difficult for both the United States and Israel. The tribe of suicide bombers will not diminish, but increase exponentially; an unending stream of Palestinian boys and girls may decide that life was worth sacrificing if such sacrifice could usher in national liberation; no sophisticated-sounding arguments are likely to hold them back.

The Americans have created their own problem and they themselves will have to sort it out. It is, however, astonishing that there is hardly a squeak around the world in protest against the atrocious Bush interdict. Here, in India, the Left have issued their routine statement; that is no earthshaking event. The rest of the political parties have been coy, as coy as coyness could be. What the Americans say is taken as law; even if it is lawless it is law, because it has been handed down by the Americans. As if the entire world has been reduced to the condition Thailand and Philippines, for instance, experienced 50 years ago. An absolute ruler is named by the Americans, the army is tutored by the Americans, the arms are sent by the Americans, the law is set by the Americans. Whether you are a Pibulsongram or a Macapagal, it does not matter: you rule because the Americans have allowed you to rule. The opposition is supposed to die a natural death; the American concept of democracy in poorer lands does not admit of an opposition which exhibits recalcitrance to the White House's views and intentions. The media too is expected to be equally servile. The latest Cabinet decision in New Delhi on direct foreign investment in the media will enormously facilitate such unquestioning obedience. And it could be an interesting guessing game how many years it will take before a Cabinet reshuffle in New Delhi has to be cleared with Washington DC. Or have we already arrived at that tomorrow?

On the other hand, this could only be a beginning. For all one can perceive, the history-has-already-ended school of thought has begun its celebrations a little too early. If there is a spurt of Edward Said wisdom in West Asia, there is no earthly reason for the non-repetition of the story in Africa or South Asia either. Latin America, in any case, has been set sufficiently on fire by the likes of Che Guevara and Garcia Márquez. In the circumstances, we ought to be agog with anticipation. History is only adjourned, it is never ended; it has turned upon itself in the last couple of decades of the twentieth century, it could still do another somersault very soon. Should you cherish a belief of this nature, depending on the prevalent system of values, you will be described as either a professional optimist or a professional pessimist.

At the same time, it will be a gross act of discourtesy not even to mention an apologia proffered in extenuation of the Bush outburst. Have a heart, the explanation runs, it is the grandeur and universality of American democracy which induces a US President to go off the rails every now and then. He is under relentless pressure: from the Congress, from the judiciary, from the states, from the media, from the public. Such pressures are the noblest attributes of the magnificent American democracy. The compulsions of the democratic process often render the President the subject of the most humiliating experiences, such as Bill Clinton's explicit description of his lurid sexual proclivities. To survive, the US President must have an outlet for his emotional pent-ups caused by such experiences. Which is why he takes it out on Castro, on Saddam, on Arafat. The rest of the world must therefore put up with the authoritarian conduct of the President. That is necessary to ensure the survival of American democracy. After all, who lives if American democracy dies?

The greater fundamentalist

1 February 2003

Have a heart, cronies need to survive; they have therefore to stay one step ahead of the boss. The Australian government has announced a fiat with no nonsense about it: henceforth any person resembling Saddam Hussein and found loitering anywhere within the precincts of the southern continent will be locked up. Saddam is evil, and, should you look like him, you are guilty by resemblance. Cronyism apart, the notification reflects a belief on the part of the Australian authorities that human cloning is already an established global arrangement. Physical similarity, it is being implied, is invariably accompanied by identical attitudes, manners and thought processes, so much so that one Saddam is indistinguishable from other ones. Or perhaps the assumption is of a slightly different genre: whether cloning is actually taking place or not, the concept underlying it, the government of Australia is convinced, is no humbug, and no chances should be taken: Saddams to the left of it, Saddams to the right of it, Saddams in front of it. Faith, after all, moves mountains; it can also create the spectre of Saddams.

The boss nation is exhibiting another manifestation of faith. Iraq, President George W. Bush is certain, has concealed weapons of mass destruction, loads and loads of them. Hans Blix and his men, bearing the imprimatur of the United Nations, may have found no evidence, but the US President will not blink; he is convinced the United Nations inspectors are wearing blinkers; the absence of evidence is actually proof of the suspected fact. Objectivity is no match for faith. The American administration believes, and would like the rest of the world to believe, that Saddam has tucked away nefarious weapons in strange sorts of places, maybe under beauty parlours, in car parks, in tunnels dug under the Euphrates and the Tigris. As everybody knows, the Americans have transmitted several warnings to the Iraqis, to no effect; no admission of treacherous crime has been forthcoming. Invasion is obviously the only option left. In airports after airports across the great United States, privates are therefore kissing goodbye to their wives and sweethearts and babies, and flying in swarm formation towards the direction of the Persian Gulf.

But, as there are wheels within wheels, deeper layers of faith are embedded in run-of-the-mill pronouncements of faith. It is an article of faith for President Bush that Saddam is hiding weapons. That is for the record. There is, at the same time, faith of a much profounder order, which too is providing inspiration to the President. Don't you know, he is on the point of launching a War of

Liberation; those of us who think he was ordering his troops to occupy Iraq purely for the fun of enslaving the people there could not be more wrong. No sir, he is, on the contrary, using the massive might of the western alliance to liberate the Iraqis from Saddam's tyranny. The Americans richly deserve to be congratulated; they have taken a leaf out of the book of the communists, who made a habit of starting wars of liberation in colonial countries one after another. President Bush proposes to beat the communists at their own game. After all, Saddam must be a crypto-communist. Every anti-American is. A national war of liberation is to free the Iraqi people; whether the latter would like to embrace freedom of the kind the US administration is offering, is a question deemed to be out of order. Here too, faith supersedes doubts: the Iraqis, the US President fervently believes, want to get Saddam out of their hair. Since the President so believes, the issue is closed. President Bush has been equally assertive about that other belief: the Iraqi scientists currently helping Saddam Hussein to develop thermonuclear and chemical weapons can be persuaded to betray him, provided the quantum of bribe offered to them is of the right magnitude and specification. Till now, not one scientist has defected from the motherland; but there is no point picking a quarrel with beliefs and faiths.

Western civilization, that is, if civilization it has to be described as, does it not follow, has turned an interesting corner. Rationality gave birth to western science, and science paved the way for technology. Science and rationality would however appear to have had their day. The country where western technology has reached its climacteric is no longer interested in facts – and rational deductions from facts. It has decided to cross over to beliefs. One cannot pooh-pooh a belief. Faiths and beliefs are self-contained entities. They do not await proof. They are taken on trust, and are as inviolable as axioms. You must examine your head before you demand proof of the rightness of a faith or a belief.

Come to think of it, such total reliance on faith is a classy case of fundamentalism. Osama bin Laden is a fundamentalist, George W. Bush is no less so. The so-called war on terrorism is essentially an instance of two fundamentalist groups flying at each other's throat. In the circumstances, the western lobby is hardly in a position to claim any moral superiority per se over Al Qaeda. Were the world asked to condemn bin Laden and his disciples, on the ground of insensate fundamentalism, a similar chargesheet should be drawn up against President Bush and his acolytes like Tony Blair too. The impending inevitable confrontation we are seemingly resigning ourselves to is therefore, by no stretch of the imagination, intended to save human civilization; it is, at most, a clash between two non-civilizations. And, at least some of the watchers from ringside seats would be inclined to act as cheerleader for the underdogs, namely, Saddam and his friends.

Never underestimate the worth of a cliché though: there is always something more than meets the eye. No contraband has yet been found in Iraq. On the other hand, leaders of the People's Republic of Korea have not at all been bashful in letting out what their intentions are. They have walked out of the Nuclear Non-Proliferation Treaty and have reiterated their determination to pursue their experiments with developing thermonuclear weaponry. The Americans are however extraordinarily coy in their reaction to Korean pronouncements. President Bush is planning no war of liberation in North Korea, nor is he looking around for a second General MacArthur. His spokesmen have only expressed regret that the Koreans have walked out of the NPT; nothing beyond that.

Both North Korea and Iraq are constituents of 'the axis of evil'. How come one constituent is belaboured, while the other one is treated with a kid glove? Is this American coyness towards North Korea because of the vast expanse of the People's Republic of China next door to that country? But, then, Iraq is not altogether vastly distant from China either. President Bush is prepared to risk Chinese annoyance over Iraq, but not apparently over Korea. This need not be that much of a puzzle though, if the focus is on certain other aspects of objectivity. Conceivably, it is not weapons of mass destruction but oil that the good Americans are in search of. Iraq has under its soil some of the largest reserves of oil. It is also one of the biggest exporters of oil, just as Venezuela is. The situation is, in a sense, dicey for the United States. Both Iraq and Venezuela cannot be allowed to go out of the Americans' sphere of influence more or less at the same time. The prospects do not look terribly good in Venezuela. Hugo Chavez is proving to be a tough nut to crack. Four coups or semi-coups have been organized under Central Intelligence Agency auspices in and around Caracas. Each one has failed. The general strike organized with the help of unlimited resources poured from American coffers has also not been altogether a piping success. A war of liberation à *la* Iraq aimed at the ouster of Chavez is also not a practical proposition. Latin America is already aflame. The wretched Castro is waiting in the wings. Brazil has voted in a Leftist president; so too has Ecuador. Argentina and Peru are wobblier than ever. An open aggression against Chavez will be too risky an adventure and could create further complications. Thank heavens, Iraq is somewhat different. The neighbouring Arab countries are still mostly under the thumb of either military dictators or corrupt sheikhs whose loyalty is still purchaseable.

An overlay of realism is therefore reposed on the base of fundamental extremism. Be a fundamentalist, but top it up with a veneer of cool judgment: this seems to be the purport of American foreign policy in the first decade of the twenty-first century. If you cannot topple both Chavez and Saddam and have to choose between one of them, do choose Saddam as the target. Vladimir Putin will look the other way, or, at most, offer a fleeing Saddam comfortable asylum, while leaders of the People's Republic of China will remain engrossed in their domestic affairs. Be a fundamentalist, but be a clever strategist too; madness will then pass for sanity.

There is, however, a snag. Suppose, as in the case of human beings, nations too begin to be cloned. That could pose a nasty problem for ever. As US army units liberate one Iraq, several other Iraqs, equally obstreperous, equally terrorist-minded, would keep bobbing up across the five continents. The United States would then have to be on a permanent liberation war binge. That could cost astronomical sums, and unnerve the Congress. Perhaps President George Bush would cross that bridge when he arrives there.

The new lexicographers

7 June 2003

Should predators double up as lexicographers? Tony Blair's side-kick, Jack Straw, has now gone on record: ferreting out weapons of mass destruction was not the principal concern behind the Iraqi expedition, it was to extricate the good people there from the clutches of terrorism.

Thereby we reach a problem. The likes of Jack Straw are self-advertising hypocrites and unblinking practitioners of falsehood. Must we depend on their authority to separate terrorists from non-terrorists? In the heydays of empire-building, the British used to dub as terrorists those whom Indians in general regarded as gems of patriotism. The list of such patriots, slandered as terrorists, included national heroes sent to the gallows by the imperial masters: Bhagat Singh, Surya Sen, Sukhdev, Rajguru, Benoy Bose, Dinesh Gupta, Tarakeswar Dastidar. Nomenclature decided upon by predators, either entrenched or aspiring, therefore deserves to be treated if not with total contempt, at least with total indifference. Till as long as Saddam Hussein followed the Anglo-American hegemonic prescriptions, he was a noble ruler; the moment he began asserting himself, he became a terrorist. Must we put up with such junk?

Several things have meanwhile happened, and are happening, in the human concourse. It is not only a wide world; it is also, thanks to the breakneck speed at which technology is progressing, an open world. An inevitable consequence of globalization, technology – and this covers the technology of mass destruction – refuses to take at face value the pretension of patent rights over it claimed by anyone. Weapons of mass destruction, big and small, and, besides, the methodology of mass destruction, are no longer the monopoly of the world's predatory powers. The Al Qaedas and Osama bin Ladens are actually the outcome of two simultaneous developments: (a) the refusal on the part of the earth's oppressed to take it any more lying down, and (b) the liberal availability of methods and modes of mass killing. It is not merely a simplistic matter of the pot calling the kettle black, or vice versa; the reality is far severer.

The British had set up the tradition. Anyone having the temerity to take to arms, to fight the alien predators occupying their land and pillaging their property, would be described as terrorists by the usurpers and mercilessly cut down. Whether it was Ireland or India or Kenya or Malaya, the story was the same. George W. Bush is not original, he has merely followed the imperial script. The invasion of Iraq was to lay hand on the largest reserve stock of oil in the world, and not in response to strain caused to this or that moral philosophy. Morality and imperialism/colonialism do not go together. Should you entertain any doubts in the matter, just ask the left-over descendants of the Cherokees still living in Tennessee and the Carolinas.

Osama bin Laden, assuming he is still around, will have every right, it stands to reason, to suggest that the charge of international terrorism should rather be laid at the door of Bush and company. And, after Iraq, it is certainly justifiable to take a second look at 9/11. Innocent lives are always lost in a holocaust. That is part of the objective of organizing a holocaust. The original author of the doctrine of mass terrorism is not, however, Osama bin Laden. Jallianwala Bagh was a British ceremonial: twenty-odd years after it happened, Udham Singh responded to it by an individual act of terror. Udham Singh was hanged. He chose to be hanged because nothing happened to the original sinners, the Dyers and O'Dwyers. Or, to change the national context, what about the Black and Tans in Ireland? The state terror unleashed by them could not ever be matched by the Sinn Fein. Even so, terror and counter-terror could still be distinguished, for the latter had a quality far more savage.

There is, it follows, little reason to continue to go overboard over 9/11. The suicide pilots who crashed into the twin towers of the World Trade Centre were Arab patriots seeking an answer, in their own manner, to the query: how to reverse an apparently interminable series of historical wrongs perpetrated by imperialists and colonialists. The principle guiding them was simple. The world's dispossessed do not have either the means or the capability to subdue the imperialists in open warfare. Apart from the enormity of the military and other resources the imperialists command, they are also actively assisted by compradors in country after country. The only way the enemy could be harried and harassed is by deploying hit-and-run tactics. What started with the hijacking of jet planes in the early 1970s is now blossoming into more sophisticated and chiselled forms of guerrilla-type activities, which the rapid spread of technology has helped. 9/11 is neither the beginning nor the end; it is a part of a process.

Two parallel premises are at work. Even in the imperial countries themselves, there is a rising spiral of rationality and ordinary, humane emotions.

Predatory adventures in distant shores have enriched the predators and accelerated the advance of capitalism in their backyard. Even if the Marxian law of motion of society is only half-operational, another mechanism starts ticking: mature capitalism leads to increasing maturity of the mind and steady unfolding of a hitherto dormant moral passion. Later generations of capitalists, give or take a span of time, are stricken by conscience; they rise in revolt against the monstrosities committed by their predecessors as also by their current seniors. Such outpouring of rationality led to the establishment of the British Anti-Imperialist League and the revolt in American campuses in the 1970s against the Vietnam war. In March/April this year too, the Iraq putsch caused an unprecedented upheaval across the six continents, including in the very heartland of the two invading countries. If anything, the anti-imperial and anti-colonial mood was somewhat less explosive in those traditional societies where anti-imperialist emotions are, by now, almost a worn-out cliché. In contrast, the thousands and thousands of protesting young people, old men and women, babies and war veterans flooding towns and cities in the western countries constituted an awesome cathartic experience.

And yet, it is impossible to back away from hard data. The anti-war legionnaires in the imperial countries are still a minority, they were not able to roll back the invasion, nor were they able to save Iraq's sovereignty for the Iraqis. Which is why guerrilla terrorism emerges as an important adjunct of the global anti-colonial war. Forget for a moment planted notions about the Al Qaedas and the Osama bin Ladens, assume for a moment that their role is no different from the role filled by Bhagat Singh and Surya Sen's Indian Republican Army: to force the British to panic and withdraw from India. These patriotic Indians, determined to liberate the land, had no standing army; whatever standing army there was, was in the employ of the British. The freedom fighters were without the resources necessary to raise an army of this kind. Nor had national awareness reached a level where the entire population would rise together and choke the British, never mind the cost in human lives. The only available option was the creation of a climate of terror: ambush the enemy here, there, everywhere; ambush the district magistrate or the police commissioner and shoot him down; raid a club where the colonials, along with their families, congregate in the evenings for relaxation. To create an ambience of terror, occasionally jack up your ambition and try to bump off a viceroy or a provincial governor. Should you fail, you will die, but terror will still make the air heavy; such terror will one day persuade the oppressors to do a cost–benefit analysis and convince themselves that the imperial game was no longer worth the candle.

9/11 was only a twenty-first century version of the Irish–Indian terror tactics. The latter achieved not insubstantial success in the earlier epochs. It was not enough, the conclusion was arrived at, to hit the imperialists at their colonial outposts; a methodology must be developed whereby terror could also strike nearer home, deep inside. The twin towers, the Pentagon and the White House were chosen for symbolic strikes. A message was intended to be conveyed: the majority of the American nation must, for dear life, arrive at the judgment that predatory imperialism was not even a zero-sum game; its impact is in fact worse – negative. The inexorable process of the rationality of the human mind will finally convince the majority of the Americans of the futility of colonial exploits as a viable long-term proposition.

Riyadh and Casablanca, both post-Iraq events, mark a resumption of the 9/11 strategy. If nuclear missile defence systems prevent, for the present, a re-enactment of 9/11 within United States territory, let the immediate targets concentrate on American installations overseas. At no stage have the imperialists suspended their acts of terror, why should the Arab insurgents do so either? Their aim is to scare the daylights out of the imperialists. It is a cruel process, but this is necessary retributive cruelty which will go on till the majority of the nation do not force their rulers to call off their predatory activities. Be fair, if the Bush–Blair affair in Iraq was not such a heinous event, Riyadh–Casablanca-type retaliatory attacks would not have been called for. The Anglo-American forces have slaughtered hundreds of innocent men, women and children. The savagery the Arab terrorists are responsible for is no worse.

Even so, there is an inherent danger in what the Islamic terrorists are experimenting with. They cannot finetune their attacks. An official Belgian building is also reduced to smithereens during the Casablanca bonfire despite the fact that the Belgian government did not approve of the Anglo-American act of insanity in Iraq. But this is an aspect of what Americans themselves call collateral damage. When 3,000-odd people were buried in the heap of the twin towers, along with American citizens, several people belonging to other nationalities perished too. This is a flaw of technology that terrorists of all hues are at present unable to correct, which is another way of saying that scientists and technicians working on weapons of mass destruction have been unable till now to correct it. The technological bottleneck can have one perilous spin-off. Just as the technology the patriotic Arabs have adopted is incapable of differentiating American from non-American whites, they could find it equally difficult to distinguish between different white groups in their thoughts and ruminations. In such circumstances, the anti-colonial and anti-imperialist guerrilla war could pave the way for a wholesale racial war. But where would you attribute the blame for that: on the Islamic insurgents, or on the imperialists who happen to be the original terrorists? While we should praise famous men, how does one know whether today's notorious terrorists could not emerge as tomorrow's famous men? What is much more ominous, are we heading towards a situation where the world witnesses a mechanistic fissure along ethnic lines? To the white segments of the human population, Osama bin Laden remains the villain because of the deeds he has sponsored or inspired. But soon he might well be the greatest hero to the globe's non-whites for precisely the same reason. The Texan buffoon masquerading as the head of the government of the only global superpower is not even capable of realizing the magnitude of the catastrophe he has chosen to preside over.

FOUR

FOUR

A friend remembers

It was the late 1940s or the early 1950s, India's was about the most glamorous name in what passed as the comity of nations. The non-aligned movement was beginning to display its clout, the average Indian citizen had reason to believe he or she was on top of the world. At least those amongst them who had a minimum degree of awareness of global realities had not the least doubt in regard to the stellar role awaiting their country in the United Nations and elsewhere.

Bunches of young Indian graduate students were flocking to the Oxbridge universities of Britain during those years: these youngsters were a part of the Anglo-Saxon world, and yet they were not. Several of them hailed from élite Indian families, some depended on scholarships or grants. They brimmed over in self-confidence. They knew which direction their country was going in, and they too along with it. After Oxbridge, they would in due course return home to civil service assignments, a few would fill prestigious slots in the up-and-coming universities. What is most remarkable, not even a minuscule minority of this lot ever dreamt of staying back in Europe or America to build a career there. India had just received her independence, she was the cynosure of the world's eyes, she was the land of vision. The youngsters scampered back home, the home was their world.

In this extraordinarily bright crowd, a slip of a girl, Dharma Venkataraman, was perhaps the smartest. A product of Bombay's hoity-toity Elphinston College, it was easy for her to get admission in Newnham. Full of charm and wit, she had no air of coyness about her. The gender war was still incipient even in the west. There was no stopping of Dharma, though. Both in university debates and late-night chirping sessions, she would floor the boys, but always with a puckish smile on her face.

Dharma was vociferously reluctant to confine herself to dull academia, specially economics. She earned her tripos at Cambridge; her mind was however always wavering from one interest to the next one and further beyond; why waste time on drab academic pursuits unless these came in handy to beguile a personable, talk-of-the-town young don?

Dharma Venkataraman conquered Cambridge. That was only a beginning. Through a seemingly inevitable natural process, she found herself, as did several of her friends, migrating to the nation's capital. New Delhi was full of bustle; the rest of the world, everybody knew, was its servitor. Jawaharlal Nehru and Krishna Menon had taken charge of the nation's global affairs; the planners were furiously at work giving shape to the country's economic future with the principal thrust on a strong public sector and a string of community development programmes. Not only was New Delhi laden with the weight of ancient history, it was also where things were happening at this moment with a concentration of glamour, power and resources. The sleepy University of Delhi was getting refurbished at a brisk pace, collecting talent from all over. The establishment of the Delhi School of Economics was a unique milestone. Many of Dharma's Cambridge contemporaries had already camped down in New Delhi either in scholastic assignments or in desk jobs in this or that ministry. The sharpness of their minds threatened to turn into instant legends. Their bearing reflected the dazzle of India's current international status. Dharma drifted into this crowd as a matter of course, like duck in water. She had meanwhile married an Oxbridge acquaintance, a Rhodes scholar, who was posted in the nation's capital with a multinational petroleum outlet. He was the only child of an exceedingly affluent *bania* family with the right connections. Dharma, too, was an only child from an Iyer family; her father was a scientist of stature and was one of the major organizers of the chain of scientific and technological laboratories set up during the decade after independence under the auspices of the Council of Scientific and Industrial Research. Dharma's interests covered a much wider range beyond conventional economics: history and sociology were of course additional components of her academic baggage. She however loved to be involved in literature, music and the arts, and had a way of developing friendship with persons who mattered in these arenas. Selective in her choice of friends, she sought kindred spirits who would share her love for mischief and gossip. This woman was an élitist, but no snob. As long as an individual, preferably from within her age-group, was clever and articulate, Dharma would draw him or her into the fold. True, she flaunted her élitism. She nonetheless had no pretences. She would pass hours on end in New Delhi's close élitist circle exchanging gossip, often malicious gossip, and confidences. She was equally comfortable, though, in the company of academic friends who hated the rich vulgar crowd she cultivated with such great loyalty.

On arrival in New Delhi, she held for a number of years a contract job with the Ministry of Finance, and was ensconced in an away-from-the-crowd bureau located on one of the top floors of the Jeevan Deep building on Parliament Street. That was, so to say, her day salon; a continuous stream of friends and colleagues would move in and out, the Ministry's chores would be shoved aside with contempt, gossip and exchange of wit would take over. Dharma had ordained a penalty for every PJ – poor joke – someone would try to market in the salon; the poorer the joke was reckoned to be, the higher was the penalty; the accumulation of these collections constituted the tea fund of the salon.

That was the specific trait in her. She refused to fit into the stylized mould even when she entertained the top echelons from politics, the civil service, industry and business. And whatever the company she was in, she would chatter away, narrating delicious stories exposing the foibles and weaknesses of eminences among her acquaintances. She had an endless stock of stories and knew how to present them to maximum effect. The space she happened to occupy at a particular moment would be converted into a gossip shop in no time. The gossip was often malicious, but there was no motive in the malice.

After jaywalking here and there, Dharma finally opted for a university career. She was not a particularly good performer in the classroom. She made up for the deficiency by her flair for story-telling. It was hardly any surprise that she created her own band of devoted admirers. They helped her to establish the journal, the *Indian Economic and Social History Review*, which survived for nearly four decades and printed first-quality stuff. This was made possible largely because of her connections with universities, research institutions and official bodies, both at home and overseas. Assembling the journal year after year was an eloquent advertisement of her grit. A further point worthy of note, she was an élitist and by instinct a fierce anti-Marxist. Even so, in the ambience she created for herself, a major chunk of her colleagues and collaborators were of Marxist inclination. She did not mind their Marxism, but that did not stop her from poking mild fun at them. A special aura of liberalism defined her: you may strongly dislike my views and I may similarly dislike yours; so what, please come home for dinner, we will have a good session of malicious banter together.

For more than four decades, Dharma lit up every venue she visited: with displays of her fickle-mindedness and passion for gossip. But there was also a certain reservoir of pride in the events unfolding around her. The *Indian Economic and Social History Review* was one loyalty she would not withdraw from: otherwise she would jump from allegiance to allegiance, which is an elliptical way of saying that she did not mind forsaking old friends and attachments, and she would do so with immaculate charm. Those whom she chose not to forsake were the object of her constant attention.

A wonderful hostess, she had without question built a niche for herself in New Delhi's esoteric circles. Her charm was formidable, her scorn was equally so. This combination of contrary blessings created the milieu that was distinctively hers and hers alone. The intellectual input the top brass of the nation's academic, political and civil service groups depended upon in that phase owed a great deal to Dharma's open-door hospitality.

But even those born with a silver spoon in their mouth cannot escape destiny. As the years advanced, domestic problems came to nag her. Her husband, polite, gentle and full of consideration, passed away. Dharma did not show it, but must have felt the loss deep inside. Her only child, a daughter, full of spirit and strong in her beliefs, looked after her mother in her own manner when the latter fell seriously ill. But, then, she had her own life to lead.

Dharma went through the learning curve and practised the art of coping with loneliness. Calamities however crowded in. A series of cerebral attacks, a series of surgeries; now all hopes are seemingly over, the latest communication suggests; she has to spend the rest of her existence as a vegetable.

Such is the irony of being. She was a non-stop chatterbox – in and out of the house, in and out of the lecture room, in and out of the office cubicle. And now she is reduced to a vegetable, beyond the frontier of all communication.

There is a wrench in the heart. Despite the chasm of ideology and beliefs, her affection and consideration had a richness of quality which defies explanation. Pardon the shocking parallel, her present state of nothingness has an eerie resemblance to the shambles the country is currently in.

A homage to Sweezy

22–28 July 2000

Paul Sweezy is 90. To celebrate the event, *Monthly Review* has issued a special number in which eminences from all over have gone into raptures while describing Sweezy's contributions to the social sciences. The contributors range from John Kenneth Galbraith and Shigeto Tsuru to Noam Chomsky and Robert Heilbroner, with a surprise in the form of Pete Seeger thrown in the middle. Seeger claims to have been Sweezy's student at Harvard and a devotee ever since.

Most of the eminences, as is obvious, were not Marxists. Some of them hold beliefs which are miles distant from Sweezy's own, yet they thought it their duty to pay homage to Sweezy's integrity and his indifference to the honours that could have been his if only he had agreed to compromise with the establishment even for a brief while. His faith in Marxism has withstood each and every buffeting over the past half a century and more. He treated with scorn the McCarthyite attempts in the late 1940s to scare him into conformity. Sweezy could not be cowed down, the annals of his career since then constitute a wondrous story of tenacity, fearlessness and loyalty to one's creed.

A man like him generates inspiration in others. As a sequel to developments in the last decade, Marxian economics and sociology appear to have been rendered irrelevant. It is possible to hypothesize further and express doubts about the viability of economic science itself as it has evolved over the past two-and-a-half centuries. It is not Marxian economics alone which, in today's context, would seem to be hopelessly obsolete. Even supposedly more respectable branches of economics would turn out to be equally out of gear with contemporary reality. Traditional macroeconomics, routinely taught in the classroom for decades on end, would now be considered as of little use, and this judgment will also cover the general theory of state intervention adumbrated by John Maynard Keynes. The entire corpus of classical political economy will be treated as a lot of garbage, with the sole exception of the doctrine of comparative costs. Much of microeconomics too will come under deep suspicion. For instance, the assumed equilibrium under conditions of perfect competition will be brushed aside as of no consequence in today's world. This is in fact somewhat bizarre, for the pretenders started out by extolling the reign of the free market liberated from all categories of regulation. It is imperfect competition, and the rule of monopoly is currently the core of economic reality. Monopoly, it is vigorously maintained, is not socially inequitous; it does not reflect exploitation and coercing the helpless innocent members of the community. Such infamy of monopoly must be discarded. On the contrary, monopoly is the embodiment of efficiency. A unit which establishes itself as of superior efficiency compared to other units will monopolize the market, and we should all sing *hallelujahs* to it. The suggestion that it is total control over a factor of production which facilitates the growth of monopoly, and that any inherent efficiency has nothing to do with it, will be treated with contempt. Efficiency, defined in a sectarian manner, is taken to be the principal architect of monopoly. The textbook lesson of how monopoly equilibrium is to the left of competitive equilibrium is to be considered as sterile wisdom. For, whatever the short-term difficulties, capital accumulation facilitated by the growth of monopoly will assure the future of economic progress.

This is new economics, if it is to be regarded as economics at all. Economic analysis, as inspired by the classical texts, will not be reconcilable with this format of reasoning. Even the assumption of super-excellence of free market activities is negated with the advent of monopoly, though a major sleight of hand is involved. Free market activism is the beginning, but the system ends up with monopoly of the most aggressive order.

Paul Sweezy, throughout his career, has belonged to a microscopic minority. Even when the Soviet Union was in a high-and-mighty state and in a position to mount effective opposition to the more outrageous postures of the United States, Sweezy, in his nook of the *Monthly Review*, was still a minority specimen. For him, the daze of globalization is not therefore an additional source of alarm. He could have slipped into the academic establishment and adorned a chair at Harvard or the Massachusetts Institute of Technology, if only he would sign some sort of a note of contrition for his erstwhile wayward ways. He did not do so and refused to deviate from his tenets. Such individuals are a rare commodity and, in honouring Sweezy, his admirers are honouring a person whose loyalty to his ideology is *nonpareil*. He has stuck to his faith and, through his example, he has invited thousands and thousands of academics and others to defy pessimism. Sweezy has battled throughout his life against the bane of monopoly capital. Nobody has, over the past 60 years, dared to ridicule him. And, hopefully, some of the professional heretics will, sooner or later, sooner rather than later, learn that sagacity derivable from economics occupies a much wider space than what is proclaimed by the haughty tribe of dim-witted efficiency-mongers.

Clichés such as hope and disappointment perhaps do not impress personalities of the timber of Sweezy. They remain ensconced in their integrity, and that is the reward they enjoy most. The social revolution they intensely wished to happen may not, they realize, eventuate even in the course of the next millennium. But such individuals too need not suffer only the prospect of pitch-dark skies. For, conscience guided by reasoning in human beings is a strange phenomenon. Consider the recent letter to *The New Republic* by Joseph Stiglitz. Stiglitz does not normally have the reputation of being a friend of the Left. That has not prevented him from speaking out when gross improprieties take place. He was vice-president and chief economist of the World Bank, and was scandalized witnessing the shenanigans indulged in by the Bank's sister institution, the International Monetary Fund, so as to do in the world's poor. Stiglitz has protested, publicly and vociferously.

Paul Sweezy has lived his 90 years till now waiting to hear similar voices of protest. The quiet satisfaction he is bound to feel is his due.

A forgotten visionary

30 September 2000

The fading of memory is an inexorable process. It is almost three decades since Pitambar Pant passed away. The new generation of economists, statisticians and left-over planners might have come across his name in hesitant footnotes of remote texts. He has no contemporary relevance. It is not just that his enthusiasm for integrated and coordinated economic planning will, at present, be considered hopelessly obsolete. Even the economics which subsumed the format of planning held dear by him has gone into disuse, and his obsession for data, *Indian data*, is bound to be treated with derision by current researchers. Data, particularly past data pertaining to the economy, it will be sermonized, have ceased to have much relevance in a globalized system. The data that are of

significance are those from overseas, the technical coefficients have to be garnered henceforth with reference to happenings taking place overseas. We must
get over our fascination for a mass of old, hackneyed statistics concerning Indian
phenomena; only foreign data, and coefficients based on such data, are lodestars
for competent economic performance.

Pitambar Pant would have been without a profession in this milieu. He
had at his fingertips whatever data were of significance to, and were culled from,
the Indian economy. His favourite expression was: '*Baba, hamse puchho*'; please
do not flounder around, do not commit howlers while opening your mouth, just
check with Pitambar, he would tell you what figures are right and what are
wrong. He had no professional grounding as such in economics; even his knowledge of statistics, he probably picked late in his academic days, when, after his
release from prison where he was detained for participation in the Quit India
movement, Jawaharlal Nehru wrote to P.C. Mahalanobis and sent Pitambar down
to the Indian Statistical Institute of Calcutta. Pitambar was a quick learner and
had an uncanny ability to sift wheat from chaff. He learnt whatever economics
he felt was worth learning from eavesdropping into the small talk by visiting
academic dignitaries at the ISI. By the time he was picked, in the early 1950s, to
be Private Secretary to the Chairman of the Planning Commission, meaning
Nehru, he was a well-rounded product and could hold his own against the Johnnys,
mostly supernumerary characters, who made up the corpus of the Commission.
His rapport with Mahalanobis had deepened, as had his closeness to Nehru. In
embarking on exercises pertaining to Indian planning, Pitambar's first act was to
plan an entente with Mahalanobis.

Even within the sphere of statistics, the Professor was a dilettante. He
could be easily persuaded that there exists a universe beyond interpenetrating
samples. The National Sample Survey was for him only a stepping stone to
national economic planning. He was already Honorary Statistical Adviser to the
government, but that, both of them concluded, was not enough; to have an effective voice in the nation's economic planning, he must have a firm, formal footing
inside the Planning Commission. Nehru agreed, and Mahalanobis was inducted
as a member of the Planning Commission.

In no time, PCM became the most towering personality in the Commission, reducing to non-entities the doddering half-senile crowd who worried their
heads over the supposedly fearful suggestion that India should plan to produce
initially 5 million tonnes of steel, and, in course of the decade or thereabouts, as
much as 20 million tonnes. Endless efforts were made by them to stop such
foolhardiness; a few of them took pride in being able to put the first spoke in the
wheel.

Mahalanobis and Pitambar launched a furious onslaught. They had the
advantage of the Prime Minister backing them to the hilt – or so they thought.
Their major stress was on the irrefutable realities that the country possessed the

157

key raw materials and natural resources essential for self-reliant growth; the country's capability to adapt, for its own needs, the technology experimented with abroad was also beyond dispute, given our huge reservoir of scientific man-power. Both the Professor and Pant were in a combative mood. They poured scorn on the mealy-mouth pronouncements of the stick-in-the-mud group of econo-mists, former civil servants and politicians who were quite content with the mod-est targets spelled out in the First Five-Year Plan. The draft outline of the Second Plan, produced by PCM and Pitambar, still firmly bore the imprint of the Indian Statistical Institute, and the clipped, short sentences constituting paragraph after paragraph of the draft reflected the precision of mind of the Professor. Once it went through the formality of receiving the imprimatur of approval of the Com-mission, the draft was an official document. Both PCM and Pitambar were truly devastating in that phase: Mahalanobis with his *hauteur* and contempt for the sheep in sheep's clothing, and Pitambar overwhelming the Commission by reel-ing off endless statistics on facets of the Indian economy. The Planning Commis-sion was conquered; Pitambar, apart from continuing to be Private Secretary to the Chairman of the Commission, was also appointed as chief of the newly set up Perspective Planning Division. He collected with care a band of statisticians and economists in tune with the mode of thought of Mahalanobis and him. Those were halcyon days and the flock of the country's economists, with the exception of a very few, capitulated all along the line.

Both politicians and hidebound economists, however, missed the cen-tral issue in the Second Plan exercise. The Mahalanobis–Pant emphasis was on national economic self-reliance which placed a low premium on foreign assist-ance. The pair of them saw little virtue in the bureaucratic obsession over the magnitude of external aid, either on the public or the private account, flowing into the country. Their point of view was simple and straightforward. Provided the nation was serious enough to build the economy on the basis of the planning model implicit in the draft outline, which laid the most stress on developing a heavy industry base, and also, provided the nation could be willed to go through a period of abstinence which would be the progenitor of savings, despite the fact that the overwhelming mass of the people were abysmally poor, there was no reason why rapid economic growth would not be the inevitable end product. Mahalanobis had been bowled over by the Feldman model which constituted the main underpinning of Soviet planning. Pitambar was not a socialist ideologue, he too nonetheless saw the logic of the proposition and went along. Once you took care of the basic needs of the people and pressed down hard on the propen-sity for lavish consumption on the part of the nation's rich, enough savings could be generated to promote capital formation and accelerate the pace of the nation's growth process. But, to ensure success of this eminently pragmatic theme, the logic of investment planning must be impeccably followed: no capital formation is to be wasted for producing luxury consumer goods, and import of such goods has to be totally banned. The pursuit of this path would not only augment the supply of investment goods; the requirement of foreign exchange too would automatically decline.

It is uncertain whether Jawaharlal Nehru understood, at the beginning, the ramifications of such a model when applied to the realities of the Indian system. Comprehension, however, soon dawned on him. Besides being a part-time dreamer, he was also a full-time practical politician. The bureaucrats could therefore easily capture his attention and convince him that six plus nine would not go into ten. Whether by happenstance or by design, the foreign exchange crisis intervened. The proponents of what Gunnar Myrdal had described as 'the soft state' took over: if the Americans were there to bail us out, why bother to toil and trouble? In a short while, the first Government of India mission to implore assistance from the US administration flew into Washington DC. They were not disappointed. The predecessor of this journal, the *Economic Weekly*, sardonically commented in an editorial note: parched earth had received the first blessing of water.

Developments followed swiftly one after another. As is easily imagined, Mahalanobis ceased to be the rage. The Second Plan premises were jettisoned. Jacqueline Kennedy tried her charms on Nehru, and John Kenneth Galbraith was the new American ambassador. The Americans – and their camp-followers in this country – had a great piece of luck in the form of the India–China border clashes. The Minoo Masanis discovered their finest hour. Mahalanobis was the target of the severest attack; his Plan model was debunked. A desolate Jawaharlal Nehru shuffled his mortal coils. Pitambar Pant was sidelined within the corridors of power. After the interregnum of Lal Bahadur Shastri, Indira Gandhi became Prime Minister. She inducted Pant as a full member of the Planning Commission. He was a diminished personality, though. He tucked in his disappointment and continued to put in solid work. His baby, the Perspective Planning Division, dug up relevant data for long-range planning. Pitambar also maintained his interest in projects involving irrigation, power, steel, fabrication and electrical engineering. He had the advantage of having a group of earnest research workers lending support to him all the way. The result was a stockpile of building bricks which promised to be in immense good stead for the nation's material advance.

With the exchange crisis persisting to loom, it was however the phase of Plan holidays. Despite his ministerial status, Pitambar was reduced to being one of the crowd of do-good men whom the civil servants could easily bypass. Once her period of tutelage was over, Indira Gandhi proved herself to be even more of a pragmatist than her father ever was. Predictably, Pitambar's links with the Prime Minister's office grew thinner and thinner. It was quite a change for someone who had lorded it over the Planning Commission barely a decade ago. The final rupture with Indira Gandhi came in the aftermath of the controversy over bank nationalization. She packed him away from the Planning Commission along with D.R. Gadgil.

Pitambar Pant was a disappointed man, more so since he was already in a frail state of health. Perhaps it is a good thing that he did not survive for long. And now, in the transformed ambience, his name has ceased to be, ceased to be even as a memory.

Should we say, such is the infirmity of history? Pitambar was a proud man, but this pride was an echo of his pride in the nation, and of the confidence he felt in the nation's ability to chart out a course of independent economic development under the auspices of the state. Did not this confidence have firm empirical roots? Or is it that relativity is all, the hard datum of the late 1950s is worth nothing forty-odd years later? If only he were around, one could debate the issue with him. He was a great one for debates, the lifeblood of a democratic polity.

One who tried to de-class himself

10 March 2001

The academic credentials were impeccable: St Stephen's at Delhi followed by King's College, Cambridge. The pedigree was equally formidable. His grandfather was in the Indian Civil Service, his father too was a top civil servant. Since it had become a matter of habit in the family, his elder brother was also in the Indian Civil Service, ending up as Chief Secretary in the Government of West Bengal. Members of the household breathed Brahmo sophistication. Whatever the expectations of the family from him, Indrajit Gupta chose to be a deviant. He went to England at the tail end of the 1930s' recession. Disgust with the system was in the air. Even so, his sensitivities need not have been any different from those of his breed. But, in such matters, accidents and happenstances play a large role. A sense of decency sometimes pushes one into realizing the gross lack of aesthetics in the existing social order; a handful are extraordinarily affluent, while the rest add to the huge load of penury and unemployment. Indrajit Gupta, at least in the beginning, flabbergasted the members of his family. Still, they had to lump it. For there was a specificity in his uprising. He rebelled against the system, the rebellion was however replete with courtesy. The family therefore was chary to say that he had gone astray; he, the household record said, had decided to be different.

The phenomenon is unlikely to be repeated in the Indian milieu. The times are changed, the sting of imperialism no longer hurts, and neo-imperialism is yet to receive its due purchase. That apart, perhaps in the particular era Indrajit found his new bearings, getting de-classed – or the endeavour to do so – was not such an arcane occurrence as it is regarded today. The conviction the mind reached, it was felt in that season, was not that difficult to follow up in actual life. After all, when Sajjad Zaheer returned from England as a red-hot communist, he abjured residence inside the palace built by his father, Sir Wazir Hasan; he preferred the commodious garage, until his mother's plaintive importunings persuaded him to be, despite being a deviant, a proper offspring.

Indrajit Gupta travelled farther. He went all the way. The party wanted him to organize Calcutta's tramway workers, as also the workers on the waterfront. Indrajit chose to live amidst the mass of potatoes whose consciousness he was pledged to arouse. He did not lose any of his graces, the aristocracy of style could not quite wear off. But he did satisfy the slum-dwellers and the precariously surviving homeless thousands that his pedigree did not matter; he could still be flesh of their flesh. He himself slummed for days on end, weeks on end, months on end, and emerged as one of the most effective trade union leaders. The Indian trade union movement, it is possible to maintain, will not really come into its own until the Cambridge–Oxford-returned professional leaders are substituted by hard-boiled genuine members of the proletariat rising from the ranks of the truly dispossessed. It is not the fault of the leaders springing from the upper classes, though, that their time is not yet past. Nature abhors a vacuum. The vacuum exists where the objective conditions would not like it to exist. The empty slots needed to be filled. The tribe of Indrajit Guptas did just that.

The persistence of this tribe, perhaps you might still say, has been the bane of the Indian working class movement; their being there could not pave the way for bloody revolution, since these leaders flinched from taking the ultimate decisions. Too much of civility was at stake; the leaders perhaps retained a whiff of emotional link with their background, a great many of them were shrouded by too much of gentlemanliness.

While you might claim that their state of de-classedness was not complete, the onus cannot be wholly placed upon them. It should be an integral aspect of what is basic reality to size up the limits of feasibility in each instance, not only with respect to situations, but also with respect to individuals. It can never be seriously alleged that Indrajit Gupta betrayed the cause; the cause was, at most, wrongly interpreted, and the tactics, as a result, got misdirected. But when one is part of a huge conclave, one has to abide by the judgment of the collective. On the evaluation of Stalin's historical role, Hiren Mukherji dared the party and continued to extol one whom he considered to be the true architect of the Soviet system. He could get away with his open dissidence because he was Hiren Mukherji, the scholar extraordinary, whom the party could not afford to lose. Conceivably, Indrajit Gupta cultivated a kind of ambivalence on the issue; he could however not make up his mind whether it was worth the hassle. In the matter of assessing the Emergency and, following the Soviet line, lending support to the Indira Gandhi regime, both Hiren Mukherji and Indrajit Gupta, it is a fair guess, had strong private views. But once having decided not to leave the ranks of the CPI along with the erstwhile comrades who went on to form the CPI(M), they were possibly of the view that, unlike in the case of the atom, there is a limit to splitting the party; they therefore followed the party's mandate. As loyal soldiers, they stood for the Lok Sabha elections in 1977 in alliance with the Indian National Congress(I), even when they knew the cause was hopeless. They lost, that was what the essence of party discipline was about. The present generation of cocky, mostly supercilious leaders take it to be the hallmark of socialist principles to breach all the norms of party discipline; they will be unable to comprehend the dimension of Indrajit Gupta's political vision.

Gupta remained a gentleman not only in his dealings with his working-class comrades, but also in his relationship with the hybrid society to which we all belong. He moved away from the family, but did not derecognize his roots. All through, the links with brothers and cousins remained strong. Even when the party fractured again and again, and the segment he belonged to shrank and shrank, he had no rancour in his heart towards those erstwhile comrades who turned out to be political adversaries. When love for a woman came to him rather late in life, he did not play footsie with his emotions. The situation was somewhat complicated, but it did not deter him from entering into nuptials with the lady. He fully integrated himself with her family, caring not a whit for gossips and backchatters. It was a most blissful union.

He had an uninterrupted parliamentary career since 1960, with a gap of two-and-a-half years from 1977 onwards. The suavity of his parliamentary performance had depth. The Lok Sabha gradually lost its lustre, it became plebeianized without being proletarianized. Gupta had little illusion about the effectiveness of setting aside precious hours that could have been used for trade union work, for silly parliamentary chores. He must have also realized in later years the anomaly of representing a constituency where his own party was a growing non-entity. But the gentleman in him was able to tuck in his unhappiness with a *sangfroid* that could not but command respect.

Did not this gentlemanliness, however, stand in the way of his blossoming into a successful and effective Home Minister in the United Front regime? Of course, by then, his physical capacity had declined considerably, but overshadowing that factor were such curses of gentlemanliness as politeness and hesitation. Decision-making he found to be an arduous task. A nagging problem was additionally posed by the puny size of his party in the parliament as well as outside. Besides, the United Front was hardly an alliance; it was, rather, a misalliance; those who could shout the most, and the hoarsest, won the day. This is a datum which apparently did not receive much weight from those who hold the view that a historical blunder was committed by the CPI(M) when it did not allow Jyoti Basu to be Prime Minister of the United Front government. It was a wild, unruly, quarrelsome, dishevelled heterogeneity that Basu was asked to head. Like Indrajit Gupta, he too might have failed, for he too is a gentleman of the mould which shaped Gupta. On the other hand, according to another school of thought, Jyoti Basu carries a grain of iron in him which Indrajit Gupta never possessed, so he might well have succeeded where Gupta failed. This debate cannot be resolved on the basis of hypotheses or assumptions, and, therefore, deserves to be adjourned.

There is a wrench in the heart, nonetheless. It is a vanishing epoch where civilization stood out as the centrepiece of attention, in sharp contrast to the uncouthness and vulgarity featuring the current concourse. The separatism of gentility from non-gentility was not merely a matter of crude class division; gentle souls could – and, even today, can – be discovered even amongst the non-rich and the non-literates. Indrajit Gupta was *sui generis*, because he spanned this divide. One would sorely miss the easy flow of his pungent Hindustani alongside his elegant Cambridge-accented English, as also his gruff Bengali diction which was a consequence of his north Indian upbringing. He was an unruffled passenger, however rough the sea or however rugged the terrain. It is quite unlikely that there will be another one like him in our morose neighbourhood.

The forgotten don

28 April 2001

Centenary celebrations these days are, shall one say, dime-a-dozen. Those prominent in national life in the first twenty-five years following Indian independence have mostly passed away. Memory, both individual and institutional, is fragile. However outstanding the contributions of these stalwarts were, few bother about them any more. They were, once upon a time, there; they are no longer there, period. Countrymen are much too concerned with the positive and negative aspects of so-called globalization; there are new names, of both heroes and anti-heroes, which are now discussed in newspapers and other media. Persons who are dead should better be dead.

It is, therefore, almost apologetically that one endeavours to put on record the fact that this is Professor D.R. Gadgil's centenary year. Half a century ago, he was a man whose importance could not be brushed aside; even a quarter of a century ago, some memory of his activities had stuck to the national psyche, more so perhaps because of the circumstances of his death a year previously. He was summarily dismissed by Indira Gandhi from the position of Deputy Chairman of the Planning Commission. He was dismissed via a messenger, and the minimum grace of calling the professor in and letting him know of the Prime Minister's other plans with respect to national planning was dispensed with. Professor Gadgil could not survive the shock of the insult; he died on the train *en route* to Pune.

At a distant epoch, he was considered nearly as indispensable to the scholarly world as P.C. Mahalanobis. Both were feudal in outlook, and, at the same time, great institution-builders. Mahalanobis set up the Indian Statistical Institute, the bulk of the responsibility for which has now been assumed by the union government. Professor Gadgil established the Gokhale Institute of Politics and Economics, which has received, over the years, much less official bounty than the ISI. The two institutions were, at a particular juncture, considered rivals to each other. When the National Sample Survey was being organized under the auspices of the Indian Statistical Institute, there was much talk on the significance or otherwise of the parallel Poona schedule evolved at the Gokhale Institute. Heated words were exchanged over the relative worthwhileness of surveys which seek recollection for a week vis-à-vis those which fall back on recollection stretching to a full month. This is a debate which has recently been revived. Fortunately for the nation and for the pool of scholars and officials caught in the middle, the controversy raging at that time was soon resolved. A political alliance between the two professors was the consequence. Some naughty ones were around to offer the suggestion that the political treaty also included in its codicils an unexplicitly stated, but implicit, actual marriage: a groom from the Indian Statistical Institute entered into nuptials with a bride from the Gokhale Institute of Politics and Economics.

There are elements of gossip which will be of little interest to today's yuppie generation. They are focused on the ins and outs of information technology at its highest level; frivolities do not detain them. Nonetheless, at some absent-minded moment an attempt could still be launched to impress on them the basic reality of the infrastructure of the academic environment which defines the contemporary phase being the bequest from Professors Mahalanobis and Gadgil.

Gadgil led a multivariate life. While at Cambridge, he wrote a path-breaking treatise on India's industrial evolution. It was strikingly original, for it veered away from Ranade and Romesh Dutt's fondness to equate the nation's history with lament for a gone, glorious past. Gadgil of course took Ranade and Dutt as his starting point, but even at that indeterminate period, he could envisage a prospect of change in the nation's industrial format. That was something later economic historians could munch into. And they did.

Cambridge did not turn him into a native *sahib*. He was of the Servants of India Society vintage; the motto 'plain living and high thinking' was not yet a joke. With the inheritance he received from his father-in-law, Gadgil set up the Gokhale Institute of Politics and Economics. The name he chose for the Institute was revealing; he shunned Tilak's extremism, Gokhale's liberal ideas inspired him to a much greater extent. He also saw, fairly early, the interconnection between political and economic issues. He collected, in the Institute, a large band of scholars–idealists who did not mind the low wages paid to them then, that is, in the 1930s. The transformation in the salary structure came in the 1950s, when economists, ahead of other scholarly tribes, learned to globalize themselves and gather the resulting pickings.

The Gokhale Institute did good, solid empirical work in social and economic fields. It also trained academics in methodological disciplines, including in statistics. One might still find all over the country scholars, active or already retired, who had some links once upon a time with Professor Gadgil's institution.

From his concerns over the problems of industrial growth, Gadgil soon crossed over to issues in regard to agriculture and allied activities, without question the principal economic sector, on which two-thirds of the working population in the country are still dependent. It was logical for him to move to matters concerning agricultural cooperation. Cheap credit for agriculture, he was convinced, was the key to rapid growth in farm output, from which, according to him, the lower stratum of the peasantry too will benefit. It is perhaps fortuitous that at the time another Maharashtrian was the Governor of the Reserve Bank of India, who, within a few years, would move on to be the nation's Finance Minister. The Reserve Bank did not, therefore, need much persuasion to set up the rural credit department. A close associate of Professor Gadgil, again with Servants of India Society roots, was named Deputy Governor of the RBI in exclusive charge of the problems of rural credit.

It is Professor Gadgil's fate that, given his feudal moorings, he failed to anticipate the kind of class-biased growth in agriculture a surfeit of rural credit would usher in. The green revolution had its own rationale; it accepted the juice which generous agricultural credit offered to affluent peasants and prepared the concoction on account of which 10 to 15 per cent of the farming population monopolized the fruits of agricultural growth. Mahalanobis, while equally authoritarian in outlook and not a Marxist himself, had at least a number of Marxist associates, including his brother-in-law, Susobhan Sarkar. Gadgil had no such ally; he watched the phenomenon of the bulk of the rural credit being whisked away by big landlords and rich peasants.

By his own volition or otherwise, he was also fated to be founder-chairman of the Maharashtra Sugar Cooperatives Federation. He became a creature in the hands of the sugar barons and had to plead for a quasi-rent to go to the Maharashtra and Karnataka cane-growers: provided you believed in a unified labour and commodity market in the country, and also in the proposition that Uttar Pradesh and Bihar growers too had the right to survive, the superior productivity of sugarcane land and superior sucrose content of cane grown in the western states had to be duly compensated for.

He had, without question, considerable influence on the country's Agricultural Prices Commission at its initial stages. One consequence is the contractors' opera in Maharashtra's sugar industry and their fabulous income, little of which is shared with the poorer farmers and farm workers. Much worse, these contractors have now moved into the educational sphere. They are setting up educational institutions; students from outside the state have to pay through their nose for admission in these institutions; quasi-rent of a different sort, one could say.

Gadgil, given his reputation for welfarism, was invited to be the working head of the Planning Commission. It was an unhappy transition. For, the jingoists and the bureaucrats had, by then, made a mess of the country's balance of payments; the result was the declaration of Plan holiday for a number of years. Even so, during his tenure at the Planning Commission, he had the sagacity to evolve a new formula for the *inter se* allocation of plan assistance to the states. He conceived the idea of Special Category States and allocated for them one-half of the total plan assistance. It was also an ingenious formula for *inter se* distribution which was popularized under his name; it placed great emphasis not only on such criteria as size of population and per capita tax effort, but also on the earnestness of the states to complete ongoing projects.

Again, Professor Gadgil could hardly be blamed if the political landscape was beyond his control. Chieftains with a shady background appropriated most of the money going to the Special Category States. Even in regard to the allocation of the rest of the funds to the other states, the prime ministerial prerogative became increasingly more vocal.

Nonetheless, there is a regret welling in the heart that men like Gadgil are so easily forgotten in the present clime. He had done some service to the state. The state does not care to remember, nor do those who have, for the present, taken over its helmsmanship. For this gross failing, you cannot lay the blame at Professor Gadgil's door.

In defence of Bihar

21 July 2001

How come Bihar has such a negative image in the rest of the country? Fingers will be pointed at the obscurantism characterizing the state, but are things any better in Rajasthan? Bihar is supposed to be riven by caste dissensions; can it, however, hold a candle in this regard to Tamil Nadu? Feudalism and social oppression are hallmarks of Bihar's daily existence; what about Madhya Pradesh, Orissa and Chhattisgarh, though? Schisms are rampant in Bihar. The state is hemmed in by Uttar Pradesh and West Bengal on either side; are these states total strangers to factionalism? According to some snooty people, Biharis are, by and large, crude. Some others would prefer to say that the people of Bihar are rooted to the soil and hate to hide their natural instincts behind pretensions; they cannot be any cruder than those populating the backwaters of Punjab.

To talk of pretensions, the Biharis are no match for the garrulous Bengalis; it is in any event not possible to judge the average by qualities attributable to those in the margin. How many leaders of national stature could or can be identified who possessed or possess the elegance, refinement and catholicity of Jai Prakash Narayan?

Make a rollcall of all state chief ministers over the past half a century; is there one who comes even reasonably close to the integrity, idealism and good-heartedness of Karpoori Thakur? In some circles, Jagjivan Ram is assumed to be a knave par excellence. But few ministers in the Union Cabinet over the post-independence span ever acquired an approximation of the sharpness of his mind and the extraordinariness of his common sense. On a somewhat lighter plane, Tarakeshwari Sinha in her salad days was unrivalled not just in glamour, but in wit and intelligence too. One also has vivid recollections of the firebrand woman-politician from Bihar, Ramdulari Sinha, who was a rage in the 1950s but who, alas, is no longer heard of. The Indian republic's first president, Dr Rajendra Prasad, who hailed from Bihar, had his failings and dark spots. Nevertheless, how many care to remember that he was one of the most brilliant alumni of that pomposity-laden academic institution, the University of Calcutta? The local scholars, ensconced in their frog-in-the-well *hauteur*, ragged him ceaselessly while he was a student at Calcutta. Was he not, after all, a Bihari dunce?

Is there not a formidable case for building an alternative hypothesis? For a full hundred years beginning with the middle decades of the nineteenth century till those of the twentieth century, the Bihar populace were victim of a vacuous, remorseless neo-colonialism enforced mostly by migrant Bengalis. The Bengali

167

babu dominated the profession of law, medicine and education. Briefless barristers from Calcutta moved to Patna and squeezed the Bihari landed gentry dry. The Bihar poor were mincemeat to exploiting Bengali medical practitioners. Any number of stories are afloat of how a *dehati* Bihari, struck down by malaria or typhoid, would approach the chamber of a Bengali quack and, after a long wait, would have his temperature taken by the condescending pretender of a doctor; the latter would not however bother to take the thermometer out of the case before thrusting it under the arm of the nervous rustic, and the pile made by such unfair means would be duly transferred to Calcutta to build palatial mansions there. Some of the Bengali educationists, to be fair, did create an ambience which facilitated scholarly aspirations on the part of the Bihari middle class. But exceptions cannot obliterate the fact of the overwhelming intellectual overlordship. Social and economic exploitation of the local population by outsiders who did not care to identify themselves with the Bihari persona was the prevailing order of the day. What all Bengalis could claim was their credentials as original British lackeys, and they thought that was a passport to exploit their western neighbours.

The second half of the twentieth century, and especially the final quarter of the century, marked a major sea-change. This was a period when the Bihari psyche began to assert itself, and in a most forceful manner. Bihar has produced, every now and then, several interesting social specimens. Take, for instance, Sher Shah. Apart from his military exploits, he was also a great builder of public works. His munificence was not run-of-the mill oriental despotism. Let us, however, cross over to more modern times and scholarly pursuits. Not that a hinterland whose past is marked by the great academic citadels of Budh Gaya, Nalanda and Rajgir was ever bereft of an intellectual inheritance. Bihar has, in more recent times, produced a great leader of the proletariat – Sahajanand Saraswati – and a scholar extraordinary of the dimension of Rahul Sankritayana. That tradition has widened and broadened in the course of the past few decades. All of a sudden, the specificity has transformed itself into a general development. Two individuals, in particular, articulated the fusion of legacy with the ethos nurtured by contemporary notions, concepts and ideas. These two, as can be easily guessed, were Pradhan Hari Shankar Prasad and Arvind Narain Das. Such a cruel coincidence that both have disappeared from the landscape within the space of the past few months.

Arvind Das had New Delhi breeding, which lent a certain sophistication to his Bihari pride. Pradhan Prasad, on the other hand, was in all respects a truly homebred product. Arvind Das combined his political activism with state-of-the-art manners of expression. Pradhan Prasad was, in contrast, raw and rustic, but he suffered from no inhibitions. He did not wear his idealism on his sleeves. He was, however, no less blunt in the outpouring of his ideological beliefs. His grounding in economic analysis was relatively weak in the beginning. He himself was fully aware of the deficiency. He was equally aware of the basic reality that to hold his own in scholarly combats, he must endeavour to reach superior levels of logic and analytical ability. Pradhan was fortunate to gain the proximity of A.K. Dasgupta, who set the standards of academic excellence for him. This bounty was not an empty box. By the late 1980s, Pradhan Prasad's foundation of knowledge and power of analysis had expanded most impressively. In other words, by then, he was a compleat economist.

One attribute setting apart the present generation of Bihar academia whom Prasad and Das epitomized deserves mention. The Bengali social scientists, almost as a class, hate to be stickers-in-the-mud; they have no ardour left for their native soil. At the very first opportunity, many amongst them would prefer to move to alien shores; of course, the first choice is the United States of America. The Bihari archetypes, on the contrary, have Bihar all the while in their minds. A further difference: their Bengali counterparts suffer from great dollops of airy-fairyness and turn their faces away from solid empirical work. Pradhan Hari Shankar Prasad and Arvind Das gathered a band of colleagues and acolytes in Bihar's university campuses and academic institutions, who did not and do not disdain such work. Their instincts are very much down-to-earth. They do not flinch from model-building if the need is there. But their models are not wild abstractions. Each of these has a contextual relationship with the country's, and Bihar's basic problems. A large proportion of the cerebral concern of both Prasad and Das was related to feudalism, semi-feudalism and the burden of emerging capitalism. They had little difficulty in discovering the locus of class interest with which to align. They had read in their formative years Wolf Ladijenski's tracts expiating on the plight of Bihari *bataidars,* and the inexorable process of immiserization which seemed to be the inevitable fate of the proletariat of the state. This self-taught duo, in their turn, tutored others on the themes of class alienation and class betrayal. Still, they did not abjure social graces. They accepted the reality of being integral elements of a multivariate democracy, where convention demanded dialogue with those whom one would otherwise consider as social vermin. Which is another way of saying that neither of them had any hesitation to respect the norms of pluralism, never mind the nonconformity of their ideological commitments.

Such men are rare in any clime and in any society. Their departure is bound to create a gaping hole in the intellectual milieu of Bihar. It will also mean a slowing down, in the immediate period, in the pace of communication of lessons Bihar might pass on to the rest of India. There could be, one dares to suggest, no acuter national loss.

Death of a gentleman

1 September 2001

Liberalization is in essence the removal of the dividing line between private and public domains. One spin-off of this is the convergence of private and public murders. Killings in any case have proliferated; violence is currently assumed to be the passport to civilized existence. And, in his hazy twilight, one can die for a private cause, but how do you know it is not a public cause as well?

An amiable old gentleman was shot dead in a Calcutta suburb a fortnight ago. He was supposed to be a man without any enemies. Belonging to the party which has been the leading political entity in the state for the past three decades or thereabouts, he was a member of the state legislative assembly for a while. Of late, he was chairman of the local municipality. In his personal life he was a medical practitioner, a do-gooder by instinct, and would charge only two rupees per visit when calling upon the neighbourhood households for succour. But the gentleman had yet another identity. He had a rich, half-baritone voice, and was a passionate exponent of the Tagore school of music. He popularized Tagore songs amongst the lower middle class and the poor. Even if he had no political pigmentation or no record of providing free medical service, he would still have been adored for his musical talent. A good party person, he was an equally good family man. Of the gentleman's two sons, the elder one had died in a traffic accident a decade ago. The rest of the family survived the shock and the sorrow mostly because of the strength of the fabric of their closeness to one another. A happy family, a loveable family, an ideal family. Now tragedy has struck them a second time in ten years, this time it is tragedy of a much more gruesome nature.

In case the gentleman did not happen to be the head of the local municipality, he would perhaps have been spared the fate of a gory death. That was not to be. He was supposed to be a man without enemies, but, there is the rub, he was not without moral principles. He was an honest man who would not compromise with chicanery, nor would he put up with shady dealings. Rumours are afloat. A bunch of fly-by-night promoters had arrived on the scene, focusing a hawk's eye on a lush piece of property falling within the jurisdiction of the municipality. The property was generally described as a 'water-body', a half-pond, half-marshy tract. These promoters wanted to convert the property into a *terra firma* on which a high-rise could come up quickly. But they had competition. Another group of supposed promoters were keen to render the real estate into a full-fledged fishery; what could be more covetable than the export of prawns to the

United States of America! So the plot around the plot thickened. Fierce competition ensued between rival sets of promoters. After all, the practice of the policy of non-principle is the best policy; that is what free market is all about.

Money is easy picking these days if one happens to be in the real estate business. Especially in urban and semi-urban concentrations, the rate of return could even be three to four thousand per cent in this sort of venture. Acquire the land you have targeted at throwaway price from this or that indigent owner; if he would not sell, remove him from the face of earth, hired killers would do your bidding. Once the non-cooperative owner is safely dead, the rest of the family can be cowed down through some means or other. Should the title deed turn out to be messy or a formal sanction be necessary from the municipality, why, in this ambience of perfect competition, the municipal clerk has a price, pay him up; if that does not do the trick, just approach the high-ups one after another.

Everything is so nice and cosy in this liberalized system. The free market is sovereign, and you bid freely in this market. X satisfies Y and Y satisfies X. One can attach a price-tag to the police constable on the beat, to the officer-in-charge of the local police station, the magic of the market may even cast a spell right at the police headquarters. As with the police, a fair number of politicians too have their services on offer. The jolly sport of profit maximization has captured the imagination of society. Each citizen has now a two-way persona, he is both the buyer and the seller. He sells his service to another person who is in a position to offer him the right price; he also purchases service by offering a bribe to the person who is capable of delivering what he wants. About everyone around, the assumption goes, nonchalantly plays a dual role: policemen, office clerks, municipal commissioners and chairmen of municipalities.

The gentleman we were talking about, the medical practitioner-cum-musician-cum-municipal chairman, was of a different genre. He was an anachronism, he was not purchaseable. He had come through the rigorous mill of a political ideology which is antipodal to the philosophy disseminated by votaries of the free market. An extremely pleasant person, but, for all that, a stubborn person too. A flutter in the dovecotes, this gentleman was a renegade to the religion of the free market; he refused to be bought. He was, it follows, no gentleman; he was a scoundrel.

Consider the absurd situation. Intense competition was going on between rival promoters eager to build an apartment block on that piece of land; similar competition ensued between rival promoters who wanted to establish a fishery, and both sets were in competition against one another. They, all of them, were prepared to pay the highest price to the chairman of the municipality so that he would accord the permission they, each of them, were seeking, severally as well as jointly. What an outrage, he would not go along. His conscience, he had the audacity to claim, is not for sale. He was, without question, an enemy of liberalization. He therefore had to die.

171

Are the above paragraphs an exercise in hyperbole? Not really. Why not turn your gaze to the shoddy affairs at present on with that biggest of real estates, Kashmir. The will of the people in Kashmir does not matter any more. Kashmir will belong to the highest bidder. The highest bidder is not an abstraction. Its identity is determined by the market process. Would India offer a superior price to the United States administration, or would it be Pakistan? The decision on the level of the optimum price is the exclusive prerogative of the superpower. The destiny of the people of Kashmir is an aspect of realpolitik, and has been reduced to transactions in the marketplace.

Perhaps on no occasion in human history did moral principles ever determine political decisions. Might has always been right, though, here too, a cycle of tumescence and detumescence is at work. Naked imperialism is no longer anybody's cup of tea. The accent is on covering up the lurid spectacle of suppression of the weak by the strong with the smokescreen of economic calculus. Troops are redundant; international financial agencies and their articles of agreement will serve efficiently the cause of the lovers of acquisition. The superpower is not greatly exercised; it controls these international agencies too. At the country level, again, the transnational corporations buy up governments one after another, be it in Senegal or Guatemala or Papua. It is an exceedingly cosy arrangement. The transnational corporations lay down the details of the terms and conditions the politicians in nominal power in each country will have to follow. Should they prove to be contrary, out they go.

Descend to the level of local governments. It is the same story but on a miniature scale, with petty potentates face to face with petty operators. For dear life, both categories are supposed to buy and sell in the marketplace. They have to buy and sell protection and integrity. The free market, it is implied, will determine the price in all instances, even where the public domain is involved.

Sailen Das, the medical man-cum-music buff-cum-political activist, refused to play the game. What a nuisance, he would not sell himself. Those who set themselves against the system do not deserve to live. Sailen Das refused pointblank to get rich quickly; he therefore had to be shot pointblank. No flowers for him!

Suicide bombs, early India edition

13 October 2001

Preetilata Waddedar. Does the name ring a bell with the present generation? Most probably not. History is a whimsical entity; historical memory is even more whimsical. It is perhaps necessary to recount this particular saga from the annals of the nation's freedom movement.

Chittagong was then a sleepy port town, kissing the Bay of Bengal, on the eastern fringes of the country, almost abutting the Arakan range in Burma. It was a picturesque little place with an aura of sleepiness about it, dotted by a series of low hillocks and demure valleys sloping down towards the bay. A schoolteacher in the town, Surya Sen, was a fierce patriot and an activist. He, a non-believer in Mahatma Gandhi's creed of non-violence, gathered together a group of young people eager to take to arms, to get rid of the British imperialist rulers. The group, sworn to utmost secrecy, styled themselves as the Indian Republican Army. Preetilata Waddedar, a slip of a girl, barely twenty-one years of age, was one of the enthusiastic recruits for the IRA. She was a bright student and exceedingly good in studies. She had her early schooling at Khastgir Government Girls' School at Chittagong, then moved to Eden Girls' College at Dacca for her Intermediate Arts, and subsequently got a BA from Bethune College, Calcutta. She was in a hurry. Nix to wasting years for postgraduate education. She must participate in armed action against the imperialist exploiters, and do so without whiling any more time.

The Indian Republican Army had already organized several actions in and around Chittagong, including the daring raid on the Chittagong armoury on 19 April 1932 at Jalalabad, which was followed by incidents at Kalarpur, Pheni, Comilla, Chandernagore and Dhalghat. Frenzy was in the air, frenzy on the part of the brats itching to liberate the country through organizing sporadic violence against the foreign masters, with intent to make a revolution. Frenzy on their part, and panic on the part of the British expatriate population. Police persecution reached a crescendo: Chittagong town was deserted by the younger elements. The parents and guardians left behind had to bear the brunt of interrogation and harassment launched by the administration. Several individuals were detained without trial as atonement for the sins of their wards and children. Preetilata Waddedar too made herself scarce. She spent most of the time in underground camps of the IRA, moving from one hideout to another. And she kept pestering Master-da, the sobriquet by which Surya Sen was known to his admirers and adherents. She was obstinacy personified. She wanted to prove a point:

women are as much capable of leading a violent anti-British action as men. She must be given a chance. The ferocity of her determination unnerved Master-da; he soon capitulated.

It was an extraordinarily wild plan of action. There was an exclusively European Club at Pahartali, on the outskirts of Chittagong. Expatriate Europeans – civil servants, policemen, army people, jute merchants and men from the customs and the rangers – used to congregate there after dusk for drinks, dance and dinner. The IRA proposed to raid the Club on a sultry September night. Seven young men were chosen for the expedition: Bireshwar Roy, Praphulla Das, Panna Sen, Kalikinkar Dey, Shanti Chakravarty, Sushil Dey and Mahendra Chaudhury. Surprise of surprises, Preetilata was selected as the leader of this otherwise exclusively male group. Each of her male comrades was senior to her in age. So what? The youngest of the lot, and the only girl amongst them, was nominated by Master-da to be the key person for coordinating the action. An even stranger decision, all the seven boys, it was decided, would disappear fast from the spot once the action was completed. They were precious property, and the IRA had other important assignments lined up for them. Preetilata, on the other hand, was to constitute a single-woman suicide squad. She would act as decoy and target herself for attention from those defending the Club, thereby allowing the opportunity to her comrades to scoot. She was to carry with her a phial of potassium cyanide and swallow it even as she was about to be apprehended. Which is to say, it was agreed that, whatever else happened, she was to die.

At this distance of time, it is pointless to question either the morality or the seeming gender bias of the decision. There was, however, enough evidence collected later which established the crucial fact: it was at her insistence that the particular decision was arrived at. In other words, she chose to die.

At nine-thirty on the night of 24 September 1932, Preetilata led the attack on the European Club, where a gala dinner and dance was on. She and her seven companions were armed with rifles, pistols, swords and the kind of bombs later known as Molotov cocktails. The power connections were first severed, the Club was plunged in darkness, and the stillness of the night was pierced by shrieks and gasps of terror on the part of the assembled European crowd. It was slaughter of an impressive proportion: thirteen Europeans were killed, another eleven were severely injured. Perhaps the manifestation of another gender bias: all the women were spared.

Preetilata's male accomplices safely disappeared in the surrounding hillocks and bushes. As per arrangement, she stayed behind and swallowed potassium cyanide. She was virtually the first woman martyr in the war of independence, in the post-Sepoy Mutiny phase. Preetilata instantly turned into a hallowed legend. The first-born daughter in every family in Bengal over the next decade was named either Preetilata or Kalpana, after Preetilata's friend Kalpana

Dutt who was a part of the Jalalabad squad that raided the armoury.

All that is moribund history. Preetilata is by now a forgotten heroine. Quite a few amongst the present generation, one can take a wager, would retrospectively ridicule her for what they would describe as her juvenile enthusiasm that turned her into an insensate mass murderer. A matter of factual detail, a last testament, scribbled in her own handwriting, was found by the police on her body. Among other things, it contained the following forthright statement:

> There are unfortunately many amongst our countrymen who would wonder why a woman should desert the noble ideals of Indian womanhood and goad herself into performing the gruesome act of killing human beings in cold blood. I beg to differ. The gender division discernible in our freedom struggle pains me no end. Why should we, the sisters, not join our brethren in the holy task of freeing our motherland from foreign bondage, even if that involves the sad task of murdering otherwise innocent people? . . . If women can join the Congress Satyagraha Movement, why cannot they participate in acts of violence against the British? In other countries, women have participated in armed struggle for emancipating their land. Why should it be any different with us? I die in the hope that many of my sisters would draw courage from my example and do their duty by Bharatmata.

Over to current reality. Globalization inevitably leads to monopolization of things and matters. The global information system has been monopolized, or at least oligopolized, in the course of the past two decades. No preaching except those by the CNN and the BBC have been permitted ever since the cataclysmic day of 11 September. America is mourning; the rest of the world too has to mourn along with her. America is seething with anger; the rest of the world too must explode in anger. America is against terrorism, that is terrorism perpetrated by others against America; it is however forbidden to raise queries regarding the hundreds of thousands of bestial deaths, and the heartless destruction of crops and habitats, at American initiative during the past decades. The visage of tears rolling down American eyes because of the cruel surcease of the lives of near and dear ones fills the expanse of the television screen and newspaper columns. America wants revenge; the rest of the world too must be revengeful. America wants war; how dare the rest of the world not want war. Anyone with a Muslim name is *ipso facto* a prime suspect. The monsters bearing Muslim names who were passengers in those ill-fated planes are, it is being taken for granted, with no shadow of doubt, mass murderers; their pictures are being flashed round the universe.

The President of the United States of America demands war, therefore it has to be war. Those who have the temerity not to join him in this war deserve to be exterminated. Better be careful not to suggest the referral of the issue to the United Nations, that could raise the global sheriff's cholesterol level.

The CNN and the BBC enjoy absolute monopoly power over the dissemination of news and opinion reports. The world, we are being assured, is in perfect unanimity: war, it has to be; you must be crazy if you are not for war; those, of whatever hue, who defy the sheriff from Texas, would be destroyed with no quarters given. The CNN and the BBC have apparently no information about the huge rallies in American university and college campuses for peace and against war, of congregations at the Union Square, New York, or of the assembly hounded out of Lafayatte Park, Washington DC. They have not heard of the Peace Action, the Students' Peace Action Forum, the American War Resistance League, the League of Artists in America and umpteen such other bodies. Nor have they bothered to mention Harry Belafonte's speaking and singing at countless sit-ins in city after city. Of course, that brave Congresswoman from California who voted against war has been duly rendered a non-person. And only the underground websites have carried the story of Phyllis and Ronaldo Rodrigues, both honest American citizens, writing to President Bush: they have lost their son in the debris of the World Trade Centre, but they want no part of any war.

In this hysteria time, not one thought has been spared for the handful of young people constituting the suicide squads who took over the planes and deployed them as missiles for destroying the Pentagon and the twin towers of the World Trade Centre. Technically, they were mass murderers. But, in their own manner, they were patriots of the first water, who had the grit and courage to sacrifice their lives for the cause they believed in.

No tributes for them. That would be sacrilege. Kindly allow us, then, to recount with trepidation the story of Preetilata Waddedar and her suicide mission so as to bring British imperialism on its knees. The times are vastly different, so too the scales of endeavour; the technology of death and destruction too is totally transformed. Could it nonetheless be that had one of those unknown martyrs decided to leave behind a goodbye note, it would have borne an eerie resemblance to the tenor and spirit of Preetilata's last testament?

You must hand it to the American administration. It has succeeded to implant a lurking sympathy in the minds of many for even the Talibans! Lest we forget, these same Talibans were, in the first place, America-begotten and America-directed.

Sarvajaya is dead

8 December 2001

The city was the venue of a film festival in mid-November. It is a globalized ambience; naturally, although dubbed the Calcutta Film Festival, it had a cosmopolitan flavour. Films reached Calcutta from all over, with Pier Paolo Pasolini's works in the lead. There were however hordes of others – from Russia, Britain, the rest of Europe, Latin America, North America, apart from the usual Bengali and Hindi ventures. The glitterati, directors, actors and actresses, film connoisseurs were present in strength from different continents.

The time for celebration was also the time for remembrance, or should have been the time for remembrance. On the day the festival was inaugurated, Karuna Banerjee passed away. In their ceaseless round of film-hopping, few people noticed, or bothered. Karuna who?

One therefore almost felt guilty for one's load of memory. In the early part of the third decade of the last century, a humble schoolteacher, Bibhuti Bhushan Bandyopadhyay, wrote an enchanting novel whose centrepiece was a rapidly crumbling Bengali village and an equally fast disintegrating middle-class brahmin household. The simplicity of the narration was gripping; the annals of nature and those of the human condition sort of coalesced in it. The family cannot make ends meet. The husband, a practising priest, is a well-meaning nincompoop. He has dreams, but that is about all he has. Whatever land he once possessed has already disappeared, earnings from peripatetic existence as a religious minstrel add up to very little. It is a living hell for the wife. Want and deprivation define her existence. She has no glimmer of hope in her daily perambulations. Arranging the skimpiest meals is a nightmare. She has not even a chance relief from the everyday grind. The husband, she realizes, cannot be depended upon. Two children, a daughter barely ten, and a son some four years younger, keep her listless company. There is also a remote granny, a distant relation, always hungry and at the receiving end of tongue-lashing from the distracted wife; she cannot throw the granny out and yet cannot decide how to keep feeding the otherwise useless bag of bones whose only capital stock is unbounded affection towards the family, particularly for the daughter Durga and her sibling brother Apu.

During his days as a commercial artist, Satyajit Ray had drawn illustrations for an abridged version of *Pather Panchali*, the Bandyopadhyay book, which translates roughly as the *Ballad of the Road*. Once Ray made up his mind to cross over to film-making, the bug of *Pather Panchali* rode with him. His first film, he decided, would be *Pather Panchali*, and the lady in the household, the long-suffering wife, would be pivotal to the story he would weave in celluloid.

Satyajit Ray's film created history. An abiding lullabyesque communion with nature animated it; Ravi Shankar's music provided an excruciating harmony. The old withered granny was magnificent; so too were the portrayals of the good-for-nothing simpleton husband and the two children. But, every time they have gone back to see the film, it is the role of Sarvajaya, the mother, which has haunted the audience. This role was played by Karuna Banerjee, the lady who died, unsung, on the day the film festival opened in Calcutta last month.

Karuna Banerjee was cast as Sarvajaya and for the next near-fifty years, Sarvajaya has been indistinguishable from Karuna Banerjee. The tragedy of the collapsing edifice of rural Bengal and the parallel phenomenon of the disintegrating middle class, both found demure expression in the film through the character of Sarvajaya. She is the mother, she is also the wife. She is hemmed in by poverty, she knows there is no tomorrow for her and yet, she has to improvise a patchwork of survival from out of sheer nothingness. Her worry is not only the husband, without any income but not without vacuous dreams. The daughter, Durga, otherwise so sweet, so helpful in domestic chores, is an equally difficult proposition. She constantly disappears amidst the lushness of flora and fauna, taking along her brother too. She visits other households in the village and is awestruck by the sudden realization that she and her family are poor, abysmally poor, even as several neighbouring households flaunt a somewhat superior level of living. Durga is not a kleptomaniac as such, but she is curious about objects and things; combining innocence with the acquisitive instinct, she cannot resist the temptation to indulge in some minor pilfering.

Sarvajaya finds the situation nearly intolerable. Day after day she is confronted by the same ignominious challenge: not a scrap of food in the house, a truant husband, children whom she cannot afford to send to school, a hanger-on of a granny who is a sheer nuisance. She will still not scrounge, she must not beg, she must mesh dignity with the wretchedness of her existence. Her daughter does not steal food, she steals trinkets. To the outside world the difference is metaphysics, and insults from neighbours fly thick and fast. It is not so much the pangs of hunger but the humiliation which singes Sarvajaya. She nonetheless cannot give in to the luxury of breaking down.

The challenge of the role was this duality: you are immiserized, you still have to retain your pride. The miracle of survival at the sub-marginal level has to be reconciled with the dignity of high-breed brahmin lineage. Karuna Banerjee came from a completely different social category, with a comfortably placed upper-class background. She had a postgraduate degree in literature from the University of Calcutta, was an activist with the fledgling Communist Party of India, and deeply involved in the activities of the Indian People's Theatre Association. In the early 1950s, Utpal Dutt enticed her into his Little Theatre Group.

All of a sudden, the overture came from Satyajit Ray to accept the role of Sarvajaya, never mind if she had never in the past acted in a film. With encouragement from the family, including the husband and the in-laws, she took the plunge.

Art did not imitate life, art in fact was the very obverse of life. But Karuna Banerjee was undeterred; she would go through the necessary transformation of personality. She might have read cursorily some Konstantin Stanislavsky, or might not have. News of New York's Method Acting could have hardly reached her. Her instinct nonetheless urged her on what to do: forget her own identity and enter body and soul into Sarvajaya. During those long months of shooting, with frequent interruptions because Satyajit Ray often ran out of funds, Karuna Banerjee forgot that she is Karuna Banerjee; she was Sarvajaya, she was the microcosm of resourceless lower middle-class Bengali womanhood, a lady at the end of her tether, yet who must assert her pride and exalt in the dignity of her existence. It was an almost absurd arithmetic, but she succeeded. She wrote somewhere that in those months she really believed the dirty, tattered sari she was in was her only apparel, the haunted look in her eyes while on the studio floor or on location were indeed her own; the misery was not ersatz, it was what she was feeling in her core. No food, no medicine, little of protection against the elements, no burden of gold or other jewellery on her frame, and she had to convince herself this state was in fact reality.

Pather Panchali won laurels for Satyajit Ray. It also rolled Karuna Banerjee and Sarvajaya into an indivisible entity. The season was right. The preoccupation of leaders and thinkers was with the problem of eradication of poverty and inequality. *Pather Panchali* acted as a stinging whip on the dormant conscience of the supposedly civilized west, even though this arousal of compassion was ephemeral. As the film claimed an international clientèle, Sarvajaya, *née* Karuna Banerjee, became the talk of the town, here, there, everywhere. Her portrayal of the character also lent credence to the premise that dignity could coexist with deprivation.

That was in another time. The obsession today is no longer the elimination of inequality but the elimination of inefficiency. And it has to be the blotting out of individual inefficiency, and not social inefficiency. The latter, according to sage economists, is a *non sequitur.*

Karuna Banerjee was an intensely private person. She took the triumph of Sarvajaya in its stride. She did the same with the near-oblivion that followed. Although she appeared in a number of other, what can be described as sympathetic film roles, she preferred to remain away from the limelight. She had been intensely ill over most of the last decade. When she died last month, the local film buffs were busy with the ongoing festival and could hardly spare a couple of minutes to offer grief-laden salute to the memory of Sarvajaya. If she were around, Karuna Banerjee, given her innate dignity, would not have minded at all.

The historical process, besides, is unstoppable. The other day, while returning to the city from Calcutta's modest airport via what is known as the Metropolitan Bypass, just beyond the stretch of gleaming waters of the fisheries earning lush foreign exchange, one had occasion to meet a mother and a daughter, Sarvajaya and Durga, if you will. Given the tide of time, immiserization is by now totally bereft of pride. Tell-tale signs of a once-and-past qualitatively superior breeding – the choice and pronunciation of words, the externalities of discourse – notwithstanding, immiserization has proceeded remorselessly, rung after rung. The mother-and-daughter pair were selling cauliflowers and radishes which they must have filched from some neighbour's field. They had avarice and cool calculation in their eyes. The dignity is ancient history, they haggled like lumpen caster-mongers. Cruelty defined their countenance. Karuna Banerjee is dead. So too is Sarvajaya.

The rebel with too many causes

26 October 2002

Post-Gujarat India could hardly care: it is ten years since Ashok Rudra's death. And he himself had no time for non-objective sentiments or emotions. Emotions were a suspect category. But, then, is callousness any better?

One could claim Ashok Rudra to be one of one's closest friends. The ardour would not be reciprocated. Ashok was too proud of his existential mindset. He hated to surrender to any externality. This was perhaps the fiercest datum defining his persona. When he arrived in Paris in the early 1950s, the cognoscenti in France were awash with two simultaneous passions. The Communist Party was very close to assuming political power, or so it seemed. The CGT could shut down the entire country at half an hour's notice. Writers, poets, philosophers, and men and women from the theatre and films had sworn allegiance to the party. At the same time, though, Jean-Paul Sartre and Simone de Beauvoir had been creating a wave of quasi-dissidence. They were with the party and yet not with it. The individual, Sartre pontificated, is his own master. He must not have loyalty to any alien force, neither to a political formation or a philosophical or literary outfit, nor to another individual. Love and friendship therefore deserve to be taboo. Head-over-heel attachments are to be avoided like the plague. A subaltern role vis-à-vis another human being is an admission of defeat: to surrender one's suzerain existence to an externality is to pave the road to perdition.

Ashok Rudra was stymied. His broad sympathies were with the Communist Party. The French maiden of Slavic extraction he was betrothed to, was already in the party. He himself had nothing but admiration for the party led by Maurice Thorez, and its domestic and foreign policies. Existentialist theory, however, cast its shadow. To be a member of the party – to be integrated with it – would be betrayal of Sartre and betrayal of the pride of one's being. Ashok, despite his Marxist instincts – he would go so far as to say, because of these instincts – was an existentialist. He could not afford to barter away his soul. After all, he was, from beginning to end, a deviationist. Dissent spelled his cerebral functioning.

The French expression *engagé* had a nuance as if specially set aside for him. Involvement invites disputation. Combats and quarrels are the hallmark of one's independence. You must, therefore, invariably pick a fight with those at the moment dear to you; you must, as a matter of course, turn your friends into enemies. These friends, wretched creatures, refused to accept the credentials Ashok would script for them. They would insist that, Ashok's disapproval notwithstanding, they remained his closest friends. Ashok was furious: he foamed in the mouth.

Such a man could not but be unhappy. The unhappiness was sourced inside him. He was a dialectician *par excellence*; that was to him an essential aspect of any coherent frame of mind. A person loyal to rationality must protest for the sake of protest. He must, under all circumstances, take up the contrary cause. Poems others liked, Ashok Rudra would disdain. Dramatic performances which sent others into raptures were rubbished by him. His economics did not run parallel to anyone else's, nor did his political thoughts. It was quite commonplace for Ashok Rudra to write a joint paper with a person whose political and economic precepts he would violently disagree with. The theory underlying his decision was somewhat breathtaking, and yet, perfectly explicable in terms of his logical structure: by forming a transient alliance with my enemy, I prove to my friends that I am nobody's slave; tomorrow is another day. Ashok Rudra was never scared of contradicting himself.

Such a person is impossible, such a person is also irresistible. Ashok could, on his own, transform the environment of an academic arena. He had a forebear. Lucknow University was putty-clay in the grasp of D.P. Mukherji, the eminent social scientist of yore. Mukherji defined the university's atmosphere; he created its milieu. Ashok Rudra possessed the same intrinsic ability to transform an academic world, or, rather, recreate it in his own image. He was a scholar of rich dimensions, but no solitary reaper of the genre described in Wordsworthian verse. Ashok would intrude upon his neighbours, he would invade their sensitivities, and he would assail them by his brilliance. It was therefore theoretically conceivable that they would come to detest him. Such a calamity would not eventuate though. The neighbours would hopelessly fall in his trap. This would happen in faculty after university faculty, in the Indian Statistical Institute, in the Delhi School of Economics, in the Churchgate campus of the University of Bombay, in Santiniketan. Ashok, you could almost take a wager, would, in all seasons, cross the barrier of subjects and disciplines. In this he was a bit like his benefactor and *bête noire*, P.C. Mahalanobis. To a nuclear physicist, Mahalanobis would pontificate on Vedanta philosophy. A mathematical statistician would be floored by passages from evocative Vaishnava lyrics. A literary hack, an insufferable bore at that, would be doled out lots and lots of gibberish on interpenetrative samples. A classical musician of the Agra *gharana* would be treated to a discourse on probability distribution of E-scale minor in Mozart. Ashok's virtuosity would traverse a near-identical concourse. The pace at which he would talk and argue would indeed be flabbergasting. This fearsome velocity of articulation was, however, only the medium which he would deploy to cross over, in bizarre, merciless non-sequence, from history to sociology, from sociology to economics, from economics to political theory, and from political theory to Trotsky's *History of Soviet Communism*. His next port of call would perhaps be French symbolic poetry, on to Picasso, on to Salvador Dalí or Paul Klee. Suddenly, a kink of a sort would develop. Ashok would be haunted by what was to him the indescribable charm of a line from a Tagore song, and explain how the mystique shrouding it was a derivative of sufi philosophy. Even that phase would be interrupted, for a painter would drop in and Ashok would speak his mind on where the visitor's crasftsmanship had collapsed in several of his works displayed in the ongoing expo. He did not know a *rohu* from a *hilsa*; that would not deter him from a harangue on either culinary arts or the vintage of French wines; be reasonable, was he not based in Paris in his early youth, hurtling from one Left Bank bistro to the next one *ad infinitum*? The only subject Ashok Rudra would stay away from was the proceedings on the cricket field; cricket was a detestable colonial pursuit. Otherwise, he would latch on to anything and everything.

But what with Mahalanobis was a dalliance – a stratagem to harass and annoy and beguile his visitor – was a matter of deep conviction for Ashok Rudra. Call it conceit, call it megalomania, Ashok did actually believe he was billeting next door to omniscience. That was his style, that was his faith as well. He would challenge both friends and enemies to join him in the bout to defy the limits of wisdom in any particular discipline. Most of the time, the challenge would not be accepted. Ashok's self-confidence on such occasions many would deride as foolhardy. He could not care less. He was 100 per cent honest when he thought Sombhu Mitra had made a hash of Bengali-izing Ibsen's *Doll's House*; he himself could do better, and immediately sat down to the task. It is a different matter that what he produced was egregiously indifferent stuff, containing little literary attributes and even less dramatic merit. Buddhadeva Bose had no business to embark on a reinterpretation of the *Mahabharata* characters; if he had any sense, he would have waited until his, Ashok's, tract on the same theme was published. To make fun of Ashok would be to miss the point. It was not conceit, but the deepest belief in oneself, which was at work.

The prowess of Ashok's intellect was awesome. Abstruse papers in scientific journals bear enough evidence of his grounding in mathematical economics and probability theory. He had prepared in the late 1950s a manual for teaching statistics. It never got published. But those who had the opportunity of going through it were struck as much by its lucidity as by its logical precision. Ashok had no formal training in economics. So what; he proved that any intelligent human being can get into the essentials of the economic science within the span of a bare couple of hours. His lack of familiarity with the history of economic analysis was a handicap; he however knew how to overcome it. And, given his passion for Marxism, he had enough hunch on the overlap of history and economics to enable him to formulate credible theoretical constructs concerning past or contemporary economic phenomena. Model-building is about the most wasteful exercise practitioners of economics in the second half of the twentieth century had indulged in, to stay in the profession. Almost absent-mindedly, Ashok chose to emulate his colleagues; he beat them hollow in this lunatic game. Nonetheless, a Don Quixote of a social scientist, he would often go horrendously wrong. For a number of years, he engaged in empirical work on the relationship between the distribution of landholdings and farm productivity. He could not show any lack of confidence in the methodology or sampling design he had himself chosen, and thus disbelieved the data he had got collected; he could not also be dishonest in his inferences. He came out with a set of conclusions which almost sought to prove that it was the sharecropper, and not the intermediaries one or two rungs above, who headed the roster of exploiters in the West Bengal countryside. On another occasion, in a foray into the morphology of the French revolution, Ashok arrived at the somber *pucca* conclusion that the lumpen class was a relatively more progressive social category than the proletariat.

His friends and enemies chose to be polite. Was not this politeness partly because they lacked the temerity to invite him to a scholastic duel? The actual truth could be more complex. Call such of his perambulations idiosyncrasies, call them by worse names, it would not have dented Ashok Rudra's integrity of purpose. Frequently uncouth in manners, abrupt in his moods, here was still a person possessing an unbounded flow of affection. He would hate well, but love with even greater fervour. He had regard for his friends, and both love and regard for his students. The simplicity of his daily habits, including his apparel, underscored his proximity to an idealized socialist paradigm. In that sense, he was a puritan.

He could also be a wild lover. He would love so intensely that sometimes it turned into a malady and gave rise to misunderstandings. Therein lay the tragedy, which had its comic side as well. He would every now and then fall deeply in love and, very soon, his being would recoil from the experience. Love and attachment are fatal diseases; they divest you of your faculty of independent judgement. Ashok would be dazzled by the charm and richness of the voice that would, at the moment, be rendering for him a Tagore song. He would feel the urge to succumb, body and soul, to the persona of the singer. That would be the end of the affair. To be shackled by affection was a matter of disgrace for a human being jealous of his suzerainty. Ashok would quarrel rudely with the person he felt enamoured about a whisker of a moment ago. Paris of the 1950s would beckon him. Ashok would discipline himself and break away from the moorings of *l'amour*.

Even so, trust Ashok Rudra to be clinical. The experience he had just gone through, he did not have the least doubt, was unique; it could offer hints to other lovers who would arrive on the scene subsequently. There is no time to waste: he would compose, at great speed, a novel or a short story on the romantic episode he had encountered. The piece would get published, causing embarrassment to a second or third party. That would not cramp Ashok's style.

These emotional encounters – Ashok surely would not have preferred such a sobriquet for them – hardly detained him. Dog day afternoon or no, come the next entrant to his portals, Ashok would be all agog. For, the visitor, he or she, was a revolutionary activist. Ashok would ply the comrade with funds and offer a few tips on the tactics of guerrilla operations. Not the fire next time or next door: Ashok could not wait; fire, like charity, should begin at home, in his own household.

It is a full decade since Ashok Rudra has been gone. There will be never another one like him.

The survival kit

26 April 2003

The saga of Saddam Hussein refuses to end. Another epithet, this time supposed to be a clincher, has now been added to the ones showered upon him over the past decade by the good Americans: what do you know, he is actually a Stalinist, he has been a consistent admirer of Stalin's authoritarianism. After this profound discovery no further debate, the American top brass assume, is called for, Saddam deservedly to the gallows.

Other lessons will be drawn, though, from the Iraq experience by masses of people around the world, including those who have made a fetish of freedom first. The ladies and gentlemen, whom Vietnam could not convince, should have now their last doubts removed. The American establishment has an outlandish perspective on the meaning and reach of the expression 'freedom'. Freedom to them is latitude for *Pax Americana* to do whatever it wants to do, and no questions are to be asked. In the light of the genocide in Iraq, even Nobel laureates obsessed with the benign virtues of freedom of thought, ideas and information should be forced to do some rethinking: how come other Nobel laureates have to go to prison for testing the waters of such freedom? Iraq proves the point: to George W. Bush, and therefore to the American administration, freedom is the obverse of life and living, it is the right to exterminate those regarded as lesser human beings. This may sound banal. But has not the superpower reduced human existence to banality?

The past few weeks have been a trauma, not just for the Iraqis but for thousands of men, women and children in the rest of the globe, including in the United States and Great Britain as well. What is even more important than the explosion of anger, revulsion and resentment, it is bound to persuade scholars to take another look at their approach towards analysing Stalin's role in history. This historiography has been frozen into a particular mould during the past half a century. Stalin was cruelty incarnate, a blood-sucker, a dictator, a sadist and all that; Stalin's passing and the gradual process of liberation set in motion in the Soviet empire by Khrushchev and brought to culmination by Mikhail Gorbachev and Boris Yeltsin, it has been the claim, succeeded in restoring eastern Europe to freedom. Such is supposed to be axiomatic truth which only the certified insane would question.

On the other hand, should not there be at least some forgiveness for an obstinate group who dare to argue that much of the ills the world has suffered from, especially in the course of the past two decades, is because of the collapse of the eastern bloc presided over by the Soviet Union, and the resulting emergence of the United States of America as the only global superpower? No countervailing power exists, and the American administration can regulate everything according to its whims and fancies. Russia, despite its nuclear capability, is in effect an insignificant power; her economic survival is the gift of the United States. Minor countries like the Czech Republic, Slovakia, Albania and Rumania have made a beeline for the NATO and American vassaldom. The Serbs entertained other ideas, and received their comeuppance. The erstwhile Asian republics such as Uzbekistan, Turkmenistan, Kirgizhistan and so on are blanketed by CIA agents flush with greenbacks; it is child's play for the outfit to buy local loyalties. The haughtiness of power has made the American masters think no end of themselves. Their word, they honestly believe, is law for the rest of the world. Capitalism is back in east Europe in vengeance. All the capitalist vices are back too. Economic growth is halting, if not downright negative, but hucksters, including blackmarketeers, are having a gala time. For a considerable majority of the people, income and employment are hard to come by. Social welfare measures have almost disappeared. Art and culture have taken a beating. Workers, including farm-hands and the middle-class salariat, cannot be paid wages on a regular basis. Thousands of young women, penury forcing them out of the countryside and demure city blocks, have little alternative but to join the world's oldest profession. Capitalist morality reigns supreme; only the profit motive matters, ideology and the rest of the old clichés are treated as garbage. The sum total of all this is freedom. Propagating this freedom, the United States is unstoppable. None ventures to stop her exercise of naked might. Not Russia, not Germany, not France, not Japan and, of even greater significance, not China. At least France, Germany and Russia have registered their protest on Iraq. True, China too expressed her reservations, but on a low, low key. Certainly, she did not threaten to cast her veto against the United States in the United Nations Security Council, in the manner of the other three countries. Perhaps China's leaders are weighing the pros and cons of a possibly more strident criticism of American atrocities in Iraq, and how it might affect China's exports to North America. Market socialism is a curious hybrid animal.

The countervailing influence has disappeared and the Americans know they are in a position to send the United Nations packing. Should the UN Secretariat learn to behave from now on, the US administration could still offer them their upkeep. Otherwise, for all one can surmise, the impressive United Nations building in Manhattan could be put under lock and key and the General Assembly ordered to disperse.

Consider the plight of the 100-odd nations which had once, high of hope, organized themselves into a movement of non-aligned nations. This has been reduced to a clowns' opera. The poor countries were listened to in the 1950s, 1960s and 1970s because the Soviet bloc acted as a ballast against western pressure. The ballast is gone and these countries of Asia, Africa and Latin America are now a nondescript herd of scattered, lost sheep. They are easy picking for the United States; the latter, however, does not need them.

The Soviet bloc was Stalin's architecture. He guided over the collectivization of Soviet agriculture in the 1930s. The freedom-lovers had described that act as savagery, which allegedly cost millions of lives. But collectivization propelled the Soviet Union to industrialize at a furious pace and enabled the country, both to resist capitalist encirclement, and to produce enough of steel and machines and tanks and planes to confront and vanquish the Nazis. The heroism of the Soviet people attained unprecedented heights in the war, because they were inspired by Josef Stalin. The freedom-mongers keep referring to the three million dead on account of collectivization, but do not deign to mention the near-thirty million Soviet citizens who sacrificed themselves in order that western civilization could be saved. To put it bluntly, without collectivization, there would have been no Stalingrad. That name, Stalingrad, has been changed to Volvograd, but that particular landmark of history is still not easy to rub out.

Stalin did not spare his family. His son had to go to war; no draft-dodger, he got killed. Stalin refused to show any special consideration for his wayward daughter, which is why she defected to the west. Yes, the man was somewhat lacking in the milk of human kindness, but was that not the key to his creativity? M.N. Roy was expelled from the Third International at Stalin's instance. He had no reason to feel generous towards this inveterate enemy. Never mind, when Stalin died, Roy wrote a perceptive obituary note. Stalin, he commented, was perhaps not a good man, he was nonetheless a great man; it was his greatness which was instrumental in thrusting the Soviet Union to the pinnacle she reached by the end of the second world war. Isaac Deutscher summed up his assessment of Stalin more or less along the same lines, and this despite the fact that Deutscher's god was Leon Trotsky. Trotsky was driven out of the country and hunted down by Stalin's men in distant Mexico. But Deutscher could not help acknowledging the fact that Stalin's collectivization was precisely what Preobrazhensky and Trotsky had once suggested, and which was then vigorously opposed by Bukharin.

It is a long, difficult, arduous task to build; it is easy to destroy. The little men who succeeded into the leadership of the USSR after Stalin made a bonfire of his great creation. The cake, of course, is taken by Mikhail Gorbachev who, as General Secretary of the great Communist Party of the Soviet Union, banned the party by his own hand, thereby ensuring the advent of the American imperial epoch.

Has the suffering of humanity gone down since Stalin was repudiated? Is there now more freedom even in the western sense of the word? Is not one justified in taking a wager that were Stalin around for some more years, the Soviet Union would have gained even greater strength in the middle decades of the twentieth century, and the American establishment would not have dared to indulge in Vietnam; that the rape of Iraq too would have been a non-event? Countries in Asia, Europe, Africa and Latin America fume in resentment at American excesses; they also quake in fear. The fear factor would have been totally absent had Stalin's architecture not been tampered with and subsequently brought down unceremoniously.

It will be nice and proper to have a reassessment of Stalin, but, let there be no nurturing of illusion, it is unlikely to take place. Even in the poor, underdeveloped lands, the conscientious few have converted themselves into short-range philosophers. Human civilization will admittedly be in danger if American insolence is not blocked along a wide barricade before it is too late. Arguments to the contrary will, however, immediately crowd in. It will take a long while, and considerable organization and determination, to neutralize superpower blandishments. Average longevity is much too short for that. Why cannot we instead join the camp of the imperial power and grab whatever titbits of prizes and gratuities are grabbable? Stalin might have been a great man, but he preached sacrifice and self-abnegation. We would rather opt for Gunnar Myrdal's soft state and subsist on American bounty.

Somebodies and nobodies

6 December 2003

A Chennai-based lawyer with a roaring practice, Govind Swaminathan, died recently. His passing became the occasion for a flurry of memories suddenly astir. True, such nostalgia is of slight significance and without market value. On the other hand, at least some species of nostalgia can tuck in a lot of sociology, and, for that matter, a smattering of economics as well.

Govind Swaminathan was the son of Ammu Swaminathan, who, by her charm and oratorical skill, outshone most others in the Indian parliament in the 1950s. It was a staunchly nationalist household despite the aura of affluence and anglicized mode of living. Ammu's husband was a formidable lawyer, just as the son later turned out to be. She, however, had credentials very much of her own. She was a firm believer in the mystique of Indian ethos despite its linguistic and ethnic criss-crosses. Devastatingly catholic in outlook, she taught her children how to take wings. Govind's sister, Lakshmi Swaminathan, was trained as a medical doctor, she got stranded in Singapore as the Japanese army swept across Southeast Asia in 1942. She happened to meet Subhas Chandra Bose and immediately made up her mind. For the next couple of years, she would head the Rani Jhansi regiment of the Indian National Army. Following the days of defeat, capture and, finally, release and the nation's freedom, Lakshmi married her INA comrade, P.K. Sahgal, and settled down in Kanpur. Another score of years, and she found fulfilment in the Communist Party of India (Marxist). Another of Govind's sisters, Mrinalini, walked away from the political ambience of the family. Groomed in Kalakshetra and Santiniketan, she blossomed into a danseuse. She too breached the linguistic divide and travelled to marry Vikram Sarabhai, the space physicist. The more interesting part of the story concerns Ammu Swaminathan's grandchildren who, with easy abandon, straddled the fencings of language, culture and religion. Lakshmi Sahgal's daughter is the present-day fiery Marxist, Subhashini Ali. Mrinalini and Vikram Sarabhai's daughter,

Mallika, has inherited her mother's passion for the performing arts and wandered even further, into social activism of diverse sorts. Govind's daughter, Srilata Swaminathan, has proceeded all the way to Jaipur; burning with Naxalite fervour, she is fixated on her goal to create, in quadruple quick time, revolutionary awareness amongst the Rajasthani tribals. Another cousin entered into wedlock with a Bengali Brahmo boy, whose mother, though, was an impeccable Maharashtrian Saraswat.

More than anything else, the Swaminathan cousins exemplified by their goings-on, an aspect of Indian nationalism which dominated the milieu in the euphoric days of the freedom movement. Indians have to be a magnificent homogeneity; the barriers of ethnicity, language, caste and communities have to be pierced, and the praxis must commence in one's own household. Of Jawaharlal Nehru's two sisters, the elder one romanced with a debonair Muslim youth, but ended up marrying a pandit from Maharashtra; the younger one preferred to marry a Hutheesingh from Gujarat. Instances multiplied. A Shanti Srivastava chose as husband a Sadiq Ali; a Litto Rai from Punjab chose an Ajay Kumar Ghosh, a Bengali domiciled in the United Provinces. Two sisters from a Muslim aristocratic family in Bombay, living in the 1940s in the Communist Party commune in the city, travelled south: one married P. Sundarayya, the Telengana hero, the other opted for the celebrated Madras lawyer, an Iyengar to boot, A.S.R. Chari. Mohan Kumaramangalam from Salem, Eton and Cambridge married Kalyani Mukherjee from Tamluk and Calcutta. His sister, Parvati, again just down from Cambridge, made up her mind to have N.K. Krishnan from Kerala as her husband. Lest we forget, much earlier, J.B. Kripalani from Sind was ensnared by Sucheta Mazumdar, a Bengali girl from Patna, J.B.'s cousin, Krishna, exchanged vows with Tagore's granddaughter, Nandita Ganguly. Nandita's first cousin, Aruna, still in her teens, eloped with the Delhi barrister Asaf Ali.

A couple of generations have gone by. Matches of this genre are no longer news-making. On the contrary, they are quite *passé*, and, to that extent, neither stir the imagination nor create waves in the media. The revolutionary dazzle has gone out of inter-provincial, inter-caste and inter-community marriages. Perhaps, in the netherlands of Uttar Pradesh, Bihar and Madhya Pradesh, such couplings still raise hackles in stray, or not so stray, quarters. But, as far as the upper reaches of society are concerned, mixed marriages are nothing to write home about. The Indian élite have accepted the occasional hybridity within their fold as a natural development. And, since the media are controlled by elite groups, the heterogeneity does not any longer stop the press. Any special emotion – for instance, that such comings-together in defiance of conventional mores are a bloom for national integration – has ceased to be either felt or articulated.

Even so, by and large, it still remains a superstructural phenomenon, the base remains unaffected. Most of the linguistically or otherwise heterogeneous families are concentrated in metropolitan centres like Delhi, Mumbai, Calcutta or Bangalore. The constituents of these families have shed awareness of their hybrid roots. Their children speak mostly English along with a smattering of Hindi; they dress alike; their cultural inclinations are nearly identical. A new breed of cosmopolitan Indians, they are barely conscious of their specificity. Given the nature of circumstances, theirs is, though, a narrow community, without even the feeblest backward linkage with processes unfolding in provincial wildernesses. They take for granted their Indianness; they are not particularly enamoured of it either. They, most of them, want to get off this what-they-consider-to-be narrow identity, and yearn instead for global citizenship.

Deviants are of course around. The handful of left-over ideologues, such as the cousins Subhashini Ali and Srilata Swaminathan, cannot understand it. They continue to be full of the idyllic dream of an integrated India detached from linguistic, ethnic, caste and religious tensions. Have they themselves not integrated, should not their example set rivers of togetherness on fire? It does not, and maybe it will not. The efforts of Subhashini and Srilata are marginalized. The new breed of metropolitan Indians, most of them, have made up their mind. They will not look back either in moral anguish or with rapid sentimentality. They have disdain for the mass of problems accumulating within the country, in region after region and state after state. Hard-boiled extroverts, they have irrevocably turned outwards, more often than not towards the United States of America.

This shift in upper-class Indian ethos has an inevitability of its own. It is difficult to stay away from the lure of the integrated market. The élite-based development model has strategic patrons. Its more negative features, such as the progressive intensification of assets and income inequalities, can, it is argued, be taken care of by special anti-poverty measures of the kind suggested by the World Bank. In any case, they are not bothered too much; they have a tryst with destiny.

Clouds of doubt nonetheless gather. Half a century ago, the Leila Sundarayyas and the Shanti Sadiq Alis wanted to spread the message of their commitment to national integration all over the country. They were only partly successful: whatever they achieved, some would even say, was only ephemeral, huge landslides of prejudice have meanwhile buried their hopes and aspirations. For the metropolitan-based integrated Indians, the country has ceased to be a relevant category. It is therefore a clash of minds, almost a clash of civilizations. The new generation ensconced in urban caves have dropped national integration from the agenda. Why, they are already integrated, they talk alike, they think alike, they dress alike. The rest of the agenda should concentrate on integration across oceans and time zones; for example, mulling over the prospect of a youngster enjoying dual citizenship of India and the US, and marrying a Guatemalan of mixed Greek–Slav extraction.

Wishful or not, speculation takes further flight. Just another half-a-dozen decades or thereabouts, the chosen people in the six continents will write the same script, speak the same language, dream identical dreams. The problem, however, lies elsewhere. Consider the Indian dilemma. The Indian oligarchs have taken care of themselves. They are already integrated nationally. The next milestone is to transit to international integration. But this does not impress those left behind in morose mufassil towns and distant villages – in the north, the south, the east and the west. These savages have their more proximate problems, whether imaginary or real, problems concerning allegedly discriminatory behaviour towards them by the centre or the neighbouring state, or economic and social exploitation of this group by that one or of this religious sect by another one. While our élite integrate with the rest of the world, our subaltern constituents – the nation's overwhelming majority – tear one another apart. Assam refuses to allow candidates from Bihar to sit for a regional competitive examination from a Guwahati centre; Bihar responds by plundering a train laden with passengers from Assam. Carnage follows. Even more frightening, the Khasis threaten Karbis and vice versa, the Nagas look askance at the Kukis and vice versa; Kasergod and Cannanore explode in fury over this or that supposedly grave non-issue; Gujarat has its perennial communal riots even as some dalits are burned regularly by the landowning *thakurs* in Unnao or Samastipur. All these provide a brilliant opportunity for police and military lobbies to swing budgetary allocations further in their favour. It also creates an opening for dirty little linguistic caste and ethnic wars. A situation might soon arrive where at one end, our decision-makers will be absorbed in playing optimum-making games over global integration, and at the other end, the national market starts disintegrating. At the level of grass roots, only the Nepalese and the Bangladeshis were till now suspect and not allowed entry into the informal markets in West Bengal. Come yesterday or the day after, it could be the turn of the Biharis or the Assamese, and the compliment would be duly returned. The philosophy of Bal Thackeray will triumph all the way, the jobs will be reserved 100 per cent for the *bhumiputras* in every nook and corner of the country. The domestic market will be increasingly sub-divided and fragmented, even as our élite will be busy passing one benchmark after another in their quest for full-scale international integration.

Nobody is bothered, or bothered too much. Fun and games are wonderful *divertissements*, such as occasional elections in this or that state, or seasonal videotapes of ministers taking bribes while invoking the holy name of Mahatma Gandhi.

FIVE

They flock together

18 September 1999

The non-sectarian regime of the Congress Party was a benign watcher when the Babri Masjid was brought down. This allegation, some will say, is by now a cliché. That does not however detract from its relevance. Between the Congress and the Bharatiya Janata Party there is really not much of a variation in the theme, at least going by the *dramatis personae* of the two parties. The leaders of both parties, by and large, come from the same social stratum, and often even belong to the same household. Mahatma Gandhi's own granddaughter chooses to opt for the BJP, the party symbiotically linked to the outfit that spawned the likes of Nathuram Godse. Madhav Rao Scindia was, once upon a time, in the BJP; he is currently a key functionary of the 10 Janpath Party. His ailing mother, however, continues to be the RSS-lining party's Queen Bee; and, irrespective of the whereabouts of the son, her two daughters, one of whom is already a union minister, are aiming for the Lok Sabha on the party's ticket. Or what about Rangarajan Kumaramangalam, offspring of one of Indira Gandhi's closest confidants, who himself was a Congress minister till the other day and has since taken a walk? Govind Ballabh Pant's son and daughter-in-law too have taken the same route. Arun Nehru happens to be amongst the very few who still bear the famous family surname. He too is no longer satisfied with his role as a non-official adviser of the Hindu revivalists; he has decided to join them formally. Switches have taken place, and are taking place, in the other direction as well. The gentleman who won the Rae Bareli seat on behalf of the BJP on the two previous occasions is now determined to find salvation in the Congress ranks. Examples of this kind of reverse movement can be easily multiplied. The conclusion is glaringly obvious. Never mind the different labels they attach to themselves at a particular moment, these politicians playing the switching and re-switching game belong to the same narrow class or coterie. Merely because they change their political label, their attitude to life and living does not alter. And the less said of ideology, the better. Stray images flashed across the newspapers and the Doordarshan screen assail the memory, images of Indira Gandhi, incumbent prime minister, hopping from temple to temple and seeking blessings from the most bigoted, sectarian-minded Hindu religious leaders. That she also simultaneously frequented *dargas* and synagogues, only compounds the confusion. Secularism should not mean treating all religious denominations alike, but keeping distance from each and all.

The rigmarole of the claim that of the two major parties, one dons the rabidly sectarian apparel while the other one does not, fails to cut much ice. Consider the overall composition of the two parties; scarcely anything distinguishes, in terms of class lineage, leaders of the one lot from those of the other. It is only outsiders who propose to either support or oppose these parties on ideological grounds who face difficulties. The possibility cannot therefore be ruled out that, once the polls are over, the secular–sectarian divide would come to a dead-end, and furious negotiations would be on to give shape to terms and conditions for supporting a stable regime in which both groups will have equitable representation. The theory of footlooseness can in fact be generalized. Nothing is any longer odd under the perennially grey Indian sky. A formidable secretary general of a so-claimed socialist party is the least bothered about his ideological pretensions: he has a private identity, which he greatly cherishes, as a loyal servitor of one of the country's leading industrial tycoons. And the leading lights of the parties claiming to represent the backward classes share a common concern to take care of their personal interests first.

The festival of hurling allegations of corruption against one another is tapering off for the same objective reason. The lady at 10 Janpath is certainly not unduly worried over the BJP's threat to import from Switzerland the final bunch of papers relating to the Bofors bribes. The threat is altogether vacuous. For, by now it is well known that, as per the verdict of the highest Swiss court, the bribe money, of which a portion has reportedly gone into the coffers of the gentleman of Verona – or is it Torino? – has been co-shared with the four famous NRI brethren settled in London. These brothers are, again as everybody knows, as close to the present prime minister as the travelling salesman from Torino is to 10 Janpath.

In fact, the convergence of interests between the two major parties is an unending affair. An official committee has gone to great lengths to unravel the mystery of the huge capital erosion suffered a few years ago by the Unit Trust of India. Its report has thrown quite a few hints regarding the authorship of the shenanigans. But, given the present concatenation of the country's superstructural politics, investigations of this nature are unlikely to go very far. Information was solicited on the floor of parliament on the identity of the parties which had benefited from huge private placements by institutions such as the UTI and the ICICI between such and such years. These placements were one principal reason for the UTI's coming to grief in that phase. The response to the parliamentary questions was uniformly fuzzy, the authorities falling back on the plea of the supposed inviolability of the statutory provision for protecting the secrecy of the relationship between banking institutions and their clients. The free market cannot be prevented from indulging in gossip, though. At least three-fifths, if not more, of those private placements, stockmarket cognoscenti are prepared to swear, had gone to a particular family business concern entrenched in Mumbai and Gujarat. The two leading political parties in the country have a common stake in protecting this business house; both parties – and some others too – are flush with funds contributed by it.

Both major parties share identical views on economic policy issues, because their leaders come from the same social background. The return of colonialism, the thinning out of government investment and privatization of existing public sector units at a furious pace define the emerging milieu. The plot, as they say, will thicken. The trickiest problems India, along with other developing economies, will face in the next decades will involve issues of trade and trade-related foreign investment. The two principal parties in the country are committed by word and deed to go along, jointly as well as severally, with the dictat of the WTO in these matters. After all, it was the commerce minister of a Congress government who signed the Marrakesh Treaty in 1994. The BJP, because it was then in the opposition, made quite a show of declaring itself against the provisions of the Treaty. But all is well that ends well. After it entered the government in 1998, a dramatic transformation took place in the BJP's stance. The amendment to the Indian Patents Act in order to make it conform to the Articles of Agreement of the WTO was a one hundred per cent joint operation on the part of the two national parties. It was a Congress MP with a formidable legal reputation who explained the amendments. The BJP Minister for Industrial Development, who had formally moved the amendments, stood up to confess that he had nothing to add to the explanations provided by the Congress luminary.

Meanwhile, though, the Ministry of Finance has gone off in its own manner. It did not worry the least whether the amending statute had been given the imprimatur of approval by the parliament. Over the decades, it has been shifting its loyalty to the international financial and trading institutions which articulate the views of the superpower. According to an article enshrined in the WTO manual, developing countries have the prerogative to maintain for an indefinite period, for balance of payments reasons, quantitative restrictions on agricultural imports. It is only when the IMF is satisfied that the country's balance of payments position has improved significantly and it so informs the WTO, that the WTO is expected to issue a directive to the country concerned to withdraw the restrictions. By convention, the IMF, before transmitting its view to the WTO, seeks the opinion of the ministry of finance of the country concerned. India's Ministry of Finance is more loyal than the royals themselves; it had, on its own, informed the Fund sometime ago, that the country's balance of payments position was excellent, so that the WTO could be advised to direct the Government of India to let go of the quantitative restrictions on farm inputs. Not a squeak of protest has been heard in the matter from the major political parties, including those who constitute the formidable farmers' lobby.

Colonialism is *passé*, so is fundamentalism. Talk of the last-ditch battle between sectarianism and secularism being fought on Indian soil would seem to be greatly overdrawn. It is all very gentlemanly. Where the situation so warrants, the sectarians will quote approvingly the sweet reasonableness of an Atal Behari Vajpayee muffling the war drums of the VHP–RSS rabble. Similarly, in due season, the Congress Party will not flinch from exhibiting film clips of a devoutly demure Indira Gandhi and her bare-bodied elder son, both lying prostrate and receiving benediction from semi-clad Hindu *sadhus.*

It is only those specially belonging to the Left, anxious to stress a sharp ideological cleavage in the behaviour pattern of the two principal political parties, who are having a trying time. Since the facts do not match, they have begun to cross over to democratic decentralism. The Central Committee resolution on electoral strategy is being interpreted differently by different state units to suit their local compulsions. Apart from the Sharad Pawar coup which took them unawares, what additionally worries sections of the Left is the prospect of a substantial segment of MPs elected on the Congress ticket breaking away from the party to join even the BJP, and share the loaves and fishes of office. Some of these post-modern converts to the communal–sectarian cause are unlikely to experience any qualms of conscience. Where opportunity fails, opportunism could beckon, and why be excessively moralistic about it? True, some of the elements the BJP has gathered under its umbrella are pretty poor examples of the human species; they might well turn out to be the greatest menace to national integrity. It is nonetheless the other sensation that brims over: haven't we given a bloody nose to the Pakistanis? Those denigrating the scale of our victory at Kargil are *prima facie* agents of the Inter-Services Intelligence, lock them up, and rough them up too. There appears to be little awareness that the joint secular–sectarian enthusiasm to discover ISI agents in every bush could provoke a major confrontation with Bangladesh. Hopefully, the superpower will then, once more, bail us out.

The colonial order is back with a bang!

Stability? Forget about it

16–23 October 1999

Shove aside the obfuscations, and concentrate on the basic features of the general election results. One outstanding outcome of the poll is the apparent inability of the two principal political parties in the country, the Bharatiya Janata Party and the Indian National Congress, to claim the loyalty of more than 55 per cent of those who voted. That is to say, at least 45 per cent of the electorate have no particular regard for the two major parties. Their loyalty is to other groups and parties, including the Left, the regional formations and the caste-based parties.

A significant corollary of the poll result is the relative diminution of strength of the BJP in relation to its allies, and, similarly, that of the Indian National Congress vis-à-vis its electoral allies. This kind of outcome is a major blow to those who had drawn up fond designs of an increasingly bipolar India, where only the two principal parties will count and the rest of the lot are dispensable. Such a design of things is very much in consonance with the concept of an emerging political set-up of the country with power and resources getting increasingly centralized. In course of time, so runs the assumption, the oddities of minor groups and parties will disappear from the scene, and India will be a perfect illustration of a two-party arrangement where other voices and views are denied any accommodation.

This species of a political model is a great favourite of Confederation of Indian Industry types. They would like nothing better than the hypothesis of an understanding reached between the two main parties in the country on the basis of a consolidated roster of economic programmes and policies. It will be essentially a CII programme. In the idyllic world the local bourgeoisie dream of, the state's economic policies are expected to be fully adjusted to cater to the Confederation's bill of goods. The poll results bring unfortunate tidings, though: the ground reality refuses to conform to the mould proffered by the Indian capitalist class. India, the election outcome suggests, continues to be a chiaroscuro of shifting patterns of minds and attitudes even as we proceed from region to region and from state to state. Those segments of the electorate who, consequent to developments over the past decade, have learnt to articulate their views via the ballot box, are indeed experiencing a whale of a time. The two big parties cannot any longer run away with the polity. Coalitions, of this or that texture, are going to be henceforth the order of the day. Even more remarkably, coalition partners will be more and more assertive with respect to the charter of rights they want the major partner of the coalition to yield to them. Call it blackmail, it does not matter. The retort of those who indulge in such practices with gay abandon will perhaps be that the blackmail is only partial compensation for the exploitation indulged in through the epochs by the social classes constituting the two major parties.

Discussion of the role the Left groups and like-minded formations could fill in this situation can, for the present, be left aside. What is, however, of tremendously greater significance is the emergence of regional parties of various descriptions. It is not just parties such as the Dravida Munnetra Kazhagam, the All-India Anna Dravida Munnetra Kazhagam, the Tamil Manila Congress, the Telugu Desam and its tributaries. It is equally necessary to take into account the role likely to be assumed by the Shiromani Akali Dal, the Nationalist Congress

Party, the Asom Gana Parishad, the Sikkim National Front, the Mizo National Front, the Gurkha National Liberation Front and so on.

The poll outcome, in other words, clinches the point that we are almost on the verge of no return. The concept of a stable administration the Indian citizenry had grown accustomed to in the 50 years since 1947, has all of a sudden lost its relevance. We are fated for confrontation with a succession of unstable regimes. No party will, on its own, be any longer able to exercise total political control over the centre, and therefore the country. Coalitions will be the order of the day, and please do not entertain any notion of the coalitions continuing for ever and ever. Such coalitions will come apart at regular, and irregular, intervals, for, the sectarian – and secular – interests of the coalition parties will refuse to abide the pretences of a still centre.

This, did you say, will be inimical to economic growth and accordingly the despair of foreign investors? Few tidings deserve to be applauded with greater cheer. Should the point of view be aired that such a state of affairs could affect the country's international political status, it would be quite in order to break out into a cynic's smile. At the rate at which we have proceeded in the recent times, other things remaining the same, our international political stature will be an exclusive gift to be decided upon by the US administration.

Given this context, a great many things can be said in favour of an ambience where neither of the two major political parties in the country is in a position to give vent to its over-centralized, medieval aspirations. Even before the sustenance of parliamentary democracy is ensured, it is, after all, necessary to ensure the sustenance of democracy itself.

And for how long more are we to continue to feign innocence of the other reality this year's poll has been compelled to reveal once more? It has been a frighteningly bizarre serenade of so-called democratic elections, the bomb and bullet blasts accompanying the gory killings. The Hurriyat Conference, the People's War groups and other Maoist formations, Bihar's caste armies, the ULFA and Boro insurgents, the rebels swearing allegiance to the Manipur United Liberation Front and the Achik National Volunteers' Council: add them up, it is yet another facet of the nation's awesome political nitty-gritty. What a cheerful thought, the CII types will have sleepless nights for some while, until they come to realize that India is not just New Delhi and Mumbai. The poll results are a slap in the face of the conspirators who thought they could walk away with the country.

The media will continue to endeavour to sustain the illusion of a stable polity. The poll results suggest the contrary: a great disorder awaits India. Is that not a lovely prospect?

The taciturn functionary

27 May–2 June 2000

There is no prospect any more of gleaning rich literature from the leaf readings. For decisions have ceased to be based on objective analysis of facts and issues. More often than not, an onrush of assumptions befuddles the structure of logic, so much so that while one ends up with a pocketful of measures which serve, albeit partially, the narrow purposes of the day, it leaves the long-term problems of the polity messy beyond words. Major elements of state policy are tackled with a degree of superciliousness that casts a shadow on the relationship between means and ends. Discontent over the ramifications of a particular issue does not dissolve on its own. The consequence is an aggravation of the rebellious mood at different layers of society. Some of these layers have never had it so good, but a vastly greater number are afflicted by clumsy roadblocks.

We are inevitably caught in the trap of a puzzle which harps on asking whether the collapse of the moral framework is responsible for the growing incompetence of the individual instrumentalities in the system, or whether it is the other way round. Even where there is general acceptance of the formula that the whole is constituted by the parts, or, alternatively, the parts combine to make the whole, such quasi-arithmetical gestures cannot cope with the outstanding social issues organically related to a framework of interdependent morality. There can, of course, be a hundred modalities of social transformation which attempt to ensure that the traditional system continues for an indefinite length of time. None of these modalities, however, provides a satisfactory explanation of the phenomenon that causally links yesterday with today and today with tomorrow. We wander about on the basis of assumptions that look reasonably straightforward but which fail, nonetheless, to answer the question whether the ingredients of ground reality do or do not influence the ethnic structure. ,

The general body comprising the social system may not be altogether keen to suggest an easy way out. The outcome can still be full of forebodings of diverse kinds. To draw up a credible picture of a stationary equilibrium after negotiating the shoals of determinants and determining variables could pose challenges of an extremely tall order. Some of the old equations would conceivably deserve to be thrown out of the window, and a number of fresh preambles persuaded to assert their presence. Who knows, through a process of trial and error, an arrangement may be reached which knocks down the erstwhile irreconcilability between a group of determining variables and a seemingly tenuous bunch of hypotheses.

It is a difficult, but not altogether intractable, sum we are asked to put together. The basic data have changed spectacularly in the course of the past decade or thereabouts. Were we to focus on our neighbourhood, it is not merely a question of internal consistencies between the pattern of entries to, and exits from, the Indian economy that have taken, and are taking, place. The harsher aspect of the arrangements is the insertion of complicated new *dhobi*-marks reflecting the stirrings of the new generation in society. Class factors are going to intervene here in a major way. A section of the hard core of the nation's middle class has been bowled over by transactions unleashed by the website and the internet. Ideology has ceased to be a part of the overall picture. The battlefield suggests an ambience where new and old aspirations with their loyalties bound to new and old ideologies come to clash with one another. A further consideration is the role to be assigned to external influences. In the old grammar, the players representing external parties were not given any recognition at all; that was a gross deficiency of the model which cries out for correction. A few other assumptions also crowd in here. The information now available on the global scale should be within the easy grasp of ordinary citizens as well, for what else does freedom of information signify? An obstinate group of individuals are bound to saunter about who will refuse to be taken for granted. The point can be easily illustrated. How the Reserve Bank of India's latest directives are, for example, likely to affect the liquidity position of domestic banks vis-à-vis that of those that have slipped under the control of foreign parties, will constitute a part of the set of questions that must have a readymade, near-glib answer, and yet there will be an elliptical recognition of the fact that the matter could hardly end there. The dialectical circumstances of an India with a huge base of natural resources, an enormous reservoir of manpower and a strong upcoming consumer goods market, are, on the face of it, not immediately reconcilable with the macroeconomics of a free market capitalism which has failed to solve the problem of a stockpile of unwanted goods at one end, and millions of unemployed workers at the other, in country after country.

Conventional solutions have not met with success. The reliance is, accordingly, on hit-or-miss measures. Maybe, those who depend on the economics of the free market characterized by untrammelled interaction with foreign goods, services and investible capital, it is indeed possible, have undying faith in the majesty of their model; they will experiment with it until the cows come home. It is not going to be a cakewalk victory; it is altogether possible that enormous sufferings will be experienced by millions and millions of our countrymen thrown out of work in agriculture and small-scale industries and other economic activities, where, till recently, the public sector had dominated. A pleasing welcome light is unlikely to wait at the end of the tunnel, and satisfactory trade-offs worked out between the quantum of suffering borne today and the quantum of additional sacrifice called for tomorrow because of the imperatives of national policies.

What is daunting, though, is the consequence of the possible intrusion of other equally formidable data. The system has admittedly too many soft spots which enable it to get assimilated, with extraordinary rapidity, to the easygoing global framework. Resistance to external forces is initially poor, and the next few years are likely to result in enormous difficulties experienced by the domestic population because of their exposure to exogenous forces. Few social anthropologists will venture to quantify the short-run sufferings, on the one hand, and the compensating gains the majority of the nation are expected to register in the course of a reasonable span of time, on the other. The losses, it is legitimate to expect, are likely to far outweigh the gains for the nation – and the reverse could be true for foreigners. The tussle between our today and the today of foreigners, and our tomorrow and their tomorrow, will therefore not terminate without incident. The prospect before us is exposure to a cheerless rotation of seasons which are rarely, if at all, blessed by the trappings of peace and prosperity. Even worse, there is every promise of the dawn of a milieu which is nasty as well as brutish.

We make our history, we also unmake it by pretending that obsession with vacuous yo-yos is indistinguishable from serious historical discourse. Two occurrences during the past fortnight would soon tend to lose their significance. Benoy Chowdhury, the taciturn functionary who was at the forefront of the struggles led by the Bengal peasantry from the late 1920s, shuffled his mortal coils. He died in a disappointed, confused frame of mind. The website crowd has shown little interest in phenomena such as land reforms and the redistribution of land, particularly at the upper end of rural incomes and assets. Himself a most mild-mannered person, the nonagenarian Chowdhury remained unflinching in his loyalty to the cause of Left radicalism. He died in a disturbed state of mind; will the strides the globalizers were registering wipe off the gains of the various class wars, stretching countries and continents, throughout the twentieth century? These were seemingly bleak days; Chowdhury was unable to connect up his and his comrades' endeavours in the Indian countryside with Ken Livingstone's defiant radical socialism. A moral debacle had characterized the daily perambulations of the once-great British Labour Party. It was the post-Maggie Thatcher era in full blast. Some machine politicians occupying strategic locations in the Labour Party took the easy way out; TINA was TINA, to tackle Thatcherism embrace Thatcherism. In fact you have to, they arrived at the conclusion, outdo Thatcherism. The formula would appear to have worked. A supposedly resurgent Labour Party did not bat an eye, it donned the mantle of the free market and approved the sale of public undertakings such as the mines and the railways, at throwaway prices. The Tony Benns and the Eric Scanlons went down fighting. Few, however, bothered about them; beliefs and ideology did not count any more, so what, are not the Labourites back in power in Britain?

A handful of protesters, amongst them Ken Livingstone, leader of the London Metro rail workers, stuck it out. London's working class, consisting predominantly of immigrant labour, mobilized its entire strength to get Livingstone elected, by an overwhelming majority, the Mayor of London. Seattle was only the beginning, now the class war across the nations has been marked by another triumph, the London Bridge has fallen down. Ken Livingstone, hail fellow well met, has sabotaged capitalism from within.

Benoy Chowdhury was already terminally ill when Livingstone hatched his open conspiracy of the dispossessed and the underdogs cutting across the colour bar. Somebody should have been around to cheer up Chowdhury: adieu comrade, there will be temporary difficulties, but the message of the Communist Manifesto is bound to endure, for, look what they have done to Thatcher's backyard.

The world's poor must take heart, conspirators are at work on their behalf too.

Uncles of brilliant nephews

24–30 June 2000

Versions of the story are widespread. That colourful personality, A.K. Fazlul Haq, had a busy time on assumption of office as chief minister of Bengal in the mid-1930s following the introduction of provincial autonomy in the country via the promulgation of the Government of India Act. He had a generous cluster of nephews who were immediately rewarded with attractive government jobs here and there. Remonstrations took place, but convictions that are held firm are not easily dislodged. The nephews got absorbed in cushy official positions in no time.

Going by the evidence, the country's current Finance Minister is a firm adherent of the subcontinent's dominant ethos: 'What can I do if all my nephews happen to be brilliant?' The Finance Minister has not concentrated attention on plying nephews with rewards. But daughters-in-law enjoying tax-exempt status for capital gains have engaged his full attention. The Minister has shown the utmost consideration for such daughters-in-law. Those who accuse daughters-in-law of shady deals in tax-exempt Mauritius – the purpose is to evade payment on capital gains – should be treated with due contempt, these people are a slur on freewheeling democracy. The Finance Minister has been outspoken, as outspoken as he could be: those running down his daughter-in-law and her friends in similarly placed positions, the Finance Minister does not have the least doubt, belong to an anti-national and anti-patriotic breed. The initiative youngsters of the present generation are displaying in the share markets and other similar financial centres is paving the way for fresh capital gains which are enriching, apart from foreign speculators, groups of comfortably placed middle-class households in the country as well. These are exciting times, and the pyrotechnics the sons and daughters and sons-in-law and daughters-in-law of these households are engaging in, are instrumental for windfall earnings of a considerable order for these families. These earnings are adding to the income and assets of politically important persons at different societal levels. There is little impact on direct foreign investment, though.

Let us strain to be what is described as level-headed. Why should you and I be unnecessarily nit-picking if the individual registering a spectacular advance in capital gains in the course of a brief weekend happens to be a daughter-in-law or son-in-law of the Finance Minister; Would it have made any difference in case she or he happened to be a daughter-in-law or son-in-law of another eminent personality? In the kind of society we have built for ourselves over the post-independence decades, the structure of income and assets distribution being what it is, capital gains, like other advantages, are mostly appropriated by the select tribe of sons and daughters and sons-in-law and daughters-in-law of those inhabiting the top of the society. In case we are not prepared to call into question the overall merits and demerits of the system, there is little virtue in latching on this or that daughter or daughter-in-law or son or son-in-law. The younger members of the wealthy households, fresh from finishing schools set up for their edification, are not easily rattled. Why should therefore the town cynic interrupt the ongoing process of money and more money accruing to him or her through pilferage, pure and simple, and income distribution further tilting the scales in favour of the right – that is to say, wrong – categories?

But another issue of substance, it will be insisted upon, still deserves to be considered at some length. You and I may get around the legal snafus, a clever solicitor can dig into the law books and prepare an impressive brief that will extricate you and me from the excruciating spell of grand morality play. What sort of society have we landed ourselves in, where ethics is dead and the dividing line between ethics and the lack of it is blurred out once and for all? The new grammar imposed on us has a single focus: we are, we live, because we love ourselves.

It is a daunting theme, the shadow will persist to fall between hypocrisy and adoration. The passing of a political leader such as Benoy Chowdhury will, on occasion, provide a mild reminder of the lack of integrity which has vitiated the towns and villages. We prevaricate, therefore we are: Chowdhury knew what he was talking about, he was conversant of the rot that has taken place in the nooks and corners of society. Those who once dreamt of a global revolution and the international brotherhood of the working class are befuddled by the latest developments. The ideologues have detached themselves, their place has been misappropriated by the mafia types. You and I soon learn that it is an integrated politico-economic arrangement. Ideology and idealism have been squeezed out of the system, but the so-called ground reality nonetheless asserts itself each season of the year.

No wonder, colossal mistakes and appalling blunders crowd the calendar. To pick a common enough illustration: direct foreign investment is refusing to rise at a rate which will satisfy the hopes and aspirations of the ruling classes. These ladies and gentlemen, however, soon travel to the edge of a fearsome realization: between the social sophisticates and the social mafia, there is hardly any difference that could enlighten us, at the end of the day, on the sociology of growth. The existing framework of society can survive only if the mafia contingents, for whatever reason, pump funds into it. But there should be no illusion; in case they do not, it will be darkness at noon.

Against this background, even foreign policy will tend to get decentralized. The two Jaswants, Sinha and Singh, will continue to toe the straight, uncomplicated pro-American line. Should the consequence turn out to be not of the expected genre, the President of the republic who, once upon a time, was a full-scale official diplomat, will be pressed into service. After all, why should he not earn his living? The dilemma, nonetheless, does not quite dissolve on its own. The forces presiding over the free market mechanism refuse to be easily cowed down.

This is the other reality we have to gradually learn to accept. You and I are not at all sure whether there is a pattern to it. Maybe there is, maybe there is not. In the heady months ahead of us, who knows, the defence lobby may choose to sound brisk and try to gobble up as much of the budgetary outlay as the media – and the mafia, they have an impressively big constituency – will approve of. We are therefore back to the crucial basic issue. Without development there will be only chaos, the fullest advantage of which will be taken by those who dislike the republic. But the environment has meanwhile deteriorated so much that no amount of increasing developmental allocations will help the nation's prospects even marginally.

Without development, the FDI index will refuse to move up. But the sensex graph will remain buoyant. There is an interdependence between the two: when one moves up, the other climbs down. Even this double-deal phenomenon cannot persuade us to move away from the objective reality of the acknowledgement of a lack of a moral climate influencing choices and decisions. Tomorrow is supposed to be another day, but who knows, are you at all sure?

The notion of inalienability

19–25 August 2000

That catechism, the unity and integrity of the nation, is wearing thin. Leave out Jammu and Kashmir, even the 'pacified' Punjab has a strong contingent of leaders who are once more referring to the Anandpur Sahib resolution. The smaller north-eastern states have always been a no-man's land, and Assam has now joined their ranks: trains blown into smithereens, ambushes, gory deaths of civilians and military personnel, are the order of the day. The Bihar countryside is an open battlefield, and Ranvir Sena goons are fighting it out with Marxist Coordination Committee cadres. Uttar Pradesh, India's most thickly populated state, hardly belongs to anybody; the 60-odd districts have been sliced up by different political groupings among themselves; even the creation of Uttaranchal will not change the quality of chaos. Because of the crude militancy of one of the partners in the National Democratic Alliance, West Bengal too promises to be unstable from now on. The nature of law and order in the two important southern states, Tamil Nadu and Karnataka, is exemplified by the continuous marauding indulged in by the sandalwood bandit Veerappan. The state governments, with occasional assistance from the centre, have tried over the past ten years to apprehend him. They have failed miserably. His latest exploit, that of kidnapping the film hero, Rajkumar, has added a grisly chapter to the tale. In Maharashtra, Bal Thackeray has once again proved to be a law unto himself, and the Shiv Sena seems to be unstoppable. That apart, large parts of the deep interior of these states and Andhra Pradesh, Orissa and Madhya Pradesh are dominated by stray Naxalite groups. Symptoms in several parts of the country betray the tension roused by linguistic, ethnic and communal passions.

It is therefore a far cry from the idyllic model of a united India. After 50 years of experimentation with a version of adult suffrage-based parliamentary democracy, we are neither united nor convincingly democratic. The persistence of illiteracy, some would say, is the main factor underlying both slow economic growth and spreading disunity. Does that tell the entire story? By taking this easy way out, we are only providing the apology of an explanation. It is altogether pointless to run away from the basic fact that the political unity which the British enforced through fiat has not stood the test of democracy as practised in the country over the past half a century. Politeness here is of little avail. From time immemorial, it has been possible to identify an Indian tradition, an Indian culture, an Indian sculpture and architecture, an Indian music and dance, even though divided into a number of strands. But history bears no witness, before the arrival of the British, of a unified Indian polity. Even the Mughal empire had only a perfunctory presence in the Deccan, and the distant east beyond Bengal was a strange foreign territory.

Our playing around with the notion of democratic sanction over the past 50 years, we should have the honesty to admit, has been a dismal failure. The Union of India is more disunited and anarchic today than it ever was since 1947. Liberalization and globalization have contributed their mite towards aggravating the problem in recent years. Thanks to denationalization and disinvestment, factories and other enterprises in the public sector have closed down one after another, creating a huge load of the unemployed. The directive to the banks and public financial institutions to deny credit and loans to corporate units in financial difficulty has compounded the hardship of the working class and large sections of the middle class. The *carte blanche* accorded to monopolies and big industrial houses to take charge of the market and the ultra-liberal import policy have struck the severest blow to small-scale and cottage industries, adding further to the burden of unemployment. The welcome mat laid out to multinational corporations has generally played havoc with the organized industrial sector because of shrivelling public investment as an integral part of liberalization policy. Capital formation has dried up in agriculture; an unusual succession of excellent rains has nonetheless shored up agriculture. But the intense pressure to raise farm prices to international levels has added to the woe of the lower peasantry and the urban poor.

The situation ought to be ripe for large-scale insurrection, which the regime in New Delhi is trying to avoid by indiscriminate deficit financing. This device adds substantially to the profit margin of employers, but devastates, through rampant inflation, the poorer classes and fixed income-earning middle groups. In the wash, organized insurrection is perhaps staved off for some while, but semi-anarchic conditions become the feature of a major part of the country.

It is important to mention yet another development. Liberalization has spawned a new upper class who are lush with funds. This surfeit of money, however, makes them even more avaricious. They want to reach overnight, by hook or by crook, the American standard of living. They can only do so, provided they come to more and more of earnings and wealth. This is possible only if they take the low road of unscrupulousness and immoral means. Since these people are also, because of their fabulous prosperity, the leaders of society, the immorality rapidly spreads here, there and everywhere, affecting the entire fabric of society. We are therefore not only a disunited nation, but a nation of crooks as well.

To be candid, the canker has entered the deepest roots, and there is little likelihood of a reversal of the trend without a total catharsis. The past cannot be reconstructed, the human mind is however unable to shut out idle speculation. Who knows, if, right from the beginning, India was divided into twenty near-autonomous states and joined together by an informal type of confederation, history could have taken a different course; or, if one dares to speculate even more boldly, when the British departed, had we carved ourselves into ten or fifteen independent states, there could have been more mutual harmony and faster economic progress for all.

The retort will come sharp and fast: in such an eventuality, the sovereign states constituting the subcontinent of India would have been the hub of activities of espionage agents and foreign conspirators. Would you say the same thing, though, about the European Community which still consists of close to twenty independent countries?

Finally, it would be no harshness to return to the issue of Jammu and Kashmir; the inheritance of this tragedy that has devolved upon us is entirely the doing of our past administrators. Misjudgment of diverse sorts was committed during the debates in the United Nations General Assembly and Security Council; the folly was repeated in 1953 when Sheikh Abdullah was put behind bars and a crook installed in his place. There was an echo of the blunder in 1984 when some Johnnys-come-lately, replete with the pretence of wisdom, got rid of Farooq Abdullah, the son. Farooq's loyalty was retrievable, but not that of the passion-laden youth of the valley. Since then it has been, in all senses of the expression, a truly lost war.

The government in New Delhi has continued to be the victim of its own illusions. About a month ago, it got into the notion that normalcy was a proximate thing in Kashmir. The indiscretion of encouraging pilgrims to march all the way to the Amarnath shrine, without arranging for even the minimal security, is the latest instance of the government's faith in its own baseless assumptions. The blood of the massacre has sullied as much the hands of the Pakistanis and 'militants' as those of the decision-makers in New Delhi. In the circumstances, the Prime Minister's near-open appeal to all groups of 'militants' to join the peace parleys comes much too late in the day. The invitation should have gone out at least twenty years ago. Now there is unlikely to be any solution to the impasse without the Government of India's admitting the essential reality that Kashmir is not, repeat, not, an 'inalienable part' of the Indian union. Till as long as that admission does not make it to the top of the agenda, the story of woes, rest assured, will remain unchanged.

The old soldier retires

18–24 November 2000

Much more than the fact of Jyoti Basu's retirement, it is the fall-out of the retirement which grips attention. The following passage is, in translation, from the editorial note of the leading Bengali newspaper which, according to the Audit Bureau of Circulation, has the largest sales in the country:

> The Leftists have been in command of the administration in the state under Jyoti Basu's stewardship for nearly two-and-a-half decades. Has that done much good to the state? Should a single party or a combination of like-minded parties be in power uninterruptedly for such a long stretch of time, any change in administration or policy is virtually impossible. Since the views of those in charge of government remain unchanged, it becomes impossible to initiate innovations and there is no scope for administrative experiments. Everything chimes in the same monotonous strain. Barrenness affects society as well as its culture too, reflecting the barrenness of politics. True, apart from West Bengal, no other state in this country has been the victim of such a misfortune in the past decades. Ruling figures in these other states have changed frequently as per the verdict of the people. Even so, the danger is inherent, in India's system of parliamentary democracy, of the prospect of continuous, uninterrupted reign in a state by a single party. The other states were saved merely because no party has been able to receive, in successive elections, the imprimatur of approval of the voters. In the circumstances, it is a moot question whether the Constitution should permit a party to rule a state almost eternally because it has continued to be blessed by the mandate of the people. To avoid the entrenchment of vested interests and also to ensure change from time to time in administrative policy and practice, it seems reasonable to introduce a specific constitutional provision. Should such an amendment be part of the Constitution, it would, in great measure, reduce the scope of political authoritarianism under the guise of democracy. And in that event it would no longer be possible for a man like Jyoti Basu to exercise unbridled con-trol over the administration, nor will there be any need for such a leader.

This is as faithful a rendering of the final paragraph of the editorial article as is possible. The purport of the article could not be more obvious. The Indian Constitution, it says altogether plainly, should move away from adherence to the principle of parliamentary democracy. A party which receives the mandate of the people should rule only for a limited period, not indefinitely. If it enjoys the confidence of the people even after the completion of two or three terms, it should nonetheless be denied access to power; this could be done by amending the Constitution.

What does the comment imply? The people, it says, have no right to respose their trust in a particular party even if they feel that reposing such trust is called for because it has done good for them and promises to contribute further to their welfare. It is therefore desirable to introduce a constitutional amendment which would deny the right of the people to be administered by a party which they prefer. The editorial writer might, of course, quote the instance of the great United States where a constitutional amendment prevents a president to be re-elected beyond two successive terms. This amendment does not however preclude a particular party from winning the elections for three or more, or, for that matter, an infinite number of times, and thereby indefinitely hold the reins of administration. The newspaper with the largest circulation in India goes much, much further. It would like the constitutional amendment it has suggested to prohibit a party from enjoying power beyond a fixed number of terms. Amateur political scientists are around who have proposed that, variety being the spice of life, a spell of socialism spanning over fifty years should be supplanted by a compulsory phase of capitalism, irrespective of whether the people of the country concerned like the arrangement or not. The leading Bengali newspaper wants to go a bit further forward along those lines.

What is remarkable is that such wise thoughts encompassing political philosophy have arisen in the minds of those responsible for the editorial article only in the context of the CPI(M) and the Left Front in West Bengal. The longevity of the Left Front in the administration of West Bengal till now is matched by that of the Indian National Congress at the centre. The Congress Party won the Lok Sabha elections successively in 1952, 1957, 1962, 1967 and 1971, that is to say, it too enjoyed five consecutive terms at the centre much in the manner of the Left Front in West Bengal. The constitutional change recommended by the newspaper, nonetheless, is intended to concern only the states. Perhaps the newspaper is unduly modest; it would, in its heart of hearts, wish the change to be introduced only in the instance of West Bengal; the other states, in the language of Matthew Arnold, are free.

Is it frustration which is being betrayed by this trail-blazing editorial comment? The CPI(M) and the Left Front, there is no question, have committed many mistakes in the course of the near-twenty-four years of their rule in the state. The government they have presided over has often been lethargic and sometimes downright incompetent. Some corruption has also crept in within the portals of administration. Because of a decision taken in 1978 to convert the cadre-based party into a mass party, the CPI(M) has increased its membership in the state by more than ten times over this period. The scrutiny and caution exercised in the past before admitting members into the fold of the party are no longer a custom; this has created its own problem. Still, a few home truths deserve to be expressed without ambiguity. The corruption that has seeped in the West Bengal administration during the Left Front regime is not a patch on what prevailed in the state during the preceding thirty years of Congress rule, or what prevails at present at the centre or in other states. In addition, irrespective of the many imperfections and blemishes in administration, a clear majority of the people in the state have continued to repose their faith in the CPI(M) and the Left Front. The statement just made does not, of course, hold for Calcutta for several reas-ons. To list a few: (a) a majority of the Calcutta population consists of migrants from other states; their mind-set follows a different route from that of the average Bengali; (b) it is in any season difficult to keep satisfied the urban electorate, more so since the priority of the Left Front is to look after the interests of the people in the countryside who have been exploited to a much greater extent in the past; (c) the Calcutta press, which exercises a predominant influence over the urban population, is under the firm control of the upper bourgeoisie, to whom the Left Front is unmitigated evil; and (d) a large section of the senior bureaucracy, including the police force, would like to see the end of the CPI(M) and the Left Front since they have been, in their view, the worst sufferers on account of the Front policy to democratize and decentralize the state administration.

These latter elements were, for the past few months, nourishing high hopes that the lady holding the railway portfolio at the centre, who flaunts the right mixture of authoritarian behaviour and vacuous populism, would be able to wrest power from the CPI(M) at the next assembly elections scheduled for 2001. These hopes were further sparked by the marked consolidation of the lumpenproletariat on the side of the lady. There is here an eerie resemblance of the description of this species, in the context of mid-eighteenth-century France, by Marx:

> the lumpenproletariat, which in all big towns forms a mass sharply differenti-ated from the industrial proletariat, a recruiting ground for thieves and crimi-nals of all kinds, living on the crumbs of society, people without a definite trade, vagabonds, *gene sans feu et sans avieu* [folk without hearth and home] varying according to the degree of civilization of the nation to which they bel-ong, but never renouncing their *lazzaroni* [declassed, lumpenproletariat] character. (Karl Marx, *The Class Struggles in France 1848–1850*)

The strong-arm methods the lady deployed, with considerable assist-ance, open and surreptitious, from the local police and the local administration, has boosted the sense of optimism of those devoutly praying for the collapse of the CPI(M). The lady herself is, it would seem, still not altogether confident about the outcome of the poll, which is why she has been vociferous in her demand for the imposition of Article 356 in West Bengal before the elections. The centre is in no position to satisfy her in this respect. In this situation, she is desperately looking for fresh issues. Her drama of resignation from the Cabinet in protest against the increase in the administered prices of petroleum products is in pursuance of the objective of not allowing the Left Front to claim exclusive credit for raising the banner of revolt against the union government's decision. There have been at least four other occasions in the past two years when the BJP-led administration had adjusted upwards prices of petroleum products. The lady did not make a squeak during those times. Her combative mood on the present occasion is, no doubt, provoked by the proximity of the state assembly elections.

The fact that she withdrew the letter of resignation without waiting for a positive response from the government in which she shares collective responsibility has already dimmed her public image. It is not certain whether, to mollify her even partially, the Prime Minister would agree to go through the motions of a symbolic lowering of the announced increases in the prices of petroleum products; both his own party and the other constituents of the National Democratic Alliance have expressed their dissent with various proposed formulae to accommodate her.

Demoralization has apparently set in amongst those who were looking forward to the lovely denouement of the downfall of the CPI(M). The realization has also dawned upon them that, despite his age and failing health, Jyoti Basu, freed from the rigours of daily administration, might turn out to be a formidable proposition as a campaigner in the poll battle. This frustration explains the purport of the editorial article: enough is enough, parliamentary democracy and the mandate of the people are all hogwash; if that mandate means uninterrupted power for the Lefties, we would rather prefer a constitutional amendment which would bar them from enjoyment of power even if they win in a free election; this may be the very negation of parliamentary democracy, and bordering on fascism and authoritarianism; so what, the people have to be saved from their own folly.

Some years ago, in order to prevent the CPI(M) and its associates from continuously winning elections in West Bengal, the suggestion was mooted to import not only poll personnel and supervisory police, but voters too, from other states on the eve of the poll. That proposal is no longer considered feasible. Hence the alternative proposal adumbrated in the editorial article: the mandate of the West Bengal electorate must not be honoured; it is time for arranging a constitutional amendment to that effect.

Calamities and classes

24 February 2001

Believe it or not, the consequences of natural calamities too have a specific class bias. In the case of floods, the low-lying areas are devoured by water. Since the poor have their abode in these low stretches, they are the worst victims of any general flooding. Never mind whether the water stays for only a couple of days or lingers for a full three to four weeks, the poor and the downtrodden are rendered even poorer and more downtrodden. Where the phenomenon happens to be famine and drought, again, the poor, who, in state-of-the-art terminology, have little or no command over purchasing power, die of malnutrition and hunger. Some of them, as happened in the ghastly Bengal famine of 1943, draw upon their last reserves of strength to trek from villages to towns and cities. But the hostility of the milieu remains unchanged. At most, as they lie stricken in the streets, lanes and bylanes, some kind-hearted individuals cart them to hospital, where their agony soon ends. The rich and the affluent, however, have an altogether different experience during famines. Not only will they be able to sustain themselves because of their superior purchasing power; should they belong to the heaven-born set of big farmers, traders and blackmarketeers, their income will soar, and soar in periods of overall scarcity of food and victuals. The adversity of the poor thereby adds a new dimension to the accumulation of wealth by the rich.

The fall-out of earthquakes, by and large, does not belong to a different genre; where awesome tremors shake the surface and sub-surface of the earth, the familiar result is calamity for the poor. They live in mud huts or ramshackle structures which are razed to the ground even when the measure on the Richter scale barely touches 4.5 or 5. On the other hand, since in fact the stone age, those with a greater share of society's resources are able to build their habitat on solider foundations. In ancient times, the basic ingredient was stone or such other equally sturdy building block; in the modern period, the affluent classes have crossed over to steel foundations, concrete layers and reinforced beams. In the habitually quake-prone regions, they have often preferred wooden frameworks which are less susceptible to damage by underground and overground tremors. In the appropriation of societal property, the richer sections have, in any case, a natural advantage over the poor. Those who have more can appropriate more; those who have more can also appropriate a greater share of wood and timber.

Whether it is famines or floods or earthquakes, the poor have therefore been till now overwhelming victims and sufferers; the affluent classes have been generally able to save themselves from the ravages of nature. If a class-wise distribution of the victims of a natural calamity were to be drawn, one dares to suggest, an eerie overlap would be noticed with the distribution of income and wealth among the different classes in society. Perhaps you would like to enter a caveat to this proposition. Perhaps you would claim that when Mount Vesuvius erupted in the first century AD, the fiery balls of lava consumed mostly the aristocracy and their property. The decline and fall of the Pompeii and Herculaneum civilization, it might indeed be asserted, coincided with the burial of the wealthy oligarchy, with their vagaries, excesses and all that, under heaps and heaps of volcanic mud and ash. But, then, is not the arrival at such a conclusion heavily influenced by the kind of historical tracts that have been written, with monotonous ardour, about earlier times, including the medieval age? To chronicle the annals of ordinary men and women, including the despicable, lowly-placed poor, became the vogue only from towards the end of the nineteenth century, following Frederick Engels' path-breaking work on the condition of the working class in England. We lament for the eclipse of Pompeii culture done in by the wrath of Vesuvius; in effect, we lament for the tragedy which, according to our perspective, engulfed princes, princesses and other noble beings. Of those who fled from Pompeii – or were unceremoniously entombed there – no historian has bothered to state what proportion constituted society's underdogs. The poor were no part of the agenda of the tradition-bound historians.

In the circumstances, it is not surprising that few factual documents exist which give details of the plight suffered by the multitude of the poor when a natural calamity took place in any epoch in any country. The poor became a whole, round number, so many thousands, or so many hundred thousands, or so many millions, who disappeared and were presumed to be dead when a natural calamity befell, or an epidemic like the Black Death struck. These devastations mostly targeted the poor, but, till about the end-point of the nineteenth century, it was the interface of the civilization which the rich flaunted that was the centre-piece of so-called human history.

The Gujarat earthquake, there is no question, has been a national calamity of a grim order. A number of small towns, such as Bhuj, Anjar and Rupar, have disappeared from the face of the earth. Politicians have started a war of words over the number of those who have been killed: it is a battle of thousands versus hundreds of thousands. The busybodies have found a new opportunity to enlarge the span of busybodiness. And criminals, always lurking round the corner, have not flinched to indulge in some pillage and plunder even as relief to the victims was chaotic, at least in the initial stage. Since the overwhelming majority of the victims were poor, relief was bound to be perfunctory. The country's Finance Minister has fallen back on the moral assurance which the earthquake has provided to propose a 2 per cent surcharge on income and company taxes. Voluntary bodies and non-governmental organizations, some genuine to the core and others ersatz – their ersatzness duly seasonally adjusted – have set to work. India, which comes to the realization of its being a nation only when a cricket series with Pakistan or some other enemy country eventuates, has now another chance to come together. In the US, at the time of the Nixon impeachment, when the nation was torn asunder, some pious ladies were known to have prayed to their Almighty: 'Please bring us together.' The Gujarat catastrophe is, on the face of it, doing for India what the Nixon scandal did to the Americans: a massive spirit of fellow-feeling, contrived or otherwise, is abroad, and the professed mission is to rebuild Gujarat, whatever that means. International aid is flowing in. These nasty people, the Pakistanis, have thrown in a monkey wrench; they too have despatched, in quick trot, relief material, including food, tents and medicines. The scoundrels also wanted to play some cricket matches; we have aborted that.

There is no need to go overboard, though. The magnitude of the calamity is, of course, worth taking cognizance of. But, this aspect apart, the Gujarat disaster is in nature no different from the usual run of famines, floods and quakes, where the poor are the silent, predominant victims. That is, nonetheless, not the entire story.

What distinguishes the Gujarat cataclysm is the fact that this case has been one earthquake where, along with the poor, affluent sections of society have also been substantial sufferers. Globalization and liberalization have come home to roost. The rich, who were agog at the marvels of western architecture, have had a rude awakening. Old structures have generally stood firm, or escaped with minor damage. But, in the city of Ahmedabad, close to 100 high-rise residential and office buildings have collapsed like a pack of cards. The new concept of gracious living is centred on penthouses located in glistening multistoreyed structures. The penthouse culture has an upper stratosphere thrust: the higher you reach out to the sky, the higher is your social status. Particularly in the course of the past decade, there has been a scampering rush to cross over from traditional feudal- or colonial-style houses and bungalows to magnificent high-rise luxuries. The great quake has, all of sudden, brought the rich down to earth – at least some of them.

Perhaps for the first time in the annals of mankind, an earthquake has shaken the confidence of oligarchs. Even those buildings which have not collapsed in a heap are still considered suspect, and must receive a rigorous appraisal by designated official architects and engineers before they could be again entered. Several luxury abodes, despite not being affected by the merciless cruelty of nature, have for the present to be evacuated for this reason. Such moves cost money. The media have joined the guessing game, whether those who have perished are to be counted in thousands or hundreds of thousands. But all such calculations are reduced to endeavours to reach a statistical integer. The number of deaths has become an exercise in commodity fetishism. The human beings, mostly belonging to the poor and lower middle classes, do not hold the interest. The survivors amongst the underprivileged, too, are not of much concern to anybody. They are suffering, but it is their ordained fate to suffer. Are they not poor? Relief reaching them may be niggardly, but this fact does not make a good enough story after a while.

The sympathy of the media has shifted to human interest stories around the rich. Few amongst the reasonably well-off have died, except for some middle-level executives and shopkeepers. It is still the plight of the comfortably placed which has captured the imagination of the media. Who knows, the consternation among the politicians is conceivably also because some of their near and dear ones have been affected, severely or mildly, by the calamity. Which is perhaps also the reason for the frequency of Cabinet meetings in New Delhi and the rush of ministers hither and thither. After all, Ahmedabad, including such of its posh areas as Navrangpura, was being advertised to the world as a prime example of the miracle globalization could do even to our ancient country. A suspicion has now sneaked in. International aid, at least on paper, is flowing in as much to cater to the poor as for refurbishing India's image. Those who bet on India are however aghast. Why should your promoters, engineers and architects be so slipshod in their work that dazzling new structures, aglow with the message of globalization, have crashed, nine out of ten, one after another, while the traditional buildings have remained more or less secure? This is a slur on free enterprise élan. There is, in the proceedings, evidently more than meets the eye. Charity and philanthropy are unexceptionable attitudes. Two and two nevertheless tend to add up to fourteen for a more basic reason. The rush of international aid, both official and unofficial, is likely to accelerate because of the deviation from asymmetry in the identity of quake victims. No nation's rich must suffer on account of a national calamity: in case they do, the American Congress would bestir itself.

It would be interesting if an earnest research student, who can gather money from some absent-minded source or has means of his or her own, does a painstaking analysis, in some twelve months' time, of the pattern of destination-wise breakdown of post-quake relief in Gujarat. It should cause no astonishment if as much as 95 per cent of the victims, dead and alive, happen to be from the downtrodden sections, while the lion's share of the funds and other *material* made available to Gujarat from external agencies is sucked in by the rich. For the first time in history, the rich can claim to be not insignificant victims of a natural calamity; they should be well catered to. Those masterminding the class-divided society know how to render such catering in the most effective manner.

Nonetheless, the Gujarat quake, shall we say, has good points. Taxes can now be jacked up with impunity, something which will gladden the heart of the phantom known as the Washington Consensus.

Crooks' opera

14–20 April 2001

Decades ago, a Hollywood film made waves. The plot revolved around the theme of how a philandering husband could still save his marriage. The technique he pursued was simple and straightforward: even if he was caught *in flagrante delicto,* the husband would pretend that the wife was experiencing a hallucination; why, there was no second woman in the room, it was all in the wife's imagination. When this ploy was repeated a number of times and, on each occasion, the husband was nonchalant even when caught mooching one young woman after another, the wife finally had a nervous breakdown and increased the frequency of her visits to the family shrink.

The goings-on in New Delhi resembled closely, at least initially, that Hollywood comedy version. The veracity of the videotapes could not be denied. The trap was admittedly laid in the name of a fictitious company. That the company was bogus did not, however, obliterate the reality that ruling politicians, ministers and civil servants are open to tempting offers from middlemen, they accept bribes and candidly discuss the price for swinging a particular contract. Politicians caught with their pants down tried to brazen it out in the beginning, much in the manner of the philandering husband in that film: who, what, when, you must be dreaming, our hands are absolutely clean. But the tension was explosive, and they soon capitulated. The spin-off of a spate of resignations is bound to be far-reaching. If the genuineness of the evidence furnished by the videotapes is to be accepted in some instances, it must be accepted in the other instances as well. To illustrate, if a middleman lets out the secret that some ministers, when bribed, will deliver 100 per cent, while a few other ministers will deliver only to the extent of 70 per cent, the credibility of such a claim will be difficult to contest. In other words, one minister, while accepting a cut of 10 per cent, will arrange to award a contract worth 100 crore of rupees, another one will award a *barat* of only up to Rs 70 crore; the amount of the bribe will remain the same, though, in the two instances. Bribe-taking on the part of ministers is to be accepted as a universal datum, even when some fulfil 100 per cent of the commitment while others do so only to the extent of 70 per cent. But, then, things have come to such a pass that a minister who satisfies only up to 70 per cent will have the audacity to suggest that he or she is actually 100 per cent non-corrupt and a paragon of virtue, in stark contrast to that wretch of a minister who delivers up to 100 per cent and therefore is corrupt through and through.

Events are unfolding at an extremely fast pace. It is at this moment difficult to guess how India's ruling superstructure is going to crumble, or whether it is going to crumble at all. For there is hardly any scope for illusion. Irrespective of the particular corner of the political spectrum you decide to depend upon, the story is the same, barring perhaps in the case of the Left. Leaders, for example, conveniently switch their loyalty from the Congress to the Bharatiya Janata Party, or vice versa. When they cross parties, they nonetheless take their baggage of venality along. Even if the present regime goes to the wall, the one which will substitute it is unlikely to prove any better. A hapless president could admonish a shell-shocked prime minister into getting rid of his defence minister. The president might even assemble a new government with a new prime minister. If the new government too soon begins to totter, he might reluctantly order a fresh election. But the chances are overwhelming that, while the new set-up would consist of recycled names, it will not represent a different genre. Crooks of the same flock, of course, stay together, but crooks have by now also learnt the trick of spreading themselves evenly over the polity and the economy.

The *Vedas* and the *Upanishads* are high-sounding tomes, full of apparently pure thoughts, but these are all a façade of the mind-set the Indian ruling class has loved either to flaunt or to conceal through the centuries. Never mind the evocation of the *mantrams*, the hard core of the Indian psyche is made up of the sternest *bania* sentiment. It concentrates on short-term gains from commerce, the fruits of long-range productive investment are not its cup of tea. To be fair, this state of mind is not specific to the Indian *bania* alone. The American middle-man who has no compunction to run over his grandmother if that will swing a luscious contract for him, does not belong to a different hegemony. It is possible to generalize even further. The free market principle is itself the quintessential expression of the *bania* philosophy. Forget the ultimate interests of the nation or of your own self, concentrate on how you can maximize your gains in the immediate period, by hook or by crook. The ambience of liberalization is actually tailormade for transactions after the heart of the *bania*; sell the wife, sell the mother, sell the daughter, sell the country, provided such activities will yield a windfall to you. Moral scruples be hanged; if the offer of a bribe will gain you a bonanza, why not offer the bribe; if the acceptance of a commission or cut money will allow you to add substantially to your assets, why should you restrain yourself? In any case, there is little risk involved, everyone around is either a bribe-giver or a bribe-taker.

The experience of the past decade has been shattering. Governments change, but the allure for so-called economic reforms does not. Over the years, the country's vital interests have been either compromised or sold to thieves and foreigners. It is no accident that, in some instances, thieves also happen to be foreigners. The sociology of globalization has, however, a fairly ancient literature. The thieves who grabbed a foreign territory and its resources got to be known as imperialists-cum-colonizers. Sometimes these foreigners could capture a country wholesale, by bribing a king or a general or a chieftain. For enlightenment, please read *The Dogs of War* by the thriller writer, Frederick Forsyth.

The writers of Greek tragedies had innovated the dramatic stratagem of catharsis. Turmoils, convulsions, frauds, betrayals, murders, suicides, fornications, adulteries, incests; at the end of it all, catharsis assumes the centrestage of the amphitheatre, a great purge of emotions becomes the instrumentality of denouement, which is what a Greek tragedy is about. The present Indian system perhaps badly needs such a great catharsis. Should it come through a general uprising all over the country across the different zones and regions? But that is an impossibility. For the country is featured by uneven development, or, if you will, uneven levels of stagnation. Some segments of the nation are straining at the leash to be an integral part and parcel of the third millennium. Several other sections exist in pre-puranic times. A revolution which will transform the Indian landscape in its totality is inconceivable. Ersatz democracy, with its appendage of adult suffrage, has led to a further complication. Those subsisting on a frame of mind which oozes pre-puranic ethos through its pores are targets of dollops of prejudice, superstition and other otiose notions. They hold in awe and esteem a large array of gods and goddesses, who are kept company by mythological figures, always larger than life. Wade through the folklore about these almighty characters. There are few sins – why beat about the bush, crimes – which they have not committed, and committed with a flourish: they have betrayed friends; they have betrayed brothers, sisters and cousins; they have cast out most virtuous and loyal wives; they have told lies, both black and white; they have stolen other people's wives without batting an eye; some of them have sucked, with immense zest, the blood of enemies they have killed in battle; they have practised polygamy and polyandry as if these were nature's ordinary events. And yet, these gods and goddesses and heroes and heroines have been, through the ages, heralded by society as role models. Overwhelming sections of the Indian population bow down to these gods and demi-gods and goddesses and demi-goddesses. Those nurturing ambition to gain hold of the ruling superstructure have to garner the votes of this vast majority through some means or other. In case they follow the mode set by these mythological figures, they will, it is reasoned, be acceptable to the multitude. If they want to attract the electoral support of the populace, they must do as the gods and goddesses and the demi-gods and demi-goddesses do. They must not flinch from donning the part of bribe-givers and bribe-takers: the *Manu Samhita*, after all, makes a not disapproving mention of *utkoch*.

The uprising at the base of society is therefore of little use if there is no holocaust taking place in the heart. If a sage person wants to save India from doom and latches on the proposition that a social transformation will do the trick, he should have another thought coming. A change of personnel in government is of little avail. A change of parties constituting the government will be equally infructuous. A change in the class composition of those who constitute

220

the ruling superstructure will also, by itself, be of little account unless there is a fundamental shift in the minds of men at relevant levels.

Do we then wait for the Waiting-for-Godot principle? Rather, should not the wait be for a milieu where Godot disbelievers have come to the fore?

A decimating thought

18 August 2001

Alfred Hitchcock had a Catholic upbringing. He had a task cut out for him to reconcile the mumbo-jumbo of the Holy Ghost and others with his innate cynicism. He solved the problem in his own manner. After all, what is God? Once the obfuscations are got rid of, God is a master manipulator of suspense and is in total control of all aspects of production; men, beasts and nature have to abide by Him. The Almighty engineers twists and turns in man's destiny; Hitchcock professed to do the same with his murderous plots. Given the surfeit of pride and self-confidence he possessed, he decided to play the role of God, no less, in relation to the characters he created. Suspense is God's writ. Suspense is also what Hitchcock considered to be his religion. Therefore he is God.

An outrageously audacious syllogism, but we have little choice. Hitchcock intimidates us and we cannot but put up with his pretensions. This frightful act of bullying defines his art. Should we say it is a load of bunk, we are at liberty not to watch the Hitchcock films. None of us are prepared to take this decision though: please, no suspension of suspense. Our pleasure is leavened by the bitter dose of unpleasantness Hitchcock serves us with.

Were India, *circa* 2001, putty-clay in his hand, Hitchcock would have been vastly disappointed. India, he would be bound to conclude, hardly provides any material to play God with. The country promises no suspense. It is through and through a downhill slide, with no twists and turns. Which is to say, all our yesterdays have lighted fools the way to dusty death. The destiny that awaits the nation can be read in advance, like the palm of one's hand. Nirad C. Chaudhuri was a show-off; his description of the continent of Circe was a bit of an exaggeration. But, at the end of almost half a century since he wrote his tract, is not India's course predictable beyond a shadow of doubt? It is a burnt-out case. Or, if you prefer another simile, this humpty dumpty can never be put together again. Even if the gaze is confined to contemporary history, what emerges is an undulating narration of misadventures impeccably foretold: the Musharraf fiasco, the Unit Trust of India skulduggery, the Phoolan Devi killing next door to parliament house, the farce of prime ministerial resignation – these occurrences fall into a pattern, and the ersatz excitement after each event is stale fare with no whiff of suspense in its unfolding. The occurrences were, and are, inevitable in the given circumstances. India shall die and nobody is in a position to salvage it, not even God, not even Hitchcock. In the context of this country, Hitchcock's occupation is spent.

Is it at all necessary to elaborate? The state is a social contract. At any particular moment, some individuals at the top of the hierarchy dictate the details of the contract. They also administer it. Those left out of their orbit of favour tend to go along. They go along out of either respect or fear. The Indian system does not command any respect any more from any quarter. The lack of respect is also the reason for the cessation of fear. Take Kashmir, for instance. Respect for the Indian republic, so-called, commenced to evaporate in the valley following Sheikh Abdullah's incarceration in 1953, and the choice of a common crook to replace him. Ups and downs have taken place since then, mostly downs. The Sheikh and his acolytes were temporarily reconciled to New Delhi in the 1970s; so did, somewhat uneasily, the people of Kashmir. The process of alienation that had set in was however without interruption. The final folly was perpetrated when Indira Gandhi decided to get rid of Farooq Abdullah. Farooq had little pride in the Kashmiri persona. His keenness was for the thrills and regalia that went with the adornment of an official position. It was therefore relatively easy to buy back his loyalty with the gift of the chief ministerial slot; he now also has a son sworn in as a minister in New Delhi's South Block. But that is about all. As far as the Kashmiri diaspora are concerned, they have neither fear nor respect left for the Indian state. Some amongst them might hanker after an independent republic of their own; some others, nursing a deep feeling of bitterness towards India, would not mind even a merger with Pakistan; the Indian nation-state is no longer their cup of tea. Those in command of the Indian state, and the majority of the Indian electorate, are unable to comprehend this reality. Such being the case, Kashmir would continue to suck India dry. Economic development could go to the dogs, but unlimited expenditure on military might and material would be persisted with in order to maintain our territorial hold on Kashmir. This attitude of mind would further weaken the polity and the economy, and, therefore, further diminish the left-over respect over there for India. Once respect disappears, fear too does. The killings would continue, but a stage would soon come when pogroms do not invoke any terror; they steel the determination of the people to resist impositions. Meanwhile, rest assured, our stylized chant over cross-border terrorism would have surcease; it would have no purchase either.

If General Musharraf has floored Vajpayee in the battle of wits, an objective exists to explain the denouement. And other things have been happening too. The nation does not exactly consist of dunces. Citizens have watched over the years the unfolding of one scandal after another in the stock exchanges; the opera of crooks, they have learnt to their cost, is being presided over directly by those in charge of the state apparatus. In some circles, the recent revelations in regard to Enron are being considered an eye-opener. Nothing of the sort. Years ago, when the power purchase deal and other agreements were negotiated, the details were known to the press and debated on the floor of parliament. The financial shenanigans were already widely advertised. So what? Those in power, never mind their political colour, could not care less. Avarice and *hauteur* constituted the ingredients of a lurid chemistry. Questions were already beginning to be asked, such as if the salt has lost its savour, how shall the earth be salted?

In any event, the loot organized through the intermediary of the Unit Trust of India is no departure. Please go through the proceedings in parliament spanning the past ten years. On several occasions, in both the Lok Sabha and the Rajya Sabha, attempts were made to ferret out the details of private placements involving the Industrial Development Bank of India, the Industrial Finance Corporation of India, the Life Insurance Corporation of India, the General Insurance Corporation of India and others. And if private placements were on the anvil, could insider trading be far behind? Once you enjoy a brutal majority in parliament, inconvenient queries and disquieting allegations directed at the treasury benches are easily shaken off, much in the manner of water off the back of a duck. Those in power would simply brazen it out, as the incumbent Prime and Finance Minister have done in the recent instance. At least, the Finance Minister has been honest enough to challenge openly the concept of accountability. Given the precedents, he is on firm ground: his predecessor, who presided over the 1992–93 stockmarket mess, had not resigned, so why should he? The Prime Minister, with his heroics, has cut a much sorrier figure. By now it is a cliché: those who threaten to resign never do.

Say goodbye for a while to stinking New Delhi and sick Mumbai; cross over to the north-east. What has happened and is happening over there since the dawn of independence is a continuum. The managers of the polity have taken it for granted that the concept of India as a nation is axiomatically valid; whoever does not agree deserves to be exterminated. Their whimsy has known no bounds. One day they have pushed the Nagas to a stellar role; the next day they have opted for the Kukis or the Meitis. No thought has been spared, nor any effort mounted, to explore the depths of diverse ethnic minds. Cash and other favours have been doled out to arrange short-term friendships; ministerships have been distributed in order to strike temporary alliances with this or that set of tribal politicians. Groups left out have immediately been up in arms against the distant, unfeeling central authority. A state of quasi-permanent insurgency has consequently been the story in the north-east over the long, lugubrious decades.

The plot has thickened. Ethnic battles have increasingly kept the company of caste and linguistic frictions, all of which have turned into zero-sum games. The pastime Indira Gandhi started to indulge in was persisted with by the subsequent occupiers of the seat of power, and centre–state relations were reduced to cynicism par excellence. This was bound to recoil. The art of cynicism can be easily mastered by other entities. Once that happens, the fat is in the fire. The bumbling regime now in New Delhi is simply not up to it. It does not dare to oust Shrimati Jayalalitha; its ability to administer pinpricks is equally in doubt. Just witness the tangle over the order of transfer of police officers from Tamil Nadu. The centre cannot but end up with egg on its face, because the lady will refuse to be cowed down; she will convene a conclave of chief ministers to discuss the issue. To re-stress, no residue is left of either fear or respect.

Is it any wonder that, having frittered away its imagination and its dignity, the regime prefers to don the mantle of comprador and sell off the country to foreigners? Saviours from overseas, the illusion is spread, will henceforth service the economy; the foreigners will also manage the country's defence, and intelligence agencies from overseas will take care of conspirators who refuse to accept the road to serfdom.

An old puzzle rears its head. If, instead of depicting the idealized portrait of a great Indian republic, those who drafted the country's Constitution had opted for eight or ten relatively modest-sized states loosely bound together in a confederation, would it not have been a vastly superior deal? The confederation could have taken charge of defence and external affairs, while the rest of the powers, functions and responsibilities could have belonged to the states. Were there no central power with total command of resources, jurisdiction and authority, the story of Kashmir would perhaps have been different. For the same reason, the stock exchanges would be a playground of blackguards of lesser proportions and financial institutions would be incapable of committing monstrous evils. The wholesale surrender of sovereignty, too, would be a much more difficult exercise.

Dreams, idle non-Freudian dreams. The reality, on the other hand, is both harsh and crude: India, a horrendously chaotic polity, is all set for a monotonic, precipitate decline. No scope here for Hitchcockian suspense, with sudden, final-moment twists of events, culminating in some rescue act or other. India shall drown and none will save her.

The new activists

29 September 2001

The judiciary has, of late, donned the robe of activism. The Supreme Court of India is fuming. It has remonstrated with the union and state governments; they must, with immediate effect, arrange to reach foodgrains to people starving in different parts of the country. The court could hardly be inert. It has been under severe pressure. A number of public interest cases have been filed with it. It could not also but take cognizance of reports in newspapers or on the television. People are dying of hunger, while government stores have stockpiles of at least 60 million tonnes of foodgrains. This, the Supreme Court has concluded, is a scandalous situation; it has accordingly issued peremptory instructions to the union and state governments to do the needful so that food reaches the starving populace.

The Supreme Court has noble intentions. It has also to be assumed that it is within the four corners of both law and the Constitution, in issuing the order. Sceptics are however around; they have always been. Quite a few fundamental rights are delineated under Article 19 of the Indian Constitution. These rights do not include, though, the right either to live or to free food. Article 21 says something about the protection of life and personal liberty; no person shall supposedly be deprived of such protection except according to procedure established by law. But that is a different kettle of fish. Please cross over to the Directive Principles of State Policy. The citizens, one such Directive Principle suggests, have the right to 'an adequate means of livelihood'. Homilies of this nature have never been taken seriously. After all, another Directive Principle states that children up to the age of fourteen years are to be provided with free and compulsory education by the state within ten years of the commencement of the Constitution. That provision has long ago fallen by the wayside. The same has been the plight of the right to means of livelihood. *Requiescat in pace.*

Are humanitarian sentiments, therefore, enough? The heart of the judges has justifiably melted at the news of citizens of this free, democratic country dying of starvation. Their cerebral instinct has guided them to ask the public authorities to redress the situation. The judiciary would appear to be within its rights, for it can draw the attention of the union and state governments to Article 282 of the Constitution: 'The union or a state may make any grant for any public purpose, notwithstanding that the purpose is not one with respect to which parliament or the legislature of the state, as the case may be, can make laws.'

Voilà, the judges may have no doubt in their minds. Article 282 has a catch-all ambit; either the centre or a state government is entitled to engage in any expenditure whose object is to cater to the succour or happiness of anyone, till as long as it is a public purpose. The judiciary has the ultimate prerogative to decide what is or is not a public purpose. Given its current mood, the Supreme Court will certainly agree that supplying foodgrains free of cost to hungry and starving people is very much a public purpose, and therefore comes within the jurisdiction of Article 282.

In view of the Supreme Court directive, the union government, suitably chastened, will have to, over the coming weeks, release larger and larger quantities of foodgrains to the state governments under food-for-work programmes of different designations with such belly-filling names as the Prime Minister's Rozgar Yojana and Antyodaya and Annapurna Anna Yojana schemes. But there is a snafu. These programmes are executed by state governments in accordance with the guidelines laid down by the centre. In some cases, the total cost of the foodgrains released by the union government will have to be matched evenly by a cash payment by the state government concerned. The state governments, by and large, are running a heavy deficit in their budgets. The devolution of taxes under the statutory awards recommended by the Finance Commission, they assert, falls for short of their requirements. The receipts from loan programmes sanctioned for them by the centre are equally disappointing. The flow of development assistance from the Planning Commission is also niggardly. In the circumstances, the state governments can hardly make both ends meet. On top of all this, the Reserve Bank of India is now rigorous in its enforcement of the limit to overdraft facilities.

Not that the state governments are heartless. But what can they do? They will plead, given this lack of funds. Under some food-for-work programmes, the union government is under commitment to reimburse the states the actual cost of food distribution; this commitment, they complain, is often not honoured, or honoured with a time-lag. Even the infrastructure for identifying 'below poverty-level' persons costs money which is not available on tap. Besides, the state governments have to survive politically; the meagre resources they have are needed to meet the demands of many pressure groups. The hungry, starving people are generally without political clout. Their voice is invariably faint; starvation renders it even fainter, perhaps to a half-whisper. True, the Supreme Court has now instilled some fear of god in the state governments. Even so, they worry about disturbing budgetary allocations already decided upon; they have to cut out some previously settled priority outlays so as to accommodate food-for-work programmes. They are bound to dither.

The union government will be experiencing still greater headaches. The shadow of the World Trade Organization looms large over its decisions and activities. The WTO is not just like the World Bank or the International Monetary Fund. The World Bank offers long-term loans to member-countries, subject to some stipulations. The International Monetary Fund similarly makes short-period advances, again under certain terms and conditions. If a country is not willing to go along with these conditions, there the matter ends: the Fund and the Bank will not lend money and, in that case, the country will have to make alternative arrangements, if it can. It will not however suffer any retributions if it refuses to agree to a loan under the stated stipulations. Even if it defaults in the repayment of the principal, along with interest, of a loan incurred in the past from either of the two international financial agencies, they will merely cut it off from receiving further loans; nothing beyond that.

The relationship with the World Trade Organization is far different and far more delicate. Our government has signed the Marrakesh Treaty and thereby has been admitted as a member of the World Trade Organization. Membership of the organization entails a number of obligations. If any of these obligations are not complied with by a member-country, disciplinary panels set up by the organization set to work. They admonish the country to correct its attitude and demeanour. Suppose the country concerned persists with flouting the rules and conditions of the international body, the World Trade Organization is then entitled to take punitive action against it. Such punitive action is, of course, subject to certain procedures that are to be followed. These procedures, rest assured, are heavily biased against poor, developing economies. The WTO can so organize things that life would be miserable for the defaulting country. For example, other member-countries could be instructed to treat this country as an outcaste and to decline to trade with it, or offer it any financial accommodation or trade concession. This is no light matter. The Supreme Court of India may ask the union government to despatch foodgrains, free of cost, to the famine-stricken people. The World Trade Organization, however, has a specific provision which prohibits the government of a member-country from subsidizing either the production or the distribution of foodgrains. Any government intervention in foodgrains trade, according to the philosophy of the WTO, is an infringement of the concept of free trade, and cannot be permitted. Therefore our government faces a roadblock. The Supreme Court may direct the union government to arrange for the free distribution of food to the people in distress. Article 282 of the Constitution may allow such free distribution, which is equivalent to a grant. But the World Trade Organization rules will say '*nyet*'. The state government may appeal to the centre for some additional financial assistance on an emergency basis so that the stipulation of providing a cash component for food-for-work programmes could be honoured. A problem will however arise here. Both the World Bank and the International Monetary Fund will look askance at such additional accommodation which might aggravate the fiscal deficit, and thereby cut across the conditions of the structural adjustment programme entered into with the two international financial agencies by the Government of India.

There is, nonetheless, a much worse dilemma ahead. Article 282 permits the central and state governments to spend funds for a public purpose. But what if such a public purpose offends a private purpose, and, in the context of the ideology of the sovereignty of market forces and free trade, harms the cause of private traders and producers? The argument here is pretty straightforward. If foodgrains are distributed free of cost, there will soon be no market where food can be sold at an adequate profit by traders and producers; the bottom will drop out of the notion of free trade. In this situation, for all one can speculate, the distribution of free foodgrains to the hungry and the afflicted, as ordered by the Supreme Court, might lead to sabotage of the conditionalities set by the World Trade Organization.

The authorities are in a tizzy. Given Article 282, the Supreme Court can certainly issue instructions to the union and state governments to sell foodgrains at zero price. But complying with this instruction could push our authorities into falling foul of international law and procedures as formulated and administered by international organizations such as the World Bank, the International Monetary Fund and the World Trade Organization. What shall the poor government or governments do? Obey the order of the highest judiciary in the country and save themselves from the ignominy and other consequences of contempt of court, or violate the rules of the World Trade Organization and be cast out of the globalized universe?

An honourable judge of the Supreme Court has recently observed that the Constitution is more important than a popular mandate. That is all very well, but is the Constitution more important than the mandate of the World Trade Organization? This is a tough nut to crack, and one the authorities are most reluctant to crack on their own. Which is conceivably why they are so desperately anxious to establish the point that the deaths in Orissa have taken place not on account of starvation because of non-availability of food, but due to food poisoning caused by fungi infection of that delicacy – mango kernels – the victims partook. Should the highest judiciary of the land buy this version, maybe it would kindly rescind its order to distribute foodgrains free of cost, thereby extricating the national government from the peril of defiance of international rules and law. This is the moment for the proper melting of the Supreme Court of India's heart.

The revolutionary departure

24 November 2001

A milestone is a milestone. The couple of amendments proposed by the Union Cabinet to the Representation of the Peoples Act constitute a revolutionary departure in the country's political annals. The Union Cabinet has taken courage in both hands and proclaimed to the world what a lovely, corrupt land India is. The amendments are an invocation of, and tribute to, national corruption.

Let us spend a few seconds to dissect the anatomy of the legislative changes proposed. The first amendment is intended to ensure that members of state assemblies, while electing members of the Rajya Sabha, will have to cast their votes openly, no rigmarole of secret ballot any more. This amendment has been mooted with a heavy heart. The state legislators, it confesses, are by and large a corrupt bunch. They are subject to monetary and other inducements. They have the cheek not to vote for the candidates set up by their respective parties, but sell their votes to the highest bidders. This causes considerable embarrassment to the parties they formally belong to. Consider the plight of the party currently ruling at the centre. It has no majority in the Rajya Sabha, and is facing enormous difficulty in passing legislation it regards as essential for the smooth running of administration. It has to depend on outside support, for instance, from the Congress Party. Such support is not always easily obtainable. If only the class interests of the Congress Party converge with those of the Bharatiya Janata Party, dicey legislations can make the grade, otherwise not. True, in most cases, the class interests of the two parties do coincide. It is however important to narrow down the corridor of uncertainty in crucial matters of this nature. In the circumstances, wayward state legislators who refuse to follow the party line, and convert their vote for electing members of the Rajya Sabha into a marketable commodity, deserve to be disciplined. No hanky-panky from now on, you must show your party whips how you cast your vote on such occasions. You have been elected to the state assembly with the party's support; you must therefore obey the party's directive in regard to whom to elect to the Rajya Sabha, and not be allowed to sell your vote to the highest bidders.

In other words, the amendment is open recognition of the fact that our legislators are a venal lot. It is also tantamount to an admission of the reality of the inability of party leaders to persuade legislators to respect the party mandate. Since exhortation has failed abjectly, compulsion, the *danda*, is the only recourse to fall back upon. The candour the proposed amendment displays is indeed breathtaking. The world is being informed, without any hide-and-seek, that the representatives of the Indian people are steeped in corruption; immoral practices are their second nature; they can be brought around only by throwing the statute book at them. Travel to every nook and corner of the world, you will be unable to discover another country whose rulers are honest to the core to such an extent as to admit that their legislators are dishonest to the core.

The second proposal is equally revolutionary. It is a different kind of path-breaking venture. It seeks to legalize corruption. The Representation of the Peoples Act has, at present, a provision whereby a candidate aspiring to be elected to the Rajya Sabha by the legislative assembly of a state must be ordinarily resident in that state. The founding fathers of our Constitution drafted the contours of the Rajya Sabha in the partial image of the United States Senate. In the United States, each state – big, moderately big, small, tiny, very tiny – sends two representatives to the Senate. This supposedly ensures the balanced distribution of legislative power and prerogatives between states of different sizes: since every state sends two senators, Hawaii and Vermont and Maine carry the same weight in the Senate as New York, Texas and California. The American constitution has, in addition, taken particular care to write in the condition that no person who is not a permanent resident of a state is entitled to be a senator from that state, with the underlying assumption that only a native son or daughter knows where the shoe pinches; carpetbaggers have no place in this scheme of things.

The Rajya Sabha in India does not have the same clout as the United States's Senate. There is also no equality of representation in the Rajya Sabha among the different states; it is the proportion-of-the-population principle which holds sway. But at least there was, till now, this specific condition spelled out in the Representation of the Peoples Act that an individual elected to the Rajya Sabha from a state must be ordinarily resident in that state; carpetbaggers are accordingly *verboten*. The presence of such a provision, the founding fathers hoped, will see to it that problems and issues confronting the different constituents of the union, whatever the size and state of their being, are effectively voiced on the floor of the upper house of parliament, and thereby pressure is applied on the central administration so that it fulfils its duties towards each constituent state.

This provision has proved to be a nuisance to our respectable political parties, barring of course the parties belonging to the Left; in any case, the Left are not regarded as respectable. Most political parties in the country believe in the unitary system. Power and influence within the parties are concentrated at the top. Those occupying the highest positions in the hierarchy of power distribute the loaves and fishes which go with this privilege. Suppose a party holds the reign of administration at New Delhi, its supreme leaders decide who will be cabinet ministers, ministers of state and all that. Unfortunately, a person cannot continue to be a minister beyond six months unless he or she is a member of either house of parliament. It is not always easy to be elected to the Lok Sabha. If an individual is particularly unpopular in his or her own state, it might be almost impossible to send him or her to the Lok Sabha from the neighbourhood. But in case the party has a huge majority in the legislative assembly of another state a thousand or fifteen hundred miles away from the state to which the ministerial aspirant belongs, the problem can be licked. Should the individual concerned be the prime minister's pet, the prime minister would call in the chief minister of this remote state and order him to arrange to elect the minister-to-be to the Rajya Sabha from the chief minister's state. In an authoritarian climate, the chief minister has no option but to obey the prime minister. There is a technical snag. The prime minister's pet is not ordinarily resident in the state that is supposed to send him or her to the Rajya Sabha; he or she has not visited the state ever previously, even as a casual tourist. So what? The person concerned will soon be named a cabinet minister at the centre; that does not mean, though, that he or she cannot be a cheat. Rush, rush, rush: he or she will buy a cowshed in a village in that state, or open a fixed deposit account with a bank in any district-town in the state. Such artifices will apparently establish his or her legal claim to be ordinarily resident in the state which he or she is yet to visit.

Necessity is the mother of invention. The necessity of assuming ministerial responsibility has induced scores and scores of eminent Indian politicians to invent residential status in distant states. All non-Left parties have gleefully participated in this marvellous game. A Bengali could thus rent a chattel in Gujarat, be elected to the Rajya Sabha from the latter state and be duly sworn in as finance minister of the country. Another finance minister who hailed from Punjab could claim to be a permanent resident from Assam; he was in a desperate hurry and put down his residential address as: care of Shrimati X, wife of chief minister of Assam. A human resource development minister, a native of Karnataka, claimed himself to be a dyed-in-the-wool son of Orissa. One of the ministers in the present Union Cabinet, born and bred in New Delhi, has no compunction about asserting that he is a backwoodsman from Madhya Pradesh.

Politicians apparently have got tired of this game of thuggery. They do not intend to live in sin henceforth; the irritant of residential provision for election to the Rajya Sabha is now proposed to be removed from the Representation of the Peoples Act. Once this condition is scrapped, our man from Punjab would not have to pretend to be a native son of Assam, nor would the men from West Bengal need to go into the bother of sharing the same mothertongue with the late unlamented father of the nation. Corruption will no longer be corruption; it will be twenty-four-carat virtue.

Come to think of it, the effective implementation of the second amendment is crucially dependent on the successful passage of the proposed first amendment. It is an unsafe world: one never knows, party leader might order party legislators in Gujarat to vote for this stranger, a Bengali from Birbhum, but a danger could still lurk in the event of persisting with the modality of secret ballot; party legislators might betray the prime minister, the party and the Bengali from Birbhum. The open ballot will be the security blanket and stop potential betrayers in their track.

And please do not ask why the founding fathers chose to insert this abomi- nable residential clause in the Representation of the Peoples Act. They were not perceptive enough; they failed to realize the importance of electing a Punjabi to the Rajya Sabha from Assam or a Bengali from Gujarat; such a measure is bound to promote national integration. Whether the nation will survive its conse- quences once the revolutionary amendment is enacted is an irrelevant issue, which need not detain us. We live for today.

Dance of the marionettes

2 February 2002

The marionettes do not fight on their own; they are not allowed to do so. So, as could have been comfortably predicted, there will be no war. Which does not matter though. The bogey of war hath its charms to make asses of men. The alibi is availed of to switch over from a regime of statutes, approved *a priori* by representatives of the people, to a regime of directives enforced from above, routinely re-issued without bothering for parliamentary sanction. The scare of war, simulated in exemplary fashion, ensures the advent of an ordinance which gives summary power to the authorities to hang you and me. Now a parallel ordinance has been enforced to tax you and me to death. The pledge which impelled the American War of Independence, 'no taxation without representa- tion', has fallen by the wayside, although with a twist in the denouement: the representatives are *in situ* all right, but it is no longer necessary to seek their approval for purposes of taxation. The power assumed to vary at will, the rates of excise duty will, have no fear, soon be followed by the authorities claiming the prerogative to raise or lower direct rates of taxation: it will be lowered for the rich and raised for the poor. Already, the chambers of commerce and industry have pressed the demand for drastic reduction in the rates of company taxation. In the given ambience, the wishes of private tycoons are as good as law to the government.

It is pointless to complain. Liberalization implies the contraction of space for the government and corresponding expansion of private space. And if some paraphernalia of the government have not yet been put out of action, it is only sensible that these are deployed for the edification of private interests who control the government besides. In any case, monetary policy, including interest rate policy, has been taken away from both the public domain and parliamentary jurisdiction long ago. The distinction between fiscal management and monetary management is, in fact, altogether metaphysical. Fiscal decisions determine the quantum, price and distribution over classes of bank credit. Bank advances are basically the same as purchasing power. If the authorities could fix the contours and content of monetary policy without leave of parliament, why cavil at the phenomenon of the institutionalization of taxation without the sanction of representatives of the people? The purists – and ideologues – should therefore pipe down.

The bogey of war has yet other advantages. It expands the ambit of liberal education. It makes us aware of the harsh reality that a pretending democracy need not waste any verbiage on popular mandate. In the American century, we must unswervingly follow American norms. *Vide* Latin America, the US administration always feels comfortable in the company of military dictators. Its preference for the Pakistan ground situation is for identical reasons. In the competitive game that is on, the Indian ruling class must outperform its Pakistani counterpart in the quest for American favour, and, therefore, in the practice of authoritarianism. When in Rome, do as the Romans do; when you worship Americans, fall in line with American mores. A beginning towards that end has now been made in India. The individual describing himself as Defence Minister, in view of his non-credentials, is unable to function on the floor of parliament; it does not matter though, he formally remains the Defence Minister.

But such nonchalance needs practice. It also calls for a lot of catching-up. The Pakistanis have a headstart of nearly 50 years over us in this respect. The challenge is, without doubt, of a formidable order. Conceivably, the generous Americans will organize a crash programme for our ministers, civil servants and military brass to accelerate the process of acculturization.

The conclusion seems almost inevitable: Kashmir is a dead and gone case. There is a logical structure impossible to get away from. The Prime Minister posts an entreaty with the US President to save us from the marauders from across the border encouraged by Pakistan. In view of the state of his health, he is perhaps considered as not very effective. The no-nonsense Home Minister therefore rushes to Washington DC and lobbies intensely with the American establishment. They can, he assures them – as if they lacked assurance – do it; they must order the Pakistanis to desist from any further hanky-panky along the border of Kashmir. The Americans oblige. The Pakistanis have to listen to them because of the TINA factor; they, the Pakistanis, have nowhere else to proceed. The superpower however believes in the most-favoured-nation principle in their treatment of lackeys – no lackey will be treated as less equal than any other lackey. No pretzel stuck in the throat will prevent George W. Bush from doling out even-handed justice. The Pakistani General can therefore legitimately look forward to some bonanza concerning Kashmir to be gifted to him as expeditiously as possible.

Have a heart, rational expectations can hardly be expected to go on a holiday on the present occasion. The Americans are genuinely foxed. Once again: according to their way of looking at things, the distinction sought to be made is overwhelmingly metaphysical; if they are asked to intercede with Pakistan so that the so-called terrorists do not disturb Kashmir, why should not the Americans be permitted to tackle the problem at its root, which is the issue of self-determination of the people inhabiting the valley! Whatever India's opposition parties might think, third-party mediation by the US has already commenced, really and truly. The Bharatiya Janata Party-led government has capitulated to the US fully and completely; the simile that comes to mind is what is associated with sackcloth and ashes. The US Secretary of State is a busy person. His visit to the subcontinent has been not to discuss weather, but to work out a deal on Kashmir. The cognoscenti know it. Even newspaper editors know it. It is a different issue that they also know which side their bread is buttered. In the circumstances, all that the New Delhi regime can hope for at the margin is a moratorium on the disclosure of the details of the deal until the ensuing series of state assembly elections are over.

The temptation to create a Pakistan, and, by implication, a Muslim phobia, was indeed very great. The stability of the government at the centre is crucially dependent upon the outcome of the assembly elections. For, should the Bharatiya Janata Party fare badly, the rats will desert the sinking National Democratic Alliance ship in scampering hurry. The anti-Pakistan frenzy has also been enormously helpful in quelling the reverberations of the Tehelka and coffins scandals. But the flip-side of the strategic design is not easily avoidable. Such is the misfortune of a globalized arrangement: to achieve a strictly domestic objective, one still needs to lodge an appeal with a distant uncle. The overall intent is to exploit, to the hilt, the spin-off of the ersatz frenzy a war bogey can create, but somehow to stop short of an actual war. This requires craftsmanship of a superior grade and, besides, the superpower to hold your hand. The superpower holds your hand, but it holds as much the hand of your neighbour. To repeat, the dispensation of infinite justice by the superpower has to be on an even keel. There is an additional consideration for the American administration. Even an accidental outbreak of full-scale war between two lackeys studded with atomic weaponry has dangerous possibilities. The Americans cannot condone an eventuality of this kind. On the other hand, both lackeys are most welcome to purchase arms, tons and tons of them, overseas. While such purchase will be for purchase's sake, it will help to overcome recession in the American economy.

All told, the prospects look grim on the Kashmir horizon. The only hope lies elsewhere. India is much too turbulent a country, with a huge land mass and an immense, heterogeneous population, which even the superpower will find it awesomely difficult to discipline. That apart, while segments of Aryavarta may be inordinately anxious to have the Republic of India enlisted as the fifty-first or fifty-second or fifty-third constituent of the great United States of America, the rest of the country could have other views. Should both the American establishment and their comprador following inside the country miscalculate, Kashmir could be rendered into much more than a question mark; a thousand violent rebellions might be declared here, there, everywhere across the Indo-Gangetic and Deccan valleys, compared to which the current turbulences in Jammu and Kashmir and the north-east would fade into insignificance.

But, then, human beings in general do not look before they leap. The Indian branch of the species do so even less. They, accordingly, have to suffer. Perhaps, in the emerging predicament, they might search for solace in the teachings of the *Gita: ma phaleshu kadachana*, never bother over the outcome of your doings, that is, your misdoings.

A disunited nation

13 April 2002

Suddenly, the realization dawns, it is no longer one, a unified nation. Many citizens are asking what appears to them the most relevant question: if these elements flaunting the Ram Rajya Parishad banner are Indians, with what heart do they describe themselves as Indians too? There is a total cleavage in attitude, belief, inclination and philosophy of life. The confrontation, some will say, is between civilization and non-civilization, and it is impossible for the two contending forces to cohabit. Gujarat seems to be a watershed. For form's sake, the heterogeneous organisms might have to exist within the same polity, but, if things remain as they currently are, a parting will be inevitable in course of time. Whether the ending will be bloody and life- and property-destroying, it is difficult to predict at this point. Acrimony will however suffocate the air. So much so that on both sides there could be realization that good riddance is good riddance, a formal split is the only way out.

Such an impression gains ground because of tidings that travel from the direction of that western state. The Bharatiya Janata Party and its 'parivar' are, according to reports, looking forward to a snap assembly elections: in the wake of the state-wide carnage, their popularity amongst members of the major community, they are confident, has reached sky-high; an immediate poll is bound to lead to a sweeping victory on their part. This is fearsome news. For it suggests that the beliefs and prejudices the 'parivar' gloats over are integrated with the psyche of the citizens concerned. And, despite the drubbing the BJP has received in the February round of elections, perhaps the situation has veered towards a direction exceedingly favourable to it. Communal savagery repels some people; it stimulates raw, base passions in some others, maybe in considerably more others.

There is, therefore, no running away from the obvious conclusion: the nation is near to arriving at the point of no return. Simple-minded neighbours may be genuinely taken by surprise. How can it be, they will raise the query, that Mahatma Gandhi's own state is rendered into such a burnt-out case? Unfortunately, they have to be disabused of their pious doubts. It may break many hearts, but let us be honest, is not the genesis of many of our present travails a direct contribution of Gandhiji's train of thoughts?

Religiosity, Gandhi taught, was the key to national revival and, consequently, emancipation of the nation from foreign rule. Self-pride and self-realization, he preached ceaselessly, should be the touchstone by which to judge a nation's mettle. Without pride and self-confidence, there could be no accumulation of the will and strength necessary to subdue the alien usurpers. Indians are by nature, he argued, reverential towards religious totems. The mythical Ram Rajya was the religious symbol he picked up. The great Indian people must remember the halcyon epoch of Ram Rajya, where justice and fair play ruled, everything was fine and excellent, the principle of morality was the over-riding code, and Lord Rama was the ruler who looked after the interests of all, of the weak and the strong, of the rich and the poor, of the proud and the self-effacing. Indians must revive their pride in that paradise which is their glorious legacy; they must prove themselves worthy of that legacy. That endeavour will draw all of them together and instil them with the strength to get rid of foreign masters without exercise of any violence. Tolerance is also a part of the ancient heritage: because in Ram Rajya everybody lived in peace and harmony with everybody else and disputes got settled through the intermediary of the grammar and ethics laid down by Lord Rama, there could be no question of resort to instruments of violence to attain individual or social objectives. Mahatma Gandhi exhorted the nation: be proud of your heritage, be humble at the same time; the invocation of the Ram Rajya spirit will enable you to make the country independent and, at the same time, to cross over once more to Ram Rajya; all you need to do is to cultivate the humility which is the offspring of pride; this humility has a family resemblance to the biblical edict of turning-the-other-cheek; it will persuade the British to withdraw, and the rich to be kindly and take care of the needs of the poor.

Fiction has raged in the country since then. It suited the Congress bosses to propagate the story that non-violence had ushered in the nation's freedom. The other political forces in the country could thereby be denied a share of the glory that was attached to the freedom struggle. The freedom movement was the monopoly of the Congress Party; it followed that the fruits of freedom too should be monopolized by the Congress hegemony. The creation of the fiction was accompanied by a few other, equally suspect corollaries. It was, alas, beyond the comprehension of both Gandhiji and his acolytes that Ram Rajya was not only a myth, it was a quintessentially Hindu myth. In due course, the Hindu revivalists stole the concept. In this particular instance, the monopoly rights were, through some accident, passed from Congress hands to the hands of the communal fanatics. Why blame separately the people in Gujarat? They had every right to take pride in the fact that Mahatama Gandhi was their very own; they might have developed weightier pride in Gandhiji's dictum of self-pride and self-realization. If the mythology was Hindu, the pride they imbued themselves with was naturally also Hindu. The other communities did not enter the picture. Or not quite. The humility part was reserved for the minority communities; they must be humble and cringing in case they want to live as a part of the nation.

The rest of the subsequent story was predictable. Jawaharlal Nehru could not quite determine whether he was a believer or an agnostic; he was one thing in the morning, a different thing in the afternoon. He expressed immense satisfaction at the fact that the idea of a secular republic could be rammed through when the nation's Constitution was being drafted. His fads and whims were law to his followers in the Congress Party; they obligingly signed on the dotted line, and on 26 January 1950, the fable was propagated about India being a secular democratic republic, the largest in the world. Why not say it, Nehru's definition of secularism went off on the wrong rails. Secularism, he explained to himself, means being equally sympathetic towards all religions. To convince the people of India of his own secular credentials, he commenced the ritual of visiting Hindu temples, as well as mosques, dargahs, gurdwaras, churches and synagogues. Since Hindus constituted the overwhelming majority in the country, Nehru could not be blamed too much for the frequency of his visits to Hindu shrines once he had latched on to the particular etymology of secularism. To be both consistent and logical, he had to mix these visits with occasional forays into sanctums of other denominations. But the populace at large reached their own conclusion: secularism equals selective sectarianism.

Jawaharlal Nehru's daughter went a bit further. Her choice of Hindu icons widened. If rumour is to be believed, she was, for whatever reason, proximate to Hindu superstitions too. Not that she dispensed with her father's guide-lines regarding the usefulness of some sort of balancing with visits to shrines belonging to adherents of other faiths. But the tilt was sharply towards Hindu rituals. Joining the thick congregation at *Kumbh Mela* was certainly no testimo-nial to one's non- or anti-sectarianism.

Jawaharlal Nehru's grandson, assuming the position of prime minister as per the rules of dynastic succession, did not even look back. That he was a son of a Parsi father did not deter him; after all, the marriage of his parents too had been consecrated according to Vedic rites. He had a Catholic wife. That also did not deter him; campaigning for popular mandate is a great antidote to sensibil-ity. Pictures were flashed on the television screen and on newspaper pages of a bare-bodied prime minister offering his homage, under the tutelage of a brahmin pundit, to Hindu gods and goddesses. The difference between private and public religious beliefs disappeared. The image that got etched in people's mind was that the prime minister was, to all purposes, a grand Hindu devotee, and in his official capacity.

The original sin began to be compounded at a very fast pace. The prin-ciple that should have been stressed in the very beginning was that secularism is coterminous with the practice of *indifference*, in an equal degree, to all religions; you stay away, scrupulously, from all of them. None apparently had the courage to pull up Jawaharlal Nehru for his gross error. The rest is the grimy story we have bequeathed.

No official ceremony, whether inauguration of a new office building or that of a government housing complex, can now be completed without perform-ance of 'Bhoomi Puja', no ship built by a public sector unit can be floated into the Bay of Bengal or the Arabian Sea without splitting a coconut shell. Ministers file their poll papers after consulting Hindu astrologers who charge a rounded one lakh of rupees for every piece of advice. And soon, the *Ramayana* and *Mahabharata* fables were turned into television 'soaps': a fantastic fusion of relaxation and religion. Television-watchers lapped it up. The television sets themselves began to be worshipped. The medium is the message.

Let us be honest, the Gujarat citizens are being honest to the Gandhi legacy, just as the BJP and its 'parivar' have drawn conclusions which are to their own advantage from the examples set by the Nehru–Gandhi dynasty. It was a Congress dynasty, supposedly a dynasty believing in secularism, it was none-theless a great believer in conspicuous religiosity of the brahminic genre.

Who can deny that it is 'karma' at work? We will be a divided nation and the polity will head towards total collapse, because our founding fathers and the political party which claims monopoly rights over the nation's freedom strug-gle, wrote a Hindu script for the nation. In the inimitable words once deployed by Sam Goldwyn, some of us would like to include ourselves out from that fate.

We hate, therefore we are

8 June 2002

Temporarily suspend disbelief. It could be the fifteenth or the sixteenth century, an ideal medieval setting against the background of the Alpine range. Two feudal entities are fighting it out over a piece of real estate. Of the two, one is a military dictatorship. That fact notwithstanding, the ruling élites there have no identity crisis. A grand homogeneity has smoothed out behaviouristic kinks: the military hegemony is drawn from the stock of feudal lords; the leaders of industry and business too have the same roots. The common people, in any case, do not matter. Nearly two-thirds of the population are without any semblance of letters. No conflict, dialectical or otherwise, therefore comes to disturb the phalanx of feudal grit. Indifference to the daily problems of the overwhelming majority of inhabitants is a datum accepted by everyone as belonging to the genre of axioms.

The circumstances are somewhat more complicated for the other polity. It is supposed to be a practising multi-party system. A system based on pluralist principles is however more often than not reduced to competitive democracy. Parties have to compete with one another for the allegiance of the electorate. That poses a substantive difficulty. Starry-eyed cheerleaders of the symbiotic attachment of democracy and freedom to each other lay admiring stress on the benefits of a free public information system featured by a multiplicity of print media, broadcast and telecast channels, and a cacophony of comments and views. All this will, it is assumed, lead to greater enlightenment at the grassroots; regaled by the privilege of alternative choices, they will learn how to decide between alternative choices and reach judgments invested with the attributes of optimality. Democracy, according to this version, spells freedom, and freedom is synonymous with welfare.

This and similar claims turn out to be a heap of gibberish. Freedom is soon revealed as freedom of competing passions and prejudices. The media disseminate ideas and opinions broached by different groups and political conglomerations. The marketplace intended to provide free information is soon transformed into a marketplace for the outpouring of frenzied, biased propaganda. The objective is to catch, by hook or by crook, the imagination of the largest slice of the electorate. Theoretically, the polity flaunts all the basic freedoms described in the International Charter of Human Rights, but, once the media build the proper ambience, competitive democracy becomes indistinguishable from competitive dogma-mongering.

The outcome is arousal of the crassest emotions of the people. Problems of hunger, lack of apparel and shelter, lack of education and nutrition are the acutest realities afflicting the masses. The media – and the management of the media – however ensure that a so-called consensus is reached that life is not worth living unless the territory over which the home chieftains are quarrelling with the chieftains on the other side is annexed, once and for all.

A further sort of enlightenment: where war hysteria is concerned, a military dictatorship and a competitive democracy are equally advantaged or disadvantaged. It is the my-patriotism-is-superior-to-yours syndrome on both sides of the divide. Those theoretically enjoying the blessing of freedom of choice are as easily provoked to a fever pitch of jingoistic emotions as the populace across subjected to the rule of army dictatorship. The freedom of choice is just a convenient modality for the freedom for spreading seeds of blind hatred towards the neighbouring people. Freedom, you are forced to conclude, whether reluctantly or otherwise, does not matter; it is incapable of persuading the democracy snobs to concentrate their efforts and resources on tackling the basic needs of the community. Few political formations dare to stand up against war propaganda lest they run the risk of being dubbed as traitors, *vide* the plight of communists in India forty years ago. The situation is also tailormade for characters eager to divert people's attention away from affairs such as Gujarat and Tehelka. The consequence is bizarre. The Montagues might be a thoroughly authoritarian set-up; civil liberties have been suspended by them; they constitute a close inbred cabal of army generals, landed gentry and gluttonous businessmen; their modes and manners could be as antiquated and reactionary as these could be. The Capulets, on the other hand, have in their midst blithe, liberal spirits who have travelled the entire trajectory of discourses beginning with Jean Jacques Rousseau, John Locke, John Stuart Mill, Edward Carpenter, Leo Tolstoy, Mohandas Karamchand Gandhi, and ending with John Maynard Keynes, Jean Paul Sartre and John Rawls. They boast of loads and loads of poets, thinkers, scientists, artists, human rights activists, women's libbers. To no avail. It is as easy for the Capulets to entice their subjects to the battlefield as it is for the Montagues. True, an interregnum separates the *alaap* from the *raga*. But rulers tend to get carried away by their own rhetoric; and cajole the following to do likewise. There is, therefore, perhaps only a little distance necessary to be covered between the phony war and the real war. Which gives rise to yet another problem. According to an anecdote fairly well publicized, if in an Irish town two sets of inebriated publicans are engaged in a bout of fisticuffs in a street corner, any third party passing by could politely inquire whether it was a private fight or whether he too could join in. Should he receive permission, he would participate in the fracas, choosing whichever side he decides to favour. Sometimes, of course, he gets confused over which party he is siding with. The result is practice of an absent-minded objectivity, widely appreciated by one and all.

Quite conceivably, though, a third party can play a reverse kind of role too. It may, for its own reasons, intervene not so much to exacerbate the fight but to limit its spread. The obvious third party in the instance under reference has to be, it goes without saying, the United States of America. The Americans may not necessarily opt for adoption of Irish civility and intervene without prior leave of either of the parties engaged in combat. They have that prerogative, because they are the world's only superpower. Since their own interests are involved, they could order both Indian and Pakistani rulers to stop the nonsense. Their geopolitical considerations may go far afield. Russia is no longer a relevant factor, but the People's Republic of China remains a question mark. Destabilizing the *status quo* may have ominous implications. Where ruling groups in the two belligerent neighbouring countries are so stoutly determined to go to gory battle, and the media in both lands are making their own humble contributions to the mess, even diehard conscientious objectors may welcome third-party meddling. The issue is straightforward enough: will cross-border warfare do more harm to people's welfare in the region than the series of spin-offs triggered by the much detested, but awesomely powerful third party? A war-like environment can act as a great enlightener even though the fruits of the enlightenment taste most sour.

A further complication clouds the picture. The establishment in both countries happen to have a stockpile of nuclear weapons. You never know, idiocy can sometimes goad itself to travel to altogether absurd directions. The starting point of contention may be that my claim to the piece of real estate is superior to your claim; it could overnight be transformed into the assertion, my bomb is superior to your bomb. One thing, it is well known, leads to another. Empty rhetoric can easily slide into atomic rhetoric. And if a nuclear implosion perchance takes place, can an explosion, with the noble goal of nuking out of existence the neighbouring land, be far behind? Unfortunately, the trouble with nuclear warfare is that, whatever the initial intent, it is almost impossible to keep it confined to the two contending parties or to a defined stretch of territory; it is bound to spill over to other powers and regions.

This, then, is another security blanket the Indians and the Pakistanis can hazard to depend upon. The big five in the nuclear club will step into the India–Pakistan imbroglio, otherwise the fate of all of them too will be at stake. It is because Indians and Pakistanis possess nuclear capability that they will not be allowed to use this capability. Their ongoing private skirmish will also not be allowed to turn into a full-fledged war.

The ultimate security India and Pakistan could, however, well boast of is their state of immiserization. One needs victuals to fight a war. Neither India nor Pakistan enjoys an infinite command over purchasing power. They lack resources to engage in a war of even moderate duration. Both ruling establishments will have to turn to the superpower for help to enable them expand their military capability. That is to say, they are in the position of dogs on a leash. If the master does not allow a loosening of the leash, a dogfight cannot really ensue. In the final count, we have to thank our stars that we are poor cringing nations. That fact will not stop either ruling establishment from starting a local riot; once it does, the other establishment will return the compliment. On their own, though, they are unlikely to indulge in any 'escalation'. People of both countries will be further impoverished even in the event of a limited war. It is, in any case, their fate to be further impoverished because of the lay of income and assets distribution in their respective societies. They will, nonetheless, be saved from worse adversity because both sets of rulers are in the final analysis dependent on the goodwill of the superpower for their survival; the war, even if it is started, will therefore soon come to a stop. The Machiavellis and the Napoleons on either side will, willy-nilly, have to eat humble pie. Hail to the superpower who gives us our daily bread – and our dose of daily poison.

A paradigm?

6 July 2002

Well, since the buzz word is paradigm, let us pay homage to it. The preliminaries to the election of the new President of the Republic of India is of paradigmatic significance; they encapsulate all that is wrong with this god-forsaken, god-infested country.

We have slaughtered thousands and thousands of members belonging to your community, we have burnt down your houses and plundered your property, we have ravished your children and women, we have gone on record stating that members of all so-called minority communities, without exception, could be permitted to stay in this country only provided they agree to follow our dictat and observe our manners and rituals. But, for the present, we have picked an individual from within your midst and decided to instal him as our puppet Head of State. You must, therefore, forget the recent gory happenings and support our mandate. We are not asking for your forgiveness; you are inferior creatures in our land, and would not have the daring to demand an apology from us for the supposedly heinous crimes we might have committed against you. It is our divine right to perpetrate such acts, and you, who are subordinately placed, have no business to question the propriety or morality of what we have done. All we are asking you is that, should you want to survive in this country, you better forget the indignities and worse you have suffered in our hands and endorse our presidential candidate who, thanks to our graciousness, is a member of your community; his nomination – and election – must fill to the brim your sense of gratitude to us. Expression of such gratitude on your part will stop, once and for all, the morons – ideologues, civil rights groups, suchlike – in their track, and, at the same time, make our sworn enemy – the Pakistanis – intensely unhappy.

The insolence does not quite stop here. It is also being taken for granted that, since the operatic team of evil-mongers and evil-doers have outmanoeuvred, in the game of picking the presidential candidate, other political formations, the latter should have the grace to give in without demur and co-adopt the individual concerned as their candidate as well. And this is precisely what is taking place. Barring the Left, it is now a desperate competition among the rest of the political stragglers to get into the opportunist bandwagon. Conventional sociologists describe the phenomenon as herd instinct. Since a member of the major minority community has been chosen by the ruling party as its candidate and others have been beaten in the game, the civilized thing, it is being hinted, is to capitulate. Two considerations are being kept in mind. First, to combat the electoral advantage the ruling party has garnered by naming a member of the minority community, it would be necessary to set up another member from the same community as his rival. This could invite the derisive epithet of copycat complex. Second, there is genuine difficulty in locating at short notice a suitable enough counter-candidate from the particular community. In the circumstances, the safest course is to opt for the myth of national consensus. Which then becomes the precursor of a lot of florid, eleventh-rate poetry. In this hour of national peril, with the wretched Pakistanis indulging in nefarious cross-border shelling along the line of control, all patriotic elements have to come together irrespective of their domestic political differences. This togetherness is epitomized by our unanimous endorsement of the ruling party candidate, who, what luck, happens to be a member of the minority community. Such a thundering endorsement will emphasize the bond of national unity even as it will amount to a comprehensive slap in the face of Pakistan. It is only small-minded people who will have the temerity to describe this wonderful gesture as an aspect of herd instinct.

A subterranean, or not so subterranean, thought is also astir. The man chosen is supposed to be a nuclear scientist who has contributed a great deal towards the development of intermediate range missiles and the concomitant delivery system that can be deployed to rain destruction on Pakistan and, hopefully, on China too. Viewed from that angle, this man must be hailed and serenaded as representing the iron will of the nation to foil foreign aggression of all kinds. He, in a way, reflects the nation's atomic *shakti*. Whoever dares to oppose his candidature is, without question, less than a patriot; in fact, the rest of us could, with good reason, accuse such a person of treason.

243

A fable is a fable is a fable. In the Indian ambience, becoming 'world-famous' is an effortless exercise, given some minimal helping hand from the media. If newspaper A calls somebody a world-renowned scientist or technologist, newspaper B is bound to fall in line. Once A and B are agreed, C, D, E and F will religiously follow the script. The other media will then take up the incantation. Someone may have an ordinary, very ordinary, bachelor's degree in a science subject. He may have subsequently entered a relatively nondescript government organization, spending uneventful years within its precincts, attaining routine promotions from one rung of the administrative ladder to the next. At some point, the organization may happen to come to a lateral arrangement whereby it is marginally involved in the programme for developing the missile delivery system. Opportunities are always wide open for those with their eyes on the main chance, the run-of-the-mill laboratory bureaucrat is, at some point of time, placed at the head of the establishment. Through sheer luck, or because he possesses the attributes essential for greasing the establishment apparatus, he overnight emerges as a nuclear scientist and, in due course, a nuclear scientist of international reputation. So much so that few, very few, in the country have the courage to inquire about his credentials, such as the number of scientific papers he has produced or the nature of technological breakthroughs he has achieved. And it would be heresy to inquire what are his original contributions, either major or minor, in nuclear physics.

A nation, a substantial section of whom holds in great deference puranic tracts, will be easily enchanted with mythology, any mythology, even that of a small-time defence bureaucrat suddenly catapulting to the status of a saint with the beatific smile. Reputation, after all, is a function of the velocity of circulation of one's name. Once the name goes into orbit, second, third and subsequent-order myths begin to pile up on top of the original myth. Biographies, let it be admitted, are not generally written; they are manufactured, and often through the assembly-line process. The consequence is a cacophony of love-you-do's: it does not matter if we have zeroed in on a Don Quixote or a Sancho Panza; he is the National Consensus, spelled in capital letters.

Myths, besides, have other crucial uses. They can be deployed to demolish the memory of harsh realities. That gruesome phase of man's inhumanity to man as depicted by the Gujarat genocide is no longer a part of the national agenda. Only stray voices are being any longer raised demanding the removal of the incumbent chief minister of that state. The distinction between what psychologists designate as synchronic and diachronic visages is commanded to silence. The presidential election season is not the humanity-extolling season. Nonetheless, a latent irony: at both points of time, the saga of national unity and integrity is invoked. This great nation abhors communal disturbances and demands Narendra Modi's head on a platter. This great nation must unite to elect a candidate who is the symbol of national unity and integrity to the post of

President, and please do not mind if, in this holy ritual, we march in step with Narendra Modi.

Pragmatic calculations do not take a back seat either. From the look of things, this fellow's election is certain. The parliamentary elections are only a couple of years away. If, perchance, there is a hung Lok Sabha, the political leader who is called first by the President to explore the possibilities of a new government will enjoy a clear advantage. Therefore, let us be, for heaven's sake, on his right side.

The wrath has accordingly fallen on the non-joiners. They have no business to ruffle the unity of the nation. It is a scandal; these rascals are, of course, adamant in their opposition to the candidate of national consensus; what is even more unforgiving, the scallywags do not actually believe in the concept of a national consensus. Their Machiavellian propensities know no bounds; they have latched on to an alternative candidate and one who has an impeccable background. She has been a legendary figure in the national freedom movement. That the candidate is a woman is an equally adversarial fact, for it is for the first time in the history of independent India that a woman has been put up as a candidate for elevation to the rank of President. She is a card-carrying Lefty, but, in view of the rest of her cv, we will bring ridicule upon us in case we seek to depict her as a traitor to the nation.

Given the situation, dialecticians have been put to work. Since all other parties are agreed on one man, the Left have no excuse for playing the role of deviant. In fact, by their foolish act, they have jeopardized the prospects of developing a solid anti-communal, anti-fundamentalist phalanx in the country. If only the Left had behaved, there would have been no falling out between them, socialists, *hawala*-loving or otherwise, and the nation's ancient party presided over by the Nehru–Gandhis. Since the Left are determined to sabotage anti-fundamentalist unity, those differing with the Left in the choice of the next President have been forced to join the fundamentalists. The villain of the piece, let it be understood by everybody, is the obstreperous, cantankerous behaviour of the Left. They deserve to be exterminated for the good of the nation. *Hamara jhanda uncha rahega.*

ISI in every bush

7 December 2002

A Bengali icon, a renowned man of letters, Annada Sankar Ray, breathed his last in Calcutta a few weeks ago. He was 98, and died full of honours. A truly versatile writer, he had authored short stories, novels, essays and *belles-lettres*, travelogues, poetry and, what do you know, even nonsense rhymes. In fact, after Sukumar Ray, Satyajit Ray's father, he is indisputably the most outstanding versifier of nonsense rhymes in Bengali. Some of these rhymes have passed into folklore. Annada Sankar Ray was, in addition, a tireless pontificator and social reformer, a liberal to the core, with a strong Gandhian bent of mind. His death will not make any difference to his role as an icon; if anything, it will add further lustre to his repute.

Way back in 1949, when the Communist Party was banned in West Bengal and Chief Minister B.C. Roy's police were looking for seditious communists in every nook and corner with merciless zeal, Annada Sankar Ray, his liberal instinct aflame, wrote an outspoken piece of political verse. It was not just ordinarily outspoken; far more than that. He was still a member of the Indian Civil Service and in the employment of the state government. He was nonetheless aghast at the witch-hunting that was on; his mortification was aggravated by the shooting down, in cold blood, by the state police of five women activists of the Communist Party, whose only crime was to have organized a public procession demanding the release of political prisoners detained without trial. The non-doggerel Ray composed had the title 'Sermon from the Missus'. A free translation will run more or less as follows:

Whatever and whenever a mischief takes place, no question, it is the communists who are behind it. No rains in Murshidabad, why, the communists must be at work. There is a devastating flood in Pabna; rest assured, the rascally communists have engineered it. I honestly wonder from which hell-hole these unspeakable beasts have suddenly arrived; they have even brought plague to our land. Our culture is gone to dogs on account of them; our civility has had its swan song. Can you think of a worse calamity: our boys, our own boys, have now joined the communists. God knows what charm our girls find in communism; they too have fallen in the trap and are facing police bullets. Communists to the right of me, to the left of me, in front of me. Which is why I am making a list of all the communists in the neighbourhood.

The sarcasm was biting in the extreme. Annada Sankar Ray, it is hardly surprising, soon quit government service, or was made to quit.

More than 50 years have elapsed, and it is a different epoch. At least some of the communists are now house-broken; some of them are even described, in private, as house-slaves, although opinions differ sharply on the issue. But have no fear, the communists might have turned respectable, they might not be held responsible any more for all the evils under the sun, surrogates are not that scarce. Thanks to the Bharatiya Janata Party-led regime, there is never a dull moment. True, the analogy is not altogether apt, but the Pakistan Inter-Services Intelligence is fast occupying the space in official lexicon the communists occupied half a century ago. Mind you, the ISI is no innocent abroad. It must have its network inside India just as our Research and Analysis Wing has its inside Pakistan. Since Pakistan, by apparently common consent, is India's inveterate enemy, we have the moral right to send our spies into the neighbouring country. And Pakistan will return the compliment. As a matter of fact, smuggling intelligence agents to foreign countries, including even friendly foreign countries, is the commonest of practices. The Central Intelligence Agency has its presence not just in Russia, but in Britain, Germany, France and even such mish-mash countries as Australia and New Zealand. This form of mutual greeting, about everybody accepts, belongs to the garden genre of activities. If you have any doubts, please ask John Le Carré.

The problem however arises with the gradual abdication of a sense of proportion in establishment mind-sets. And why blame the establishment alone? It is a national propensity. Our love for exaggerating things defines our existence. The border skirmish with China in long-distant 1962 continues to be described by our politicians and journalists as the Great Chinese Invasion. When, through some not-often-occurring miracle, the Indian hockey team defeats Pakistan, it is considered to be a millennium event. A middle-class Bengali householder discovers, to his horror, that the supply of fish has temporarily dried up in the local market; it is to him *sarvanash*, the apocalypse, no less. Given our extravagant ways of giving vent to our feelings, there is therefore no batting of an eye if the Inter-Services Intelligence is ascribed to be the perpetrator of all kinds of probable and improbable misdoings. The ISI is here, there, everywhere. Its agents are along our northern border, along our eastern border, in the Bay of Bengal, lurking in the Western Ghats, in the Arabian Sea, across the Rann of Kutch; they are hiding in New Delhi, in Hyderabad, in Srinagar, in Calcutta, in Guwahati, in Manipur. They are training the United Liberation Front of Assam contingents in Bhutan camps; they have also taken up the additional assignment of putting into ship-shape the Kamtapur Liberation Organization. Furthermore, New Delhi has *pucca* information that there is a tie-up between the Nepal Maoists, in the habit of infiltrating into Darjeeling from Birnagar and other spots, and the ISI. According to latest official briefings, an understanding between the Marxist Coordination Committee in Bihar, the People's War Group in Andhra

Pradesh and stray poets-cum-revolutionaries in West Bengal, on the one hand, and the ISI, on the other cannot be ruled out either. Our intelligence apparatus is invariably wise after the event. The Aksharadham episode in Ahmedabad was, of course, the handwork of two ISI urchins; so too was the sabotage which caused the derailment of the Howrah–New Delhi Rajdhani Express last September. As embellishment to the stories, with imagination running riot, General Musharraf's ISI is confidently bracketed with bin Laden's Al Qaeda.

This fondness for discovering an ISI-in-every-bush can be hugely counter-productive. Government leaders love such a *simpliciste* solution to the difficulties they encounter; they can then feed the same version to the populace. Credulousness expands its empire with every day: it is as if at last an earnest attempt is being made to discover the scourge which is trying to do our nation in. No such thing, though. The police and intelligence agencies are going through a flustering time. Their attitude is understandable. They have to handle too many problems. If easy make-believe solutions can save their day, they will not be at all reluctant to buy such options. A kind of mutually trusting concordat is developing rapidly between the ruling politicians, the army brass, the top civil servants and the police and security personnel. They tend to take one another's washing. Molehills are duly turned into mountains. Gossip reigns supreme and soon assumes the form of hard datum; the dividing line between illusion and reality is increasingly obliterated.

The disease can be, and is, infectious. Statisticians begin to doctor figures to please politicians; the rate of economic growth suddenly jumps up or down. Occasional cutting of corners by all and sundry becomes a way of life. Accountants help out business executives to manufacture imaginary figures of rates of return: high rates publicized to shareholders and major losses to be revealed to the tax-collectors, or the other way round. Contractors are quick learners, they use inferior material and submit claims for superior ones, besides discovering other methods to water their estimates. A nation of fiction writers is soon rendered into a race of congenital liars. As long as it is a close-circuit game, that is, untruths are told to lull into comfort our own people, the particular deficiency in character can perhaps be put up with, at least up to a point. The awkwardness lies elsewhere. Credibility is a major factor affecting international transactions. If our statements are found out to be of low credibility by the cognoscenti in international quarters, very soon a credibility rating agency will perhaps be set up in New York or Tokyo to weigh our deeds and claims; our words on oath will be taken not with pinches, but gobbles of salt.

Not merely that, either. The propensity to blame external parties for all the travails we face can have even a worse consequence: it can make us slide into unthinking jingoism. Consider the fiasco that marred the first three one-day cricket fixtures with the West Indies team. What happened were no ordinary pranks. Marauders in the watching crowd would not put up with any Indian setback. At the match at Jamshedpur, 18 runs conceded by India's leading off-spinner was the harbinger of unquiet. Defeat was apparently staring India in the face; such a misfortune must be averted. Play was immediately disrupted: foreigners, who are inferiors to us by definition, have no business to worst us either in game or in war. If a disaster nevertheless threatens, sabotage the proceedings. The story was repeated in Nagpur and Jodhpur. The incident in Jodhpur is particularly obnoxious. That blackie of a bowler, Drakes, or whatever his name, had the cheek to get our captain out; he must be taught the appropriate lesson; the decision was taken in a jiffy to throw a stone aimed at Drakes' backside; India would not yield an inch of ground to any adversary.

The Inter-Services Intelligence is certainly working overtime to do this country harm. Conferring omnipotence upon it is however an exceedingly foolish, even suicidal, pastime. Such demeanour is bound to turn us, in due course, into a nation of excuse-seekers and, ultimately, habitual weavers of untruth.

Crime and punishment

21 December 2002

Even wretched Ecuador has crossed over to the Left. The ruling junta in Colombia is understandably jittery. It is thinking of initiating a move of some imagination: air-dropping a bevy of nubile bikini-clad damsels over the terrains infiltrated by Marxist rebels. The insurgents are bound to find the allure irresistible; they will be much too busy fornicating to devote themselves to the business of making revolution.

No question, hope springs eternal in the human breast. The United States establishment proposes to do even better than the Colombian army bosses. The American Congress has just passed a legislation empowering President George W. Bush to offer a package to Iraqi scientists in the service of Saddam Hussein who would be willing to desert to the United States: they have been promised instant American citizenship for themselves and their families, cushy job opportunities and maximum security blanket for life. The underlying logic is charmingly simple: money talks; Iraqi scientists, engaged in developing thermo-nuclear and chemical weapons for Saddam, could not but be enticed away by the huge offer made to them. It is beyond official American imagination that, in the case of some people, patriotism is not, and will not be, up for sale. But, then, a desperate situation calls for desperate measures. You never know, the United Nations inspection team might give Iraq a clean chit, the international environment might not be suitable for a unilateral American strike. In such eventualities, other stratagems would become necessary, including, for example, the special legislation to seduce the best Iraqi scientific talents. The US President will surely be reduced to tearing his hair, should the Iraqi scientists turn down his overture.

Nearer home, similar legislative endeavours are under contemplation, albeit for a slightly different purpose. Grandiloquence and India's ministers are usually inseparable. Of late, though, they have been excelling themselves. The Deputy Prime Minister of the country has proposed a new legislation which will make the death penalty mandatory for crimes against women. The Defence Minister, instinctively irrepressible, has chosen to go one better. Let us quote him verbatim: 'I will support the Deputy Prime Minister's thinking on this. I will also insist that it should be done as the Chinese do.' It has taken exactly forty years to the day from Bomdila for our current Defence Minister to fall in love with the Chinese. He proceeds to expound what he has in mind with regard to following Chinese procedure in the matter:

> If a person is caught today in China, he is produced in court the next day and allowed to cool for a day. He goes for an appeal, the appeal is heard and dismissed and then he goes back to the cell where he is kept. Then the family of the man is asked to pay for the bullet that will be put in his head to kill him, to send him out of this world.

The Defence Minister is impeccably correct. The course of treatment he describes so succinctly is however applied in China not just for rapists, but for criminals of all categories, including those found guilty of diverse acts of corruption. You indulge in blackmarketing in China, you are shot. You steal government money, you are shot. You provide a job to one of your kinfolk, you are liquidated. You doctor the accounts of your firm, you are removed from the world. You may be a minister or vice-minister and have built a nest egg by doling out government contracts against which you received a hefty commission, you are summarily despatched to death. Dear Defence Minister, this is precisely where the problem arises. China has arrived where she has because her laws are applied uniformly to all citizens, including highly placed public officials, ministers not excluding. A thoroughgoing social revolution constitutes the underpinning of contemporary Chinese jurisprudence; the resulting catharsis has been of a staggering dimension. What China has attempted and succeeded in is, for the present, beyond both our imagination and our capability. The Defence Minister will therefore be wise to cut down on his hyperbole; this is, he will well appreciate, dangerous territory.

The Minister should cut down on his hyperbole and concentrate on relatively small matters, such as mull over the nightmare Shrimati Bhuvaneshwari, a twenty-seven-year-old housewife, resident in the village of Balaghat in the district of Jabalpur in Madhya Pradesh, has been going through since last July. She was offered employment as a teaching assistant by a kindly headmaster in the village primary school. For a women to venture out of her private precincts and teach at a school was unheard of in the feudal milieu. The village panchayat was hot with indignation: stories were circulated insinuating an improper relationship between the young housewife and the elderly headmaster. The panchayat chief convened a meeting of the full panchayat and summoned the lady to stand trial. Some false charges were posted against her; some false witnesses were routinely produced. The panchayat sat in judgement; the verdict was ready in less than ten minutes. The young woman was found guilty of improper behaviour. The punishment was stern: the lady was to be subjected to mass rape; she would be violated in public, and within the next hour, by four villagers nominated by the panchayat head; the panchayat head was magnanimous enough to make himself one of the four nominees. As the public spectacle, somewhat reminiscent of the hoary *Mahabharata* scene depicting the unrobing of Panchali in the court of the Kauravas, was being readied, the husband arrived at the nick of time in a car accompanied by some friends. They just managed to rescue the lady. Bhuvaneshwari, foolish woman, did not want to take the horrendous experience lying down. She tried to lodge a complaint at the local police station. She was refused. After several abortive attempts, she approached the subdivisional police officer. The officer, a reluctant journeyman, agreed after many appeals to accept a complaint against the panchayat chief and his associates, but not for attempt at mass rape, only for verbal abuse. Four persons were routinely arrested and immediately set on bail. Nothing further has happened since then; no formal prosecution has been launched. Bhuvaneshwari has meanwhile been transferred, on account of social opprobrium, to a primary school 12 kilometres away from her village. She has to trudge the distance, an uneven, rugged, wild, shrubbery-infested stretch, on a wobbly cycle. She can be attacked any day at any time during her journey to and from the school; no security has been given to her.

Mr Defence Minister, could you not kindly forget for the moment the idea of any fresh legislation and use the power and resources at your command, and at the command of the Deputy Prime Minister, to ensure that Bhuvaneshwari receives justice at least within the ambit of what the present structure of legality allows? Or would you please consider the case of this other woman in another remote village in holy Aryavarta who was similarly violated by four sturdy neighbours bent on having a spot of fun? She was raped not once, but several times. The village panchayat was seized of the matter. It has duly given its verdict. The four guilty persons have been fined a total sum of two thousand rupees, which, if and when realized, is to be handed over to the woman as compensation for the annoying experience she has undergone. (Even though equally relevant, it is best to leave out from these comments any reference to the horrific experience of women owing allegiance to 'wrong' denominations in post-Godhra Gujarat.)

Ministers are omniscient, they must know that cases are not heard for years on end or cases are not registered at all or cases are registered not on account of the heinous crime actually committed but, as in the instance of Bhuvaneshwari, for a nominal, ridiculously minor offence. The rule of law has not broken down in the country; it has never operated where the downtrodden and the socially oppressed are concerned. The rich and the influential can commit a thousand rapes and murders and steal thousands of crores of rupees from the public till; they will remain untouched. Such beyond-the-pale-of-law mode of existence on the part of the rich assumes many forms. Only the other day, the Finance Minister was explaining on the floor of parliament some of the provisions of the rules framed with respect to eligibility for bidding for the equity of nationalized banks that are sick and are proposed to be a target of disinvestment. These banks might have gone sick because tycoons who had borrowed huge amounts from them have walked away without repaying a single paisa. The tycoons have used the money looted from the banks to accumulate huge personal wealth. Nothing prevents these accumulations, the Finance Minister has informed the nation, from being used by the tycoons to purchase majority shares in the banks, thus setting up almost a new law of economics: to buy a bank, at first borrow from it.

In terms of the details furnished by our Defence Minister, non-repaying borrowers of this sort will be shot in China. Instead, in India, each of them will be presented with a bank. Several instances have occurred of official functionaries, including ministers, found guilty of corruption being summarily executed in China. In India the custom is to kick them upstairs, with or without the investiture of a Bharat Ratna.

Why whimper, however, over criminals not being brought to justice within the country? Flouting the rule of law is now most honoured international practice as well. Consider the American arrogance over Iraq; Geneva and Vienna Conventions be hanged, international law is what the US President holds it to be. The Australian Prime Minister too has now climbed on the bandwagon: international law is for the birds, he will order pre-emptive strikes against Indonesia or the Philippines or Malaysia or Thailand, once he suspects terrorists to be hiding in any of these countries. It is the rule of illegality everywhere.

Borderline cases

1 March 2003

History books are replete with references to the Silk Road, the 4,000-mile-long trade route which, from ancient times onward, used to transport silk from China to the Mediterranean countries, and wool and precious metals in the reverse direction. It came to wider prominence when Marco Polo rediscovered it at the tail end of the medieval period. The Silk Road is now in disuse, but its historical significance is beyond obliteration.

Another trade route, lesser known but once upon a time equally vibrant, straddled, for nearly 2,000 miles, along South Asia. It was the Cattle Route starting at Baluchistan and winding its way through Sind, Punjab, Rajputana, Vidarbha, Oudh, and Varanasi–Sasaram into Bihar; from Bihar it would finally meander across into Bengal and come to a surcease on the banks of the Ganges. For close to 3,000 years, it carried cattle in repeated deals from Baluchistan all the way to Bengal. Sturdy cattle would be picked by traders from the Quetta market and brought via the Cattle Route to what is now Hyderabad in Sind, where Baluchi cattle would be sold off, but cattle locally procured, of less healthy breed, would be taken north into Punjab; once again, the imported cattle would be sold and local stock, of a slightly emaciated breed, would join the Route. The Route would then sidle into the Jaipur–Mewar–Udaipur terrain. At each point, the process would be repeated, superior cattle would be sold and local stock picked for disposal at the subsequent stop: Quetta cattle would be delivered in Hyderabad, Sind cattle in Multan, Multan cattle in Chittorgarh, Chittorgarh cattle in Indore or Gwalior, Gwalior cattle in Agra. Cattle picked in Agra would be taken to Gorakhpur, the Gorakhpur cattle exchanged for local cattle in Pataliputra, and the final lot from Bihar would find its destination in Bengal.

The *modus operandi* would involve the constant switching of not just cattle but also of traders. At no stretch did any herd of cattle travel more than a few hundred miles. That was equally true for the tradesmen. The Cattle Route was an integer, but it was also segmented. A fresh group of traders took over at every halt. And as traders travelled eastward, the quality of cattle, defined in terms of their effectiveness as draught animal and source of supply of both milk and meat, progressively declined. Not unreasonably, the prices at which cattle were disposed of also fell steadily even as the merchants proceeded in the easterly direction. That did not create any disequilibriating situation. The peasantry and townspeople in Bengal were generally an extremely poor lot and could afford only the most emaciated cattle, providing less milk, inferior-quality meat and weakened power to pull carts or draw the ploughshare.

The commodities transported in the reverse direction were, not surprisingly, demand-determined. The eastern regions were lush, the western lands received lesser bounty of nature. Mostly foodgrains, cotton as well as clothing, farm implements and household utensils were carried along the Route from east to west. In this case too, the ambit of buying and selling was localized and regionalized, never extending beyond 50 or a 100 or at most 200 miles. Traders who hailed from Quetta turned back from Sind, those travelling from Sind to Multan duly returned to Hyderabad after completing their transactions, and so on all the way. Cattle were exchanged at every market, often described as a cattle fair; the nature of goods exchanged against cattle however varied.

The Cattle Route survived the vicissitudes of political geography. Empires rose and fell, kingdoms popped up and disappeared, tribal chiefs asserted their authority here and there, occasionally war raged or anarchy took over, but the Cattle Route was considered inviolable. Cattle were *laissez-passer*.

Till the end of the nineteenth century, most of the exchanges in the market centres covered by the Route took the form of barter. Once the East India Company asserted its dominance over the entire stretch of the Route, a common medium of exchange, the rupee and its lesser denominations, emerged as legal tender.

Such arrangements were comfortably *de rigeur* till the middle of the twentieth century. The Partition and, more than the Partition, the Punjab–Delhi–Garmukhteshwar carnage, drew the curtain over the hoary annals of the Cattle Route. Cattle from Baluchistan and Sind and Multan no longer travel to India; they cannot; Indian wares and foodgrains do not take the traditional westward route beyond the Wagah–Amritsar border either. The inalienable parts of Pakistan belong to Pakistan, the inalienable parts of India belong to India, and the twain are supposed not to meet.

It has been however a different sort of story on the eastern fringe of the Cattle Route around the Bihar–Bengal border. The partition had sundered the nether flank of the Indo-Gangetic valley. The Ganges was taken to be the rough demarcation between the two countries by the Radcliffe Commission. Country boats could not be stopped from plying across the Ganges and its tributaries. Further north, dirt roads continued to join upper Bihar and upper north Bengal with East Pakistan, now Bangladesh. In this neighbourhood, the border between the two countries has remained porous. It could hardly be otherwise, for the vagaries of the Commission's award had sometimes split a Bengal house-site clumsily into two, the main building or hutment falling in India and the kitchen perhaps in Pakistan, or the homestead in one country and the arable land owned by the family in the other. It took several years even to introduce a formal system of passports for travel between India and East Pakistan.

The residue of the Cattle Route has survived longer and happens to be a contemporary reality. A Rajasthani merchant settled in Bihar and otherwise an ardent follower of both the Bharatiya Janata Party and the Vishwa Hindu Parishad, does not mind smuggling for profit sickly cattle for consumption by the Bangladeshi poor. He smuggles back into West Bengal rice, vegetables and contraband foreign goods. And it is not just cattle and merchandise. Labour too moves both ways: masons, carpenters and weavers regularly travel from Bangladesh to Malda, Nadia or Murshidabad in West Bengal, even cultivators on daily wages. Skilled workers specializing in this or that craft, in demand as operatives in small engineering workshops, move from West Bengal to Bangladesh. Over the decades, such cross-country travellers have included fishermen, snake-charmers, wandering bards, professional holy men and, of course, thieves and small-time crooks. By and large, they have consisted of decrepit, down-and-out marginal men and women.

The implicit principle has been one of live and let live. Those belonging to the lower stratum of the social scale have traded and travelled across the West Bengal–Bangladesh border. They have not bothered about rules or passports, but then they have caused no political harm to either country. Governments in both countries have chafed at the phenomenon. Nevertheless, at least till the advent of the Bharatiya Janata Party regime in New Delhi, neither side had lost much sleep over it. Some Indians have also had the sagacity to remember that without such an informal border, India could not have succeeded in its campaign against Pakistan in 1971.

Stray groups of Bangladeshi migrants belonging to all communities, who had penetrated into West Bengal, have occasionally travelled further, such as to Delhi or Mumbai or Ahmedabad, in search of a living, as their forefathers had been wont to do in the past. Their number cannot possibly exceed a few thousands. Borders are imposed by political fiat. Social exchanges indulged in by human groups, however, transcend such artificial divisions. That is the great historical truth.

The BJP government in New Delhi appears to be in right earnest to destroy that truth. Given the primitive animal urge which impels it and the accompanying philosophical stance, it is not content with having only Pakistan as an active enemy. It must also invest Bangladesh with the same infamy. It would not like to make a distinction between the Pakistan and Bangladesh administrations: a Muslim regime is a Muslim regime, why bother about linguistic and ethnic specifications? Pakistanis and Bangladeshis are accordingly being tarred by the same feather. Pakistan's Inter-Services Intelligence and Bangladesh's espionage network are being ascribed a common identity. The objective could not be more transparent: by hook or by crook, the Bangladesh government must be forced to embrace the clasp of Islamabad; it would then be easy to mobilize the wild ones back home against Islamic global conspiracy, of which India and the US are common victims.

The thesis has been carefully built over the months. ISI agents, with the connivance of the Bangladesh army and police, have allegedly set up camps inside Bangladesh, where spies are being trained to infiltrate across the border into Tripura, Meghalaya, Assam and West Bengal so as to carry out sabotage. Most of these stories are an amalgam of hearsay, semi-truth and fiction, and are being put together by central intelligence agencies and assiduously passed on to the state governments concerned.

We are no friends of Pakistan. Pakistanis too are no friends of ours. It is, therefore, altogether conceivable that the ISI is trying its worst to harm our interests across the globe and attempting to send across saboteurs and conspirators into our territory, just as our Research and Analysis Wing is bent on returning the compliment in diverse ways. What is however somewhat suspect is the story of a link-up between Pakistani and Bangladeshi agents. By making such statements in public without caring to discuss them in *tête-à-tête* sessions with the Bangladesh administration, the Government of India is perpetrating what many would consider to be a major folly: it is alienating the government as well as the people of Bangladesh to an extent where they would feel like welcoming back Pakistani overlordship. New Delhi is also breathing down the neck of the governments of the eastern states of the union and admonishing them to intensify their own efforts to thwart Pakistani infiltration via Bangladesh. Nothing is supposed to be beyond the capability of the ISI: it is at the root of all the evils that beset India. Hunting down ISI conspirators has been raised to the level of a Great National Pastime: a Bengali-speaking Muslim, be he in Matunga in Mumbai or Mayur Vihar in Delhi, is *ipso facto* a Pakistani spy unless he or she can prove otherwise.

Is there no scope for at least raising the query whether a mountain is not being sought to be made out of a molehill, and with expansive flourish? The BJP has a stake in waging permanent war with Muslim-majority countries. The build-up of the scare over ISI infiltration, it is possible to suggest, is an integral part of the *parivar's* long-term strategy. Should the governments in the eastern states, several of whom have a political philosophy and a moral culture radically different from the BJP's, fall for the trap? Is there any ground for taking at 100 per cent face value, versions of sabotage and espionage doled out to them by central police and security authorities, including RAW and CBI?

The issue can be posed even more categorically. The BJP may declare any Muslim-majority country as its sworn enemy. Will that however also be the point of view of a Left Front-led state government in West Bengal or Tripura, or of a Congress regime in Assam or Arunachal Pradesh? Should these state administrations, either consciously or absent-mindedly, convert themselves into tools of the BJP regime at the centre and hound, in the name of war against terrorism, poor innocent people who happen to have Muslim names, and, furthermore, incite countrymen as much against Bangladesh as against Pakistan? On the other hand, has not the time arrived for seriously putting forward the proposal that should the NDA government in New Delhi persist on treading this dangerous path of creating an enemy out of almost every neighbouring country, states constituting the union of India should then have the prerogative of insisting on a separate foreign policy of their own? Such a proposal could indeed be necessary for ensuring the integrity of the nation. For, unless foreign policy is federalized, the BJP could well discover, maybe in a score of years or in even lesser time, that a unilaterally imposed foreign policy, to go with a monogamous religious philosophy, is the swiftest road to the liquidation of India as a political entity as it has existed since 1947.

The police *über alles*

21 June 2003

An incident ten years ago, perhaps comprehensively insignificant, not worth *eine kleine nachtmusik*. The sequel of developments around it still epitomizes the current state of the democratic republic of India.

A dishevelled looking, small, worn-out building owned by a middle-aged lady, Banimala Naskar, at 170/2 Picnic Garden Road on the eastern fringes of Calcutta. Banimala lived alone; she had however rented out in the preceding February, a two-room bit of her house to a young Punjabi couple: the husband was Lachhman Singh – in some versions, Lachhmi Singh – and the wife, Rani Singh, or so they called themselves. They were a quiet couple and kept to themselves. They had paid three months' rent in advance. Banimala had no complaints.

The eerie early hours of 19 May 1993. Daybreak was still at least two hours away. Two different narrations of the story exist. In one narration, a helicopter landed in a nearby field where boys of the neighbourhood used to practise football. Five shadowy characters emerged from the chopper. Two cars were waiting for them. They got in the cars and sped to the doorstep of Banimala's house. The other narration does not mention the chopper and only refers to the sudden arrival of the cars. Whatever it be, the strangers rudely knocked at Banimala's door and woke her up. They enquired of the Sikh couple. Banimala pointed at the flatlet she had rented out. The five intruders, Kalashnikovs already blazing, barged in; no questions asked, the man and the woman were summarily shot several times over, and the severed limbs flew in different directions in a *danse macabre*. But the gun-toting gang kept their cool. They gathered together the sundered limbs, loaded the carcasses in their cars, and, engines and guns roaring, disappeared amid the foggy darkness.

The facts got unravelled bit by bit. The intruders were a special contingent of the Punjab anti-terrorist police force. The Khalistani agitation was at its peak in Punjab in the late 1980s, and the union and state governments coalesced to build a crack division of security personnel to mow down misguided youth who, it was presumed, were on foreign payroll. The police boss hand-picked to head this special division was a man of many laurels. A celebrated swiller of hard drinks, he was once convicted by the state high court for assaulting a serving IAS woman officer and outraging her modesty. Despite the conviction, nothing happened to him. He was precious merchandise, highly connected, and regarded as saviour of the nation, rescuing Punjab from the clutches of the despicable terrorists, even if that involved liquidation of thousands of young people in fake encounters and grim midnight ambushes. Given his sparkling other virtues, occasional pinching of women's bottoms was small beer. This same person was commissioned last year by the Bharatiya Janata Party bigwigs to be their 'security adviser' in Gujarat in the wake of the grisly genocide in the state; he did such a wonderful whitewashing job on their behalf that few or no witnesses now dare to appear before the judicial enquiry commissions and narrate the bestialities perpetrated during those nightmarish weeks.

This super police boss was above the law, he assumed his menials too were likewise. Lachhmi or Lachhman Singh was claimed to be a Sikh insurgent who escaped the dragnet of the Punjab police, travelled all the way to Calcutta with his wife or companion, and took shelter at Picnic Garden Road. To add flavour to the story, it was even alleged that Lachhmi or Lachhman Singh was actually Bashir, a Pakistani aiding the Khalistanis. The Punjab security police received information about Bashir's fleeing to Calcutta and seeking refuge in Banimala Naskar's house. The quarry, they decided, needed to be immediately hunted down: Expedition Picnic Garden Road was organized with the greatest speed.

The Punjab police, however, had no jurisdiction over the state of West Bengal. If they wanted to gather their prey in the manner they did, they, the law demanded, had to seek permission from the authorities over here. Under the country's Constitution, even Indian army personnel cannot enter the territory of a state unless that state has been specifically brought under the purview of the Disturbed Areas Act. But the Punjab police and their history-sheeter of a head were not in the habit of abiding anybody else's question. Damn the law, hang the Constitution; whether by helicopter or by other means, in the wee hours of 19 May, the contingent from Punjab's special task force reached the eastern fringes of Calcutta, launched a smashingly successful raid, and cut down the militant

258

they were in search of. They also summarily disposed of the wife or companion, and decamped with the severely sundered bodies of the two victims.

Thereby they, the Punjab police, committed a number of grievous offences under the law. They entered the territory of West Bengal without permission from the local authorities. They shot down an alleged suspect in cold blood even when not under attack. They killed a young lady who was either his wife or his companion, even though she had absolutely no police record. On top of committing the two murders, they were also guilty of whisking away the corpses, which amounted to concealing incriminating evidence, a major crime.

A public outcry ensued in West Bengal, and elsewhere as well. In the beginning, the government of Punjab tried to bluff its way through: it was not aware of any such action on the part of its police force. The pretence could not be kept up for long. A reference was made to the Supreme Court of India and the Punjab authorities caved in. As directed by the Chief Justice of India, a CBI enquiry was arranged. The underlying facts were fully exposed. The five culprits – including an IPS officer – were finally apprehended and sent up for trial at the Alipore Sessions Court in Calcutta. All of them were found guilty. An appeal against the judgment pending in the high court, the convicted persons got bail.

But the judicial process has little clientèle these days. Other moves were afoot. All seasons are, according to some quarters, seasons of amity and goodwill. Roughly a year ago, the state government of Punjab reportedly approached the government of West Bengal: please, have a heart, these five policemen on our roll are gems of humanity; they no doubt committed an indiscreet act, but they did so in the cause of the country, to deliver it from terrorism; they are patriots of the first water; so why cannot you, the government of West Bengal, kindly forgive and forget, and grant these five cold-blooded murderers a free pardon?

The government of West Bengal, reports suggest, promised to examine the case sympathetically. The West Bengal authorities, according to further reports, promised additionally to consult the Ministry of Home Affairs in New Delhi in the matter. Things proceeded fast from then on. The Ministry of Home Affairs advised the government of West Bengal that it was a most fit case for exhibiting the quality of mercy William Shakespeare was so charmingly effusive about. The West Bengal authorities, seemingly anxious not to spoil their reputation as good boys, responded positively to the entreaty of the Punjab authorities and the advice of the centre. The state government's recommendation was forwarded to the West Bengal Governor, who has since signed the order of pardon. To be fair, he was not exercising any gubernatorial prerogative, but complying with the properly elected government's recommendation. Everything is fine and excellent; once the formal announcement is made, the story of the gruesome murders committed ten years ago on Picnic Garden Road, Calcutta, would get obliterated from the record books.

Questions nonetheless keep nagging. Suppose some lion-hearted Vishwa

Hindu Parishad partisan, feverishly ideology-minded, arrives in Calcutta, makes a beeline for the famous Nakhoda mosque in the city centre, organizes a shooting spree there and, in the process, kills a dozen innocent bystanders before being apprehended. Suppose, after arrest, he is charge-sheeted, undergoes the appropriate trial and is given the death sentence. Suppose the sentence is upheld by the Supreme Court. Suppose further that, at that juncture, the Ministry of Home Affairs advises the government of West Bengal to grant pardon and release the murderer. What would the state government then do? For, New Delhi would hoist the state government on the petard of the precedent it has itself set up in the Punjab policemen's case.

Other questions too would rear their head. One of them is closely linked to the confusion the Punjab pardon is bound to cause in regard to the dividing line between legality and illegality, and deciding which is to be preferred. Once upon a time Bertolt Brecht wrote some biting poetry to suggest that, when the push comes to the shove, an authoritarian-minded state apparatchik, when faced with popular discontent, would rather dissolve the people. The predicament in the present context is slightly different, to determine whether the intent of the authorities in this great democratic republic of India is to dissolve the law. Memory rankles. Way back in the early 1950s, a judge of the Calcutta high court found the Preventive Detention Act, under which several communist leaders and workers were detained without trial, to be bereft of legality. When it was argued on the government's behalf that should the Act be declared *ultra vires*, these dangerous communists would have to be released, which would pose a major threat to the security of the country, the judge quoted the Roman edict: *fiat justitia ruat coelum*, justice has to prevail even if the heaven collapses. He did not relent, he ordered the release of the illegally held communists, whose list included Jyoti Basu and Indrajit Gupta.

Times change, moods swing. Law and justice now need to be dissolved so as to protect policemen who indulge every now and then in sprees of calculated, cold-blooded murder.

Other things aside, may one place, with humility, for consideration by the powers-that-be, an issue not altogether irrelevant? Neither brevity nor coyness is the soul of wit in a competitive democracy. The state government, for its own sake, ought to take the public into full confidence concerning the details of this pardon of convicted murderers. The Left Front regime in West Bengal has numerous enemies. That does not mean that it should, with generous absent-mindedness, let go of its friends either. Already a suggestion, snide or otherwise, is afloat: the Left Front in West Bengal is attempting to emulate Enrico Berlinguer's efforts two decades ago in Italy to effect a 'historic compromise' with the Catholic church. That did not save that country's communist party, once Europe's largest, from disintegrating, though.

The carpetbaggers are a-coming

30 August 2003

Idaho, up in the Rocky Mountains, is one of the 50 states constituting the United States of America. In ordinary reckoning, it should be of little importance. It has barely 2 per cent of the total land mass of the US; its population is less than even one-half of 1 per cent of the total national population. It has some minerals, such as silver and antimony, but is mostly agricultural. Its potato is well known, and obese Americans are, on the sly, often referred to as Idaho Potatoes. While one can afford to make snide comments on Idaho, one cannot ignore it. For it has two senators in the US Senate as every other state has: area, population, level of economic activity, none of these matters. Whether it is New York or California or Texas or Massachusetts, each in this instance is in the same league as Hawaii, Maine or Idaho. The constitution of the US lays it down that big, small or medium-sized, all states will have the same representation in the nation's upper house, exactly two for each of them.

And there is more to it. Irrespective of the state you are from, should you happen to be a US Senator, you come to exercise enormous clout in national decision-making. In any event, the Senate is much more powerful as per the US constitution than the House of Representatives. The different committees of the Senate can veto proposals mooted by the administration, and the chairman of every committee has, in course of time, accumulated enormous power in his or her hands. Besides, since the chairmanship of Senate committees is decided by seniority, a person from even a relatively insignificant state, in case he happened to be a senator of long standing, could behave like a proper czar and turn out to be a walking nightmare for the administration; the administration, of course, includes the office of the President.

Idaho's population may comprise less than one-half of 1 per cent of the total US population, but a senator from Idaho, it follows, is something different. Larry Craig is one of the two senators from Idaho. Of late, he has come into the news. He held up Senate approval for a large number of US air force promotions till an additional fleet of four cargo jet planes was supplied to strengthen Idaho's National Guard contingent. The air force fumed, the Pentagon went into shivers, Defence Secretary Rumsfeld was in jitters, President George W. Bush was bemused. They could do little about Senator Craig's tantrums. True, Larry Craig is a Senator from a state which covers a measly 2 per cent of the total land mass of the US. He is nonetheless a Senator, and a Senator in the US competes with the Almighty God.

Joe McCarthy of Wisconsin proved the flip-side of senatorial divinity; his rampaging witch-hunt in the 1950s of supposed communists in every nook and corner of the country remains a permanent blot on US history. At the same time, significant economic benefits, who can deny, have got showered on the states by string-pulling Senators, thereby spreading the growth of income and employment relatively evenly all over the country. Infamy has stuck to senatorial 'pork-barrels', but they have also been major levellers of inter-state economic opportunities. The Larry Craigs thus can lay a fair claim to glory.

Come away 10,000 miles and consider Meghalaya, one of the constituent states of the Republic of India, tucked in the remote north-east. In terms of size, population and national endowment, it should be, in the Indian scale of things, on a par with Idaho in the US. But the similarity ends rather brusquely.

Of close to 250 members in India's upper house, the Rajya Sabha, only one represents Meghalaya. The writers of the Indian Constitution had fallen between two stools while giving shape to the contours of the Rajya Sabha. They could not quite make up their mind whether the upper house of the legislature should be in the image of the House of Lords in Westminster or the American Senate. The thought of vesting the Rajya Sabha with the power and grandeur of the US Senate tantalized them. Inhibitions are however inhibitions. Post-colonial reflexes are really indistinguishable from colonial ones. The die was so cast as to pattern the Rajya Sabha more like the decorative British upper house, with the emphasis on 'classiness' and maturity but little authority. Despite the provision that most members of the Sabha are to be elected, the American principle of the same number of representation from each state was deviated from. Members are elected to the Rajya Sabha in varying numbers from the different states on the basis of population. A second departure: in the US, Senators are directly elected by the voters; members of the Rajya Sabha are elected by state legislators. To dilute the composition further, the Indian Constitution has provided for nomination of a certain quota of members by the President, in effect by the union council of ministers.

Even so, the pious hope continued to be entertained in some hearts that the Rajya Sabha, honouring its nomenclature, would emerge as the forum where discussion concentrated on the specific problems of the states rather than of the nation as a whole. Paying homage to this hope, the Representation of the Peoples Act, enacted in 1950, indicated that those wanting to get elected to the Rajya Sabha from a particular state must be 'ordinarily resident' in that state.

For a while, the statutory admonition worked all right, only persons 'ordinarily resident' there were chosen by the political parties to fill the Rajya Sabha seats from each state. The criterion for establishing the status of 'ordinarily resident', generally accepted by the Election Commission as well as the judiciary, stressed ownership of a piece of property or, failing that, long-standing client–customer relationship with a financial institution based in the state. Hassles were few and far between till the 1970s: members of the Rajya Sabha elected from a state were fully conversant with the problems of the state, and of course also with its languages. Even if, in some cases, they could not claim the principal language of the state as their mother-tongue, they could use it with great felicity.

With Indira Gandhi and her reign, a sea-change took place in the landscape. Indira Gandhi was a great believer in bending the law or, where necessary, ignoring it. She took a dim view of the provision of 'ordinarily resident' status for election to the Rajya Sabha. What nonsense, she herself should decide who would come to the Rajya Sabha from which state on behalf of her party; what have constitutional or statutory provisions to do with it? Thereby got planted a gigantic poison tree. It has been since then a continuing defiance of the Representation of the Peoples Act, with someone 'ordinarily resident' in West Bengal getting elected from Gujarat, a Malayali from Kochi getting elected from Rajasthan, a Kannadiga hailing from Bangalore getting elected from Orissa, a Punjabi from Hoshiarpur getting elected from Assam. Barring the Leftists, all parties became enthusiastic participants in this great national sport. The legal difficulty was easily circumvented. Your party has decided that you, a permanent resident of Hissar, Haryana, are to be elected to the Rajya Sabha from Arunachal Pradesh; you are not even sure where Arunachal Pradesh is; never mind, just purchase a map of India and locate the teeny-weeny distant state and hasten to buy an address in Itanagar; if the nominations are closing tomorrow, and you do not have the time to buy a postage-stamp-sized plot of land in Arunachal Pradesh, just give your address as: 'c/o Madam so and so, wife of Chief Minister, Arunachal Pradesh'. It has happened in the history of the Indian republic that such a nomination paper was duly accepted. Seasoned politicians viewed it as a game of politics, hence did not flinch from playing the game to the hilt. How does it matter if you declare your address to be the apron-strings of the wife of the state's chief minister; a charade is a charade is a charade.

Decades rolled by. Conceivably for seasoned politicians too, the falsehood started to hang heavy on their conscience. They decided to remedy the situation. They hit upon a brilliant idea. After all, legality is a function of how the law is defined. Were the rider of 'ordinarily resident' status excised from the Representation of the Peoples Act, politicians would be saved the discomfort of playing the role of imposters, and a Kannadiga 'ordinarily resident' in Bangalore could represent Orissa in the Rajya Sabha ensconced in the cleanest of consciences.

In other words, if the law pinches, just abolish the law. Indian politicians are about to do that. Legislation to abolish the nasty provision is on the anvil and maybe passed in the current session of parliament itself. Once that happes, whatever minimal chance there is of a counterpart of Senator Larry Craig of Idaho getting elected to the Rajya Sabha from the backyards of Meghalaya would be crushed for ever: the states doing poorly would continue to fall behind, no 'pork-barrels' to help them out; the members they would elect to the Rajya Sabha would belong to the species of carpetbaggers, without any sense of loyalty to the electing states, and no prick of conscience to bother them either.

The trend is towards transiting from a federal-type polity to a closely knit, centre-dominated national administration; leaders strutting on the stage in New Delhi must wield power mindlessly, and no questions are to be asked. No equivalent of a Larry Craig would be there to state that unless Meghalaya or Arunachal Pradesh or Tripura were blessed with a rail network of 5,000 kilometres crisscrossing the state, the railway budget would be stalled, or that if an immediate decision were not taken to grant a steel plant, a heavy machinery plant and an IT village to the state, appropriations for the Ministry of Commerce and Industry would be vetoed. There could however be second- and third- and further-order consequences stemming from such purposive snapping of the nexus between 'ordinarily resident' status and membership of the Rajya Sabha. Meghalaya would not develop, and more and more natives of Meghalaya would join the insurgents, as they would do in Assam, Nagaland, Mizoram, Arunachal Pradesh, Tripura and Sikkim. The defence and security budgets would accordingly have to swell and swell even more, so much so that there be no economic development not only over the region of the Seven Sisters but practically across India as a whole.

Several underground organizations operating in the north-east have recently announced a boycott of Hindi films from Bollywood; they intend to enforce the boycott. The seasoned politicians have no time for such small news items though. They also know how to comfort themselves: much of all this is the doing of ISI agents.

Remember Zohra and Uzra?

27 September 2003

Layers of oblivion. Even Uday Shankar's name would sound strange to the current crowd. He, some kindly soul would explain with just the right dash of condescension, happened to be the elder brother of the sitar maestro, Ravi Shankar. Uday Shankar should have been served better by chronicle writers. Once upon a time, he did for Indian music and dance what Ananda Coomaraswamy did for India's art and archaeological history. The early 1930s constituted his high noon.

The European bourgeoisie, ravaged by the first world war and, subsequently, by the great depression, were badly in need of diversions. They found one in Uday Shankar and his troupe. In the beginning, it was almost a family episode: the brothers, Uday, Devendra and Ravi, and the cousins, Kanaklata and Lakshmi. As Uday Shankar's imagination gained wings, others joined in, including old *guruji* Allauddin Khan, Vishnudas Shirani and Timirbaran Bhattacharya. A young *belle* of perhaps half-Hungarian, half-French antecedents – a discard from Anna Pavlova's ballet group – also found herself in the company. They held Europe in thraldom, with dance rituals that were a blend of Bharatanatyam, Kathakali, Kathak and Manipuri, the accompanying music a fascinating pot-pourri of Hindustani and Carnatic classical and non-pretentious folk. The choreography was done carefully with advice from connoisseurs and scholars of reckoning, the dress and the ensemble were dazzling. The Uday Shankar troupe were like a callow band of wandering minstrels; they still doled out a version of oriental culture whose sophistication bowled over the European aristocracy as well as diehard colonials.

Two pretty damsels of solid upper-class Muslim stock were soon inveigled into being members of the team. They became instant celebrities. They had a natural flair for dancing, wafting their bodies magically in the air, instant liquid shapes, the tinkling of *ghungroos* harmonizing with the quiver of their arms and the deep mystery of their eyes. Zohra and Uzra maddened the crowd almost as much as Simkie did.

That was in the worn-out 1930s. Uday Shankar gradually fell from grace, his troupe dispersed, the second world war was followed by the ravages wrought by Partition. The two sisters, Zohra and Uzra, got separated. Zohra Sehgal stayed back in India and, in course of time, moved into prominence in the world of theatre; she combined her creative activities with a raging social conscience. Uzra Butt found herself in Lahore. She too prospered in diverse spheres of the fine arts. Both sisters had wide connections and could claim a number of close friends in the establishment of either country.

That did not help. The political divide was the principal reality. Rational thinking would have suggested that, once the scars of bloodshed, plunder and trans-shipment of populations were over, the people in both countries would be allowed to settle down to tranquillity which spelled affection, understanding, civilized exchange, and expanding social and economic welfare of the broad masses on either side of the border.

That hope was shot down almost immediately. Kashmir intervened, and Kashmir refuses to be a defunct issue. As if Kashmir were not enough, on the Indian side there was an additional factor at work, Chinaphobia. It has therefore been, strictly speaking, no normal existence for Indians in the 56 years since independence. The situation in Pakistan is about the same, if not worse. The army brass soon took charge of that country. Anti-Indian sentiments have been their survival kit; the issue of Kashmir evoked passion and fuelled the spark of further militarization: the two set-ups became the spitting image of each other. The Indian establishment has, for most of the time, prospered on the basis of the capital stock of the febrile ideology of finish-off-Pakistan-once-and-for-all. The establishment in Pakistan has reciprocated with vigour bordering on frenzy. The consequences have been glaringly evident. Development has remained merely as an essential political cliché; actual development has not proceeded beyond the thin circle at the top in both countries. The budgets of both have grown increasingly defence-oriented. A third of the population may, in fact, be starving; so what, the priorities have got topsy-turvied with single-minded emphasis on creation of nuclear capability and delivery systems. At a certain juncture, foreign powers with superior might have found it profitable to act as mentor as well as ringside *kibitzer* for this country as much as that. They have had a genuine vested interest. The more resources poor nations spend on defence and security, the lovelier it is for arms merchants with domicile in the industrially advanced western countries.

Chasing the crooked shadow of nuclear superiority, started off by the dispute over Kashmir, has been worse than pursuit of the will-o'-the-wisp. The populations in both countries have paid a heavy price for the sake of Kashmir. The price paid by the people in Kashmir is, no question, much, much heavier. They have been without civil liberties for the past couple of decades or more. It should hardly be a crime to nurture patriotic emotions. But the Kashmiris have been penalized on that score; the penalty has often assumed a ghastly pattern, turning the Kashmiris even to a greater extent than before against the interlopers. Of late, they have been offered cellular telephones, presumably considered an appropriate substitute for self-determination.

The sacrifice the rest of India – and, let us have the grace to admit, of Pakistan too – has been called upon to make is of no mean order. Since no political party has the courage to call the Kashmir bluff, a great concordat has been reached at the national arena: all parties swear to Kashmir being an inalienable part of India. Because this claim is by now a vacuity, it has needed to be backed up by larger and larger outlays in the name of defence and security, which in turn has meant goodbye to economic and social development for the nation's majority. Development has ceased to be any part of the formal official agenda. The political leadership has cultivated a rather out-of-the-ordinary frame of mind: let foreigners look into that particular aspect of the matter, we ourselves cannot be bothered; we have to concentrate on keeping Kashmir; in order to keep Kashmir, we have to give a bloody nose to Pakistan; to facilitate the achievement of this objective, the population must be bled to the limit, or even beyond the limit, so as to ensure that the defence build-up was optimal.

Every now and then, the Americans, in the interest of their own geopolitics, remind the Indian and Pakistani authorities of Winston Churchill's picturesque phrase: jaw-jaw is superior to war-war. A thaw follows. Once that happens, there is a flurry of exchange of delegations of various descriptions between the two countries: parliamentarians, jurists, journalists, society women, table tennis and basketball players, student and youth groups, poets and writers. But the mood and manners soon change. For, the superpower has several other axes to grind, and the pressure mounted by it eases. As a result, the tragedy of separation continues for ordinary people in both lands, such as those who are without contact with other members of the family residing in the other country. The two sisters, Zohra Sehgal and Uzra Butt, did not see each other for decades and were re-united only last month, courtesy the current season of ersatz camaraderie. Zohra Sehgal and Uzra Butt are not unusual cases; there are hundreds of instances of brother separated from sister or brother, father separated from son or daughter, wife separated from husband.

The problem has deeper implications. Hindustani music is a unified foliage. Its roots were ruptured at the time of Partition and, since then, vocalists on either side have been able to exchange ideas and learn from one another only fitfully. The predicament is no less for the corps of academics and literature buffs now bisected into two. These pangs apart, what about humble men, women and children along the political border whose economic activities had been organically interlinked over centuries? A fiat from above does not automatically change the content of reality at the base. Newspapers have recently been full of tales about children herding goats or sheep, or playing *kabaddi*, straying accidentally across the border and getting locked up in alien prisons, while their families pass their days laden with sorrow and worry. There have been reports too of fishermen in wobbly country boats from both countries breaching the fictional divide between national and international waters without being aware of it, and getting caught. It is obviously not a question of retarded economic development alone. What is involved is a much more comprehensive calamity, taking a walk away from humanity and humanism. And what for? It is beyond the capability of India to demolish Pakistan, or of Pakistan to destroy India, never mind the magnificence of defence preparations on either side. Insensate hatred, by itself, does not ensure military triumph, and, in any event, powerful neighbours are bound to intervene before the final round of confrontation ensues. Kashmir may be, as per the slogan, inalienable, but it is unwinnable too: even if cross-border terrorism, so described, stops, forces are being constantly released from within, and they cannot be tamed by deployment of force. The futile search around Kathua must have brought that realization home.

So what is proposed to be done next? We have written off the right of secession from the Constitution, but it is not for us to deny the right of self-determination even if the United Nations charter is regarded as hooey. True, the political bosses would not like Kashmir to be dropped from the agenda. They have a vested interest in Kashmir, for they have a vested interest in defence and security outlays; commissions from contracts and purchases make the where-withal of their good living. Is it, though, not time for revolt? Some events and incidents only cause dismay, for example, the pompous story of how the Nuclear Development Authority met for three or four hours to chalk out future programmes and decide on budgetary appropriations, and thereby guarantee increasing immiserization of the national population. Or consider the newspaper photo of the country's Defence Minister fondling with dreamy eyes an assault rifle manu-factured in our ordinance factories. Could not a sufficiently large number of people in both countries rise in unison and register their protest at these obscene goings-on? Why cannot the powers-that-be be told that enough is enough, their daily perambulations are a hokum, a great confidence trick intended to cheat the common people, but the people will no longer be cheated? Both Indians and Pakistanis have been much too polite, listening patiently and credulously to what-ever garbage the establishment has passed on to them. In the first half of the twentieth century, conscientious objectors were taken seriously; during wartime they were now and then imprisoned, but nonetheless held in high regard. Maybe it is time to start a Society of Conscientious Objectors who will say baloney to Kashmir. Recruits must come from both countries and a certain number of indi-viduals from amongst them must be prepared to get up and be counted – and, if necessary, go to prison. It is time perhaps for another freedom movement, but the freedom demanded should be to extricate the national budget from the tyranny of fake syndromes, such as that of Kashmir.

Detailed arithmetic exercises can be left to the hacks. But Kashmir- and Pakistan-related defence and security outlays in this country have been mostly financed by sacrificing development. It is not too far-fetched an assumption that in consequence, over the past half a century, India's GDP has, on the average, been set back at least 1 per cent every year. Compound the loss and it would be legitimate to claim that had there been no Kashmir imbroglio, our per capita income today would have been at least double of what it is. Similar estimates should be possible for Pakistan too.

Has the game been worth the candle? Have the leaders of the two coun-tries ever bothered to present the problem before their people in such stark terms?